Hiking Waterfalls in New England

HELP US KEEP THIS GUIDE UP TO DATE

Every effort has been made by the author and editors to make this guide as accurate and useful as possible. However, many things can change after a guide is published—trails are rerouted, regulations change, techniques evolve, facilities come under new management, and so forth.

We welcome your comments concerning your experiences with this guide and how you feel it could be improved and kept up to date. While we may not be able to respond to all comments and suggestions, we'll take them to heart, and we'll also make certain to share them with the author. Please send your comments and suggestions to the following address:

FalconGuides
Reader Response/Editorial Department
246 Goose Lane
Guilford, CT 06437

Or you may e-mail us at: editorial@falcon.com

Thanks for your input, and happy trails!

Hiking Waterfalls in New England

A Guide to the Region's Best Waterfall Hikes

Eli Burakian

FALCONGUIDES

GUILFORD, CONNECTICUT
HELENA, MONTANA

FALCONGUIDES®

An imprint of Rowman & Littlefield
Falcon, FalconGuides, and Outfit Your Mind are registered trademarks of Rowman & Littlefield.

Distributed by NATIONAL BOOK NETWORK

Copyright © 2015 by Rowman & Littlefield
Photos: Eli Burakian
Maps: Alena Joy Pearce © Rowman & Littlefield

British Library Cataloguing-in-Publication Information available

Library of Congress Cataloging-in-Publication Data available

ISBN 978-0-7627-8685-5 (paperback)
ISBN 978-1-4930-1442-2 (electronic)

∞™ The paper used in this publication meets the minimum requirements of American National Standard for Information Sciences—Permanence of Paper for Printed Library Materials, ANSI/NISO Z39.48-1992.

The author and Globe Pequot Press assume no liability for accidents happening to, or injuries sustained by, readers who engage in the activities described in this book.

Contents

Acknowledgments x
Introduction 1
    How to Use This Guide 2
    Safety and Preparation 4
    Leave No Trace 6
Trail Finder 7
    Author's Favorite Waterfalls 7
    Least Crowded Waterfalls 7
    Most Popular Waterfalls 7
    Interesting Gorges / Chasms / Ravines / Geologic Formations 8
    Roadside / Almost Roadside Falls (<0.1 mile) 8
    Challenging Hikes (length >3.0 miles or difficult terrain) 8
Map Legend 10

CONNECTICUT 11
    1. Indian Well Falls 12
    2. Spruce Brook Falls 15
    3. Buttermilk Falls (CT) 18
    4. Kent Falls 20
    5. Wadsworth Big and Little Falls 23
    6. Chapman Falls 27
    7. Bailey's Ravine 29
    8. Blackledge Falls 32
    9. Enders Falls 35

RHODE ISLAND 38
    10. Stepstone Falls 39

MASSACHUSETTS 41
    11. Campbell Falls 42
    12. Race Brook Falls 45
    13. Bash Bish Falls 49
    14. Wahconah Falls 52
    15. Windsor Jambs 55
    16. March Cataract Falls 58
    17. Money Brook Falls 62
    18. Twin Cascade 64
    19. Tannery and Parker Brook Falls 67
    20. Doane's Falls 70
    21. Spirit Falls 73
    22. Royalston Falls 75

Overview

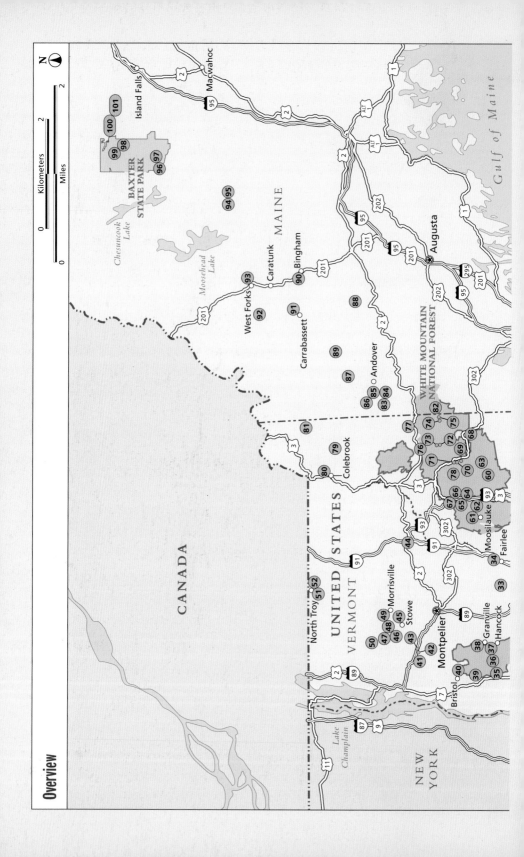

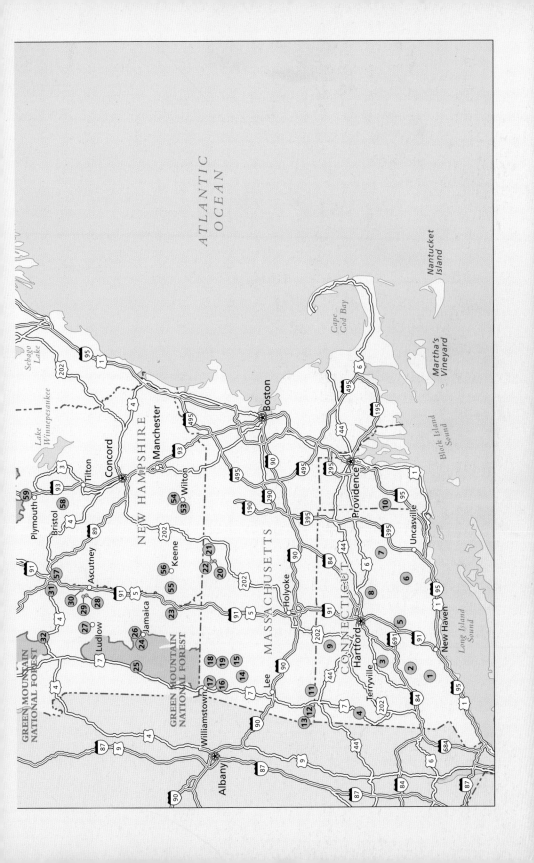

VERMONT **78**
  23. Jelly Mill Falls / Old Jelly Mill Falls 79
  24. Pikes Falls 81
  25. Lye Brook Falls 84
  26. Hamilton Falls 89
  27. Buttermilk Falls (VT) 92
  28. Cascade Falls (VT) 95
  29. Hidden Falls 98
  30. Gerry Falls 101
  31. Quechee Gorge 103
  32. Thundering Falls / Thundering Brook Falls / Bakers Falls 107
  33. Old City Falls 110
  34. Glen Falls 113
  35. Falls of Lana 116
  36. Bailey Falls 119
  37. Texas Falls 122
  38. Moss Glen Falls (Granville) 125
  39. Abbey Pond Cascades 127
  40. Bartlett Falls 130
  41. Huntington Gorge 132
  42. Honey Hollow Falls 134
  43. Bolton Potholes 136
  44. Emerson Falls 138
  45. Moss Glen Falls (Stowe) 140
  46. Bingham Falls 143
  47. Hell Brook Cascades (Lower) 146
  48. Sterling Falls Gorge 149
  49. Terrill Gorge 152
  50. Jefferson Falls / Brewster River Gorge 155
  51. Jay Branch Gorge / Four Corners 158
  52. Big Falls 160

NEW HAMPSHIRE **162**
  53. Garwin Falls 163
  54. Purgatory Falls 166
  55. Chesterfield Gorge 169
  56. Beaver Brook Falls (Keene) 172
  57. Trues Ledges 175
  58. Profile Falls 179
  59. Livermore Falls 182
  60. Waterville Cascades 185
  61. Beaver Brook Cascades (Moosilauke) 189
  62. Lost River Gorge 193
  63. Sabbaday Falls 196

64. Flume Gorge / Flume Pool Loop 200
65. Basin–Cascade Trail Falls 204
66. Falling Waters 207
67. Bridal Veil Falls 210
68. Diana's Baths 213
69. Nancy Cascades 216
70. Arethusa Falls 219
71. Ripley Falls 222
72. Glen Ellis Falls 224
73. Crystal Cascade (NH) 227
74. Eagle Cascade 230
75. Brickett Falls 234
76. Appalachia Falls 236
77. Giant Falls 240
78. Zealand and Thoreau Falls 243
79. Huntington Cascades / Huntington Falls 248
80. Beaver Brook Falls (Colebrook) 251
81. Garfield Falls 254

MAINE **257**
82. Bickford Slides 258
83. Screw Auger Falls 262
84. Step Falls 265
85. The Cataracts 267
86. Dunn Falls 270
87. Angel Falls 274
88. Mosher Hill Falls 277
89. Smalls Falls 280
90. Houston Brook Falls 283
91. Poplar Stream Falls 286
92. Grand Falls 291
93. Moxie Falls 294
94. Gulf Hagas 298
95. Hay Brook Falls 302
96. Big and Little Niagara Falls 304
97. Katahdin Stream Falls 307
98. Howe Brook Falls 309
99. South Branch Falls 312
100. Sawtelle Falls 314
101. Shin Falls 317

Hike Index 320
About the Author 321

ACKNOWLEDGMENTS

First and foremost, I'd like to thank my wife, Julia, who has been so supportive throughout the process of putting this book together. She was pregnant for most of the time I was doing my fieldwork and dealing with our son at night while I was at the computer cranking away. She inspires me with her energy and love. I'd also like to thank my son, Levon, who in his few short months of life has brought us many smiles. I can't wait to visit these waterfalls with him someday.

My parents have always supported me throughout my life, and their energy and joy of life is something I hope I can maintain as I age gracefully like they have. My grandmother, whom I lovingly call Bana, is someone else who has inspired me throughout my life. She got her bachelor's and master's degrees well into her senior years and has shown me that nothing is ever beyond our reach.

Greg Parsons and Kate Watson's book *New England Waterfalls* and Dean Goss's website northeastwaterfalls.com helped provide so much information in the research for this book; I owe them a big thank you.

And finally, thank you Otis and Tigran, who, with their combined eight legs, are always enthusiastic hiking companions.

INTRODUCTION

Over the course of this project, I have driven thousands of miles, from the southern part of Connecticut to northern Maine. (Thank you, audio books, which were my saviors on many of the longer excursions.) Undoubtedly, I saw many beautiful waterfalls, however I quickly came to realize that the journeys through New England were just as rewarding as the waterfalls themselves. I followed miles of meandering streams and rivers and passed through quaint towns and rugged mountain vistas.

I garnered a new appreciation for Connecticut, with its rolling hills, jagged coastline, and numerous beautiful waterways. The Berkshires in Massachusetts are as beautiful as any sub-range in the Appalachian Mountains and at times can seem worlds away from the coast and the greater Boston region. Vermont truly is the "Green Mountain State" with dramatic forests blanketing every hillside and interesting towns sprinkled throughout. The character of the landscape varies dramatically throughout the state, from the calm Connecticut River Valley, to the remote Northeast Kingdom, to the shores of Lake Champlain and all the high peaks in between.

New Hampshire is characterized in the north by the dramatic alpine summits of the White Mountains and hikes to waterfalls that climb steeply up rocky slopes through dense forests. In the southern part of the state, a more populated and mellower landscape speaks to the coexistence of man and nature and a history of rivers as a part of an industrial heritage. Maine has a little bit of everything, but most of the waterfalls can be found in the rural central portion of the state. Far beyond the rocky coastline, Baxter State Park encompasses Mount Katahdin, the state's highest peak. This far north you really can feel the vastness and power of nature. And let's not forget Rhode Island, with one waterfall in the book, the state is worth visiting for the many attractions including hundreds of miles of beautiful coastline.

When I told people that I was working on this project, I'd often get the question, "Are there really that many waterfalls in New England?" Well, let me tell you, yes there are—and then some. In fact, there are so many waterfalls that it was difficult to choose which ones to include in this guidebook.

So how did I end up with these 101 waterfalls? First, I included the waterfalls generally accepted as the premier waterfalls in New England. But it was important that I include some lesser known waterfalls too. I looked for geographic diversity in an effort to include waterfalls that are at least a reasonable distance from most points in New England. I also included a number of waterfalls with desirable swimming holes, where you can have a good time taking a dip. As a professional photographer, I also tried to include the most photogenic waterfalls; that wasn't too difficult, as I find most waterfalls visually appealing. Being that I'm also an avid hiker, it was important that some of these hikes would provide a measure of solitude and tranquility. Finally, I made an effort to include hikes and falls that are just plain fun.

Many of the hikes in this book are perfect for children, and I think waterfalls are a great way to get your kids excited about the outdoors. There are waterslides and pools for playing in. There are rocks to climb on, and places to take great photos. As a new father myself, I look forward to sharing many of these special places with my son.

You might think that waterfalls would be more interesting either in spring after the snowmelt or after a big rain. And, in many instances, you would be correct. However, even in late summer and fall (or winter for that matter), waterfalls can be just as interesting. When the water is low, there is a much better chance that you can climb on the rocks all around the falls, as well as get up much closer to the falls, providing interesting photographic opportunities. Drier conditions usually mean the hiking is easier and less muddy, and fall in New England turns the forest into a kaleidoscope of colors, making your hike rewarding in other ways. Few waterfalls in this book are very seasonal, and most have at least some flow throughout the year.

Also note that bigger isn't always better, as many of the most beautiful waterfalls happen to be smaller falls. Sometimes a small waterfall is located in a geologically interesting location, such as an area of sculpted rocks or a deep chasm. Every hike in this book is rewarding in some way, and by visiting these waterfalls at different times of the year, you are bound to have entirely different experiences.

So be safe and have fun!

How to Use This Guide

This is by no means an exhaustive compendium of all the waterfalls in New England. However, what makes this book unique is that it is comprehensive. I have provided driving directions to each waterfall, descriptions of the falls and the hikes, and step-by-step mileage for each hike. This includes the latitude and longitude of all trailheads and most waterfalls as well. (If you don't have a GPS device, don't worry. You don't need one.)

The "specs" for each hike are listed too. These include my highly subjective "beauty" rating (Good, Very good, Excellent, and Spectacular), as well as the difficulty (again, subjective), distance, hiking time, and elevation gain. The county is listed for each hike, as well as the land status and trail contact whenever possible. I have also noted any special considerations, such as if the hike is wheelchair accessible and if there is a parking or admission fee.

Each hike, unless it is roadside, also has a map. This should be all you need to safely complete each outing. However, I have also included two more pieces of information. First are the page number and location of the waterfall in the appropriate *DeLorme Atlas & Gazetteer*. I cannot recommend these publications highly enough. If you plan on doing any driving in unfamiliar locations and want to get an idea of the terrain, surrounding features and towns, or pretty much anything else, get the appropriate atlas. There is one each for Maine, New Hampshire, Vermont, and Massachusetts and a combined atlas for Connecticut and Rhode Island. These were invaluable in my fieldwork. I have also included "other maps," which are recommended hiking maps

for the area. If you're like me, you may want to know what other trails are in the area, and the suggested topo maps will give you a good idea of the surrounding terrain. Keep in mind, though, that these are suggestions; everything you need to do these hikes is included in the book.

The overview map in the Table of Contents shows the location of each waterfall so you can see what other waterfalls may be nearby. The photos will show you the waterfalls, among other things, and will hopefully inspire you to get out there and see them for yourself. There are also a few "Tidbits" offering relevant information you may find interesting, as well as "Photography Tips"—you may want to take photos of all the wonderful places you visit.

Throughout the book I use a number of terms to describe waterfalls. I'll define a few of these terms to help you more readily ingest the information contained here. Cascades are waterfalls that consist of a series of small drops that descend at a low angle. The water is usually in contact with the rock. Horsetails are very large cascades. Plunges fall off ledge and therefore freefall away from the rock surface before reaching a pool or rock below. Block and Sheet falls are wide falls, usually wider than they are tall, and Fan falls are wider at the bottom than the top. I use Step to describe waterfalls that go from one rock outcrop to the next and generally look like they are going down steps or a staircase.

I would be remiss if I didn't note that there are many other great waterfall hikes throughout the region. I highly recommend checking out Greg Parsons and Kate Watson's website (newenglandwaterfalls.com) as well as their book *New England Waterfalls* and also Dean Goss's informative site (northeastwaterfalls.com); they will provide you with many other waterfalls to visit near the hikes in this book.

Safety and Preparation

A safe hike is an enjoyable hike. The most important thing to remember is that if you use common sense to prepare for a hike, you most likely will be just fine. Make sure to look at the weather ahead of time. If it's going to be raining, be prepared by bringing not only a rain jacket but also rain pants and a pack cover of some sort, as well as a change of clothes in case you get wet.

Hiking to and around waterfalls carries with it extra responsibilities. Never swim anywhere where you are not absolutely sure it is safe, and don't jump into the water unless you have verified that the water is deep enough. People die at waterfalls all the time, and have at many of the waterfalls listed in this book. When climbing on wet rocks, be extra careful. Remember to bring sandals or crocs if crossing a stream, as nothing is worse than hiking in wet shoes. Most of the rivers, brooks, and streams mentioned in this book are cold all year long. Bring a towel and extra layers in addition to the change of clothes.

Make sure that everyone in your party is prepared; one unprepared hiker can ruin a trip for everyone. Obviously, make sure you have the proper footwear—nothing ruins a hike more easily than blisters. Be sure you have enough water, either by bringing multiple containers on a long hike or by using purification tablets or a water filter

A viewpoint above Giant Falls provides a direct shot to the northern Presidentials (hike 77).

if you plan on refilling while out. None of the waterways covered in this guide are guaranteed to be safe to drink.

Here is a list of items to consider bringing on any hike.

❑ Backpack
❑ Hiking boots or sneakers
❑ Rain and/or wind gear
❑ Extra clothing for warmth
❑ Sunglasses
❑ Hat
❑ Water bottle
❑ Snacks
❑ Map (and possibly a compass and/or GPS device)
❑ Insect repellent
❑ Sunscreen
❑ Towel (if swimming)
❑ Mobile phone
❑ Emergency kit containing fire starter, knife, bandages, antibacterial ointment, personal medications, headlamp, and water purification tablets

Most important, especially if you are alone, make sure to let somebody know where you will be hiking and when you plan on returning. Although many of the hikes in this book are in the forest and/or are remote, many areas have good cell reception, so be sure to bring along a cell phone. Additionally, a smart phone can be used in multiple ways, including functioning as a GPS and map.

Be aware during hunting season. Make sure everyone in your party is wearing bright clothing, and put hunter's orange on any dogs. Check with state fish and wildlife divisions for specific dates, and be sure to stay on the trail when hiking during hunting season.

Leave No Trace

Leaving no trace of your passing is extremely difficult. It is made more so by repeated disregard of these principles. Most people would agree that a primary reason for going on a hike is to enjoy nature. Unfortunately, we humans adversely impact nature more than any other species, and the true natural places are becoming less numerous. In order to continue to enjoy what nature provides and to allow future hikers to enjoy it as well, along with just doing what is decent, all hikers should strive to make as little impact as possible while traveling through these natural places.

By following the basic principles listed below and using common sense, you can ensure that the places you visit will remain in their current state, however "natural" that may be.

Pack out all your trash, including biodegradable items like apple cores, which have as great an impact as other trash. When possible, pick up and remove trash that you come across.

Avoid going off the trail whenever possible. This keeps soil damage and erosion from spreading beyond the narrow route. It takes just a few hikers to create a new route, and when this becomes obvious, it turns into a trail. You'll also decrease your chances of getting poison ivy or picking up ticks by remaining on the trail.

Use outhouses and restrooms whenever possible. When it is not possible, make sure you go well away from the trail and water sources (at least 200 feet) and bury waste 6 to 8 inches deep in the soil.

Don't pick flowers or destroy wildlife, and don't remove natural objects.

Don't feed or approach wild animals.

Be courteous on the trail, allowing people moving in the opposite direction or at quicker speeds to pass. If you need to get off the trail to do this, try to stand on rocks or wood so as not to disturb the trailside plant life.

For more information visit LNT.org.

Author's Favorite Waterfalls

4 Kent Falls

9 Ender's Falls

12 Race Brook Falls

13 Bash Bish Falls

14 Wahconah Falls

18 Twin Cascade

28 Cascade Falls

35 Falls of Lana

36 Bailey Falls

41 Huntington Gorge

42 Honey Hollow Falls

45 Moss Glen Falls (Stowe)

57 Trues Ledges

62 Lost River Gorge

63 Sabbaday Falls

64 Flume Gorge / Flume Pool Loop

65 Basin-Cascade Trail Falls

68 Diana's Baths

69 Nancy Cascades

76 Appalachia Falls

78 Thoreau Falls

80 Beaver Brook Falls
   (Colebrook)

82 Bickford Slides

84 Step Falls

86 Dunn Falls

87 Angel Falls

88 Mosher Hill Falls

93 Moxie Falls

94 Gulf Hagas

Least Crowded Waterfalls

5 Wadsworth Little Falls

7 Bailey's Ravine

10 Stepstone Falls

18 Twin Cascade

28 Cascade Falls

29 Hidden Falls

36 Bailey Falls

53 Garwin Falls

69 Nancy Cascades

75 Brickett Falls

88 Mosher Hill Falls

95 Hay Brook Falls

100 Sawtelle Falls

101 Shin Falls

Most Popular Waterfalls

3 Buttermilk Falls (CT)

4 Kent Falls

5 Wadsworth Big Falls

6 Chapman Falls

9 Enders Falls

13 Bash Bish Falls

26 Hamilton Falls

27 Buttermilk Falls (VT)

31 Quechee Gorge

32 Thundering Falls

35 Falls of Lana

37 Texas Falls

38 Moss Glen Falls (Granville)

40 Bartlett Falls

45 Moss Glen Falls (Stowe)

51 Jay Branch Gorge / Four Corners

59 Livermore Falls

62 Lost River Gorge

63 Sabbaday Falls

64 Flume Gorge / Flume Pool Loop

66 Falling Waters

67 Bridal Veil Falls

68 Diana's Baths

70 Arethusa Falls

72 Glen Ellis Falls

73 Crystal Cascade (NH)

80 Beaver Brook Falls (Colebrook)

83 Screw Auger Falls

89 Smalls Falls

93 Moxie Falls

96 Big and Little Niagara Falls

Interesting Gorges / Chasms / Ravines / Geologic Formations

2 Spruce Brook Falls

8 Blackledge Falls

15 Windsor Jambs

18 Twin Cascade

19 Tannery and Parker Brook Falls

22 Royalston Falls

31 Quechee Gorge

35 Falls of Lana

37 Texas Falls

41 Huntington Gorge

43 Bolton Potholes

46 Bingham Falls

48 Sterling Falls Gorge

49 Terrill Gorge

50 Jefferson Falls / Brewster River Gorge

55 Chesterfield Gorge

57 Trues Ledges

62 Lost River Gorge

63 Sabbaday Falls

64 Flume Gorge / Flume Pool Loop

83 Screw Auger Falls

85 The Cataracts

89 Smalls Falls

94 Gulf Hagas

Roadside / Almost Roadside Falls (<0.1 mile)

4 Kent Falls

5 Wadsworth Big Falls

6 Chapman Falls

10 Stepstone Falls

14 Wahconah Falls

15 Windsor Jambs (top)

20 Doane's Falls (top)

23 Jelly Mill Falls

31 Quechee Gorge (view from bridge)

37 Texas Falls

38 Moss Glen Falls (Granville)

40 Bartlett Falls

41 Huntington Gorge

42 Honey Hollow Falls

44 Emerson Falls

46 Bingham Falls

51 Jay Branch Gorge / Four Corners

52 Big Falls

55 Chesterfield Gorge (top)

57 Trues Ledges

80 Beaver Brook Falls (Colebrook)

83 Screw Auger Falls

89 Smalls Falls

Challenging Hikes (length >3.0 miles or difficult terrain)

7 Bailey's Ravine (very short steep section at beginning of loop)

12 Race Brook Falls (vertical gain, some route-finding, steep)

13 Bash Bish Falls (route described is short but very steep)

18 Twin Cascade (climb over wall, climb over dam, roots and mud)

22 Royalston Falls (only difficult if exploring ravine below falls)

25 Lye Brook Falls (long)

28 Cascade Falls (only steep if going to base of falls)

33 Old City Falls (only difficult if going to upper falls and/or middle of stream)

35 Falls of Lana (only difficult if scrambling down south side of falls)

36 Bailey Falls (bushwhacking)

60 Waterville Cascades (fairly long)

61 Beaver Brook Cascades (Moosilauke) (steep, vertical gain)

66 Falling Waters (vertical gain, fairly long)

67 Bridal Veil Falls (fairly long, scrambling to base of falls)

69 Nancy Cascades (long, steep, vertical gain, minor bushwhacking)

70 Arethusa Falls (steep climb up from Bemis Brook, fairly long)

74 Eagle Cascade (long, steep, vertical gain)

78 Zealand and Thoreau Falls (very long)

81 Garfield Falls (only difficult if crossing stream and climbing other side)

82 Bickford Slides (difficult route-finding, some scrambling)

87 Angel Falls (numerous stream crossings, easy when dry)

91 Poplar Stream Falls (route described is long, some route-finding)

94 Gulf Hagas (long, rocky, vertical gain)

Maple leaves rest atop a rock below Ripley Falls (hike 71).

Map Legend

93	Interstate Highway	Boat Ramp	
3	US Highway	Bridge	
110	State Highway	Building/Point of Interest	
	Local Road	Campground	
	Unpaved Road	Capital	
	Railroad	Cave	
	Featured Trail	Dam	
	Trail	Gate	
	State Line	Lodging	
	Boardwalk/Steps	Parking	
	Small River or Creek	Peak/Summit	
	Intermittent Stream	Picnic Area	
	Marsh/Swamp	Rapids	
	Body of Water	Scenic View/Viewpoint	
	National Forest/Park	Town	
	National Wilderness/Preserve Area	Trailhead	
	State/County Park	Tunnel	
	Miscellaneous Park	Visitor/Information Center	
		Waterfall	

CONNECTICUT

A number of small falls are visible just above the bottom section of Bailey's Ravine (hike 7).

1 Indian Well Falls

This short, flat hike leads to a 15-foot waterfall tucked into a small circular gorge. Indian Well State Park also has a nice beach along the Housatonic River, as well as a picnic area and boat launch. The trail to the falls is part of the 9.2-mile Paugussett Trail.

Start: Parking lot on Indian Well Road
Distance: 0.3 mile out and back
Hiking time: About 15 minutes
Approximate elevation gain: 25 feet
Difficulty: Easy
Beauty: Good
County: Fairfield
Land status: Indian Well State Park
DeLorme map: Page 24, G-2

Other map: Indian Well State Park Map, www .ct.gov/deep/lib/deep/stateparks/maps/ indianwell.pdf
Trail contact: Connecticut State Parks and Forests (part of the Department of Energy and Environmental Protection); (860) 424-3000; www.ct.gov/deep/indianwell
Special considerations: Parking is free for the falls but not for the beach.

Finding the trailhead: (From CT 8) Take exit 14 in Shelton and follow CT 110 / Howe Avenue north for 2.2 miles. Turn right onto Indian Well Road, following signs for "Indian Well State Park." Park in a lot on the right in 0.4 mile.

(From I-84 near Danbury) Take exit 11 and follow signs for CT 34 East. Continue on CT 34 for 13 miles and turn right onto Bridge Street in Derby, which heads to Shelton. Across the river take CT 110 / Howe Avenue; follow this for 1.8 miles and turn right onto Indian Well Road, following signs for "Indian Well State Park." Park in a lot on the right in 0.4 mile.

The trail begins across the street and follows the stream. **GPS:** N41 20.280' / W73 07.416'

The Hike

Although the waterfall here is a single 15-foot horsetail, the gorge that encompasses the waterfall is very interesting. The falls pour into a circular pool surrounded by tall vertical walls. The trail is part of the 9.2-mile Paugussett Trail, which crosses the brook here and climbs steeply before traversing all of Indian Well State Park. There are nice views of the Housatonic River from farther along the trail.

To get to the waterfall, cross the road from the parking area. The trail begins to the left of a bridge and follows along the edge of Indian Hole Brook, reaching the falls in 0.15 mile. Return to the parking area on the same trail.

Indian Well Falls

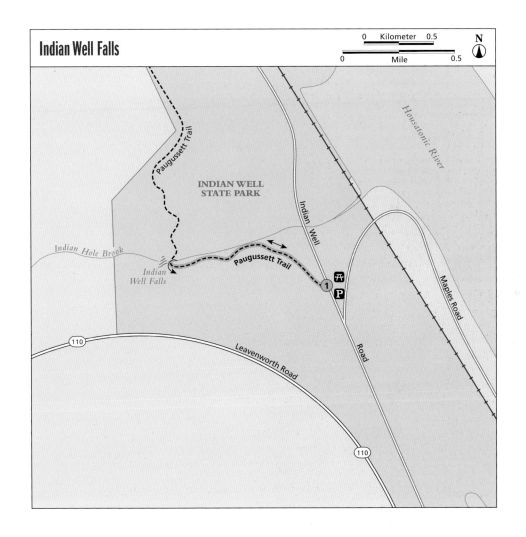

0   Kilometer   0.5

0   Mile   0.5

N

Paugussett Trail

INDIAN WELL
STATE PARK

Housatonic River

Indian Hole Brook

Indian Well Falls

Paugussett Trail

Indian Well

Maples Road

110

Leavenworth Road

Road

110

Miles and Directions

0.0 Start from the parking area. Cross the road and take the trail that starts next to the bridge and heads upstream.

0.15 Reach Indian Well Falls (N41 20.319' / W73 07.587'). Return the way you came.

0.3 Arrive back at the parking area.

Although the waterfall at Indian Well Falls isn't huge, the surrounding rock walls create an interesting moss-coated cavernous pool.

2 Spruce Brook Falls

This short hike follows a cool mossy stream through the Spruce Brook Ravine in a forest filled with towering trees, where a number of falls, the largest at 15 feet, tumble into pools of various shapes and sizes.

Start: Clearing at left fork at end of Cold Spring Road
Distance: 1.0 mile out and back
Hiking time: About 20 minutes
Approximate elevation gain: 200 feet
Difficulty: Easy
Beauty: Excellent
County: New Haven
Land status: Naugatuck State Forest

DeLorme map: Page 33, L-17 & L-18 (unmarked)
Other map: Naugatuck State Forest Map, ct.gov/deep/lib/deep/stateparks/maps/ NaugatuckEastWestBlocksTrailMap.pdf
Trail contact: Connecticut State Parks and Forests (part of the Department of Energy and Environmental Protection); (860) 424-3000; www.ct.gov/deep/stateparks

Finding the trailhead: (From the north) Take exit 24 off CT 8, 8 miles south of Waterbury. Turn right onto North Main Street then take the first right onto Depot Street. After crossing a bridge, turn right onto Lopus Road and in 0.1 mile turn right onto Cold Spring Road, which becomes a rough dirt road. Travel for 1 mile; bear left at the fork and park in a clearing at the end of the road.

(From the south) Take exit 23 off CT 8, 8 miles north of Derby. Turn right onto CT 42 / South Main Street; follow this for 1 mile and turn left onto Depot Street. After crossing a bridge, turn right onto Lopus Road. In 0.1 mile turn right onto Cold Spring Road, which becomes a rough dirt road. Travel for 1 mile; bear left at the fork and park in a clearing at the end of the road. **GPS:** N41 27.318' / W73 03.801'

The Hike

The falls here are nice, but the cool ravine with its steep walls, giant boulders, and moss-covered walls makes this area worth a visit even when the water is low. Do note, however, that in late summer or times of extended dry periods, the falls all but disappear.

From the parking area, take the trail that heads down to the right. This will curve around to the left as it begins heading upstream in the ravine. At 0.25 mile, you will reach the largest waterfall, a 15 foot plunge. Travel for another quarter mile, passing by multiple cascades, some of which are split by one or more boulders. Return back to the parking on the same trail.

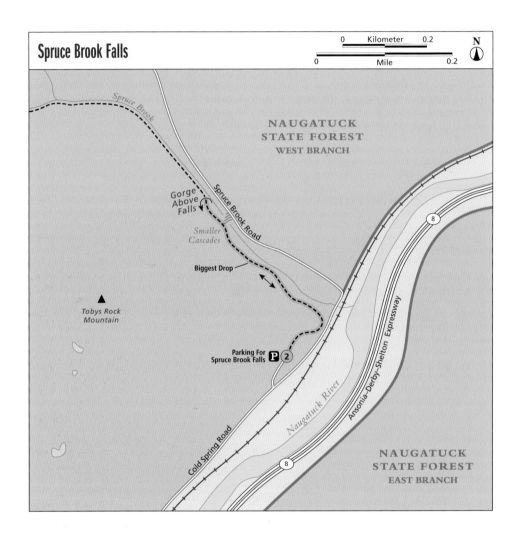

Spruce Brook Falls

0   Kilometer   0.2

0   Mile   0.2

N

Spruce Brook

NAUGATUCK
STATE FOREST
WEST BRANCH

Gorge
Above
Falls

Spruce Brook Road

*Smaller
Cascades*

Biggest Drop

▲
*Tobys Rock
Mountain*

8

Ansonia-Derby-Shelton Expressway

**Parking For
Spruce Brook Falls** 🅿 ②

Naugatuck River

Cold Spring Road

8

NAUGATUCK
STATE FOREST
EAST BRANCH

Spruce Brook flows through a narrow canyon filled with round eroded rocks almost entirely covered by moss.

Miles and Directions

0.0 Start at the parking area and take the trail down to the right. It will curve around a bend and begin following the ravine to the northeast.

0.25 Reach the 15-foot plunge waterfall, the largest in the ravine.

0.5 Arrive at a pool farther up the ravine, where the terrain becomes less rugged and more of a traditional brook through a forest. Return the way you came. (**Option:** Continue on to explore more of the ravine.)

1.0 Arrive back at the parking area.

3 Buttermilk Falls

Buttermilk Falls consist of a series of falls, pools, and cascades located just yards from a road, yet invite visitors to explore up and down the stream through a beautiful forest filled with rocky ledges. The largest falls is 55 feet.

Start: Parking on right (south) side of Lane Hill Road
Distance: 0.2 to 0.6 mile out and back, depending on how much exploring you do
Hiking time: About 5 minutes (or more)
Approximate elevation gain: 0 to 200 feet, depending on how much you explore
Difficulty: Easy to moderate
Beauty: Very good
County: Litchfield

Land status: Owned by The Nature Conservancy; Mattatuck Trail maintained by Connecticut Forest and Park Association
DeLorme map: Page 33, A-21 (marked)
Other maps: None
Trail contact: Connecticut Forest and Park Association; (860) 346-2372; ctwoodlands .org; e-mail: info@ctwoodlands.org
Special considerations: Parking is tight, but there are numerous spots along Lane Hill Road.

Finding the trailhead: (From the south) From Waterbury, take CT 8 North for 3.6 miles and take exit 37. Follow signs for CT 262 East as it makes a number of turns. After about 2.5 miles from CT 8, turn right onto Greystone Road / Waterbury Road and follow this for 3.1 miles. Turn left onto South Main Street; in a few hundred feet turn right onto Lane Hill Road. There will be a number of small parking spots on the right, with the best one about halfway up the hill. All spots provide access to the falls.

(From the north) On US 6, 0.5 mile west of the intersection with CT 72, turn south onto South Main Street in Terryville. Follow this for 2.6 miles and turn left onto Lane Hill Road. There will be a number of small parking spots on the right, with the best one about halfway up the hill. All spots provide access to the falls. **GPS:** N41 38.687' / W73 00.442'

The Hike

As long as there is a good amount of water flowing, there is no doubt you will be impressed by the 55-foot waterfall here. There are many other plunges and cascades here as well. Even if the water is low, the hemlock forest, shimmering pools, and moss-covered rocks make this feel like another world. Unfortunately, some people have spray-painted a number of the rocks, detracting somewhat from the beauty here.

From the parking lot, head straight into the woods, following a trail with blue rectangle blazes over a small bridge. (This is a small section of the longer Mattatuck Trail.) In a few hundred feet you will be at the top of the main falls. A short steep trail leads down to the bottom, and you can continue to explore both above and below the main falls. Return on the same trail.

Miles and Directions

0.0 Start from the parking spot along the road and follow the blue-blazed trail over a small bridge.

0.05 Reach the top of the falls. Head down to the bottom for the best view.

0.1 Reach the bottom of the falls. Return the way you came. (*Option:* Spend some time exploring!)

0.2 Arrive back at your parking spot.

Above Buttermilk falls, small pools reflect the late day sun.

4 Kent Falls

Although located at a popular roadside picnic area, these falls are not to be missed. A partially paved path leads to numerous excellent views of the falls as they tumble 250 feet down a steep hillside in waterfalls of all shapes and sizes.

Start: Covered bridge next to the parking lot on US 7

Distance: 0.8 mile out and back

Hiking time: About 30 minutes

Approximate elevation gain: 300 feet

Difficulty: Easy to moderate

Beauty: Excellent

County: Litchfield

Land status: Kent Falls State Park

DeLorme map: Page 40, E-8 & E-9 (state park marked)

Other map: Kent Falls State Park Map, www .ct.gov/deep/lib/deep/stateparks/maps/ kentgis.pdf

Trail contact: Connecticut State Parks and Forests (part of the Department of Energy and Environmental Protection); (860) 424-3000; www.ct.gov/kentfalls

Special considerations: No swimming or alcohol allowed; parking fees are charged on the weekends.

Finding the trailhead: Kent Falls State Park is located on US 7, 5.1 miles north of the town of Kent and the intersection with CT 341. It is 21 miles south of North Canaan and the intersection with US 44. There is a large parking lot on the east side of the road with a sign for "Kent Falls State Park." The paved trail begins at the covered bridge next to the parking lot. **GPS:** N41 46.605'/W73 25.007'

The Hike

Kent and Enders Falls are the two waterfall hikes in Connecticut that should be at the top of your list. Here the falls drop 250 feet. There are wide horsetails, narrow plunges, and examples of block and fan falls as well. As soon as you pull into the parking area, you will be impressed. A nice maintained footpath parallels the brook, and there are plenty of great viewpoints along the way. Be sure to hike to the top to get the whole experience. With picnic tables and a giant field for playing, this is a great place to spend some time and enjoy a picnic lunch.

From the parking area, follow the paved path through the small covered bridge. You will see the bottom half of the falls ahead, with beautiful examples of block falls. Continue following the paved path as it winds up along the side of the brook, eventually becoming a dirt path partway up. The trail is graded, but a decent climb, so take your time and stop at all the viewpoints. At the top is a great example of a two-tiered plunge. Return back down the same trail.

Kent Falls

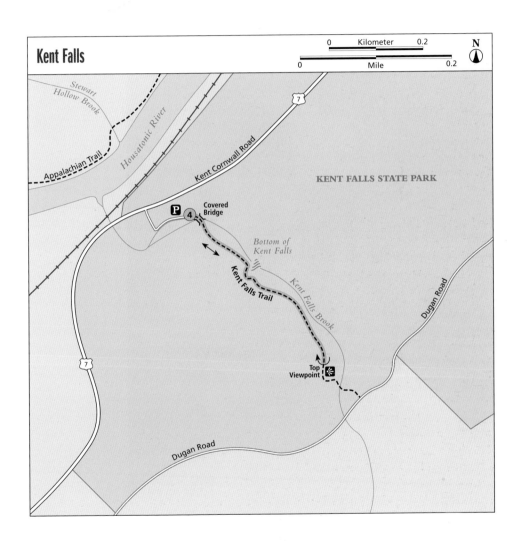

0   Kilometer   0.2

0   Mile   0.2

N

Stewart Hollow Brook

Housatonic River

Appalachian Trail

Kent Cornwall Road

KENT FALLS STATE PARK

7

P 4 Covered Bridge

Bottom of Kent Falls

Kent Falls Trail

Kent Falls Brook

Dugan Road

7

Top Viewpoint

Dugan Road

Miles and Directions

0.0 Start on the paved path and go through the covered bridge.

0.1 Arrive at the bottom of Kent Falls. Continue following the paved path up to the right. It becomes dirt partway up.

0.4 Reach the top of the falls. Return the way you came.

0.8 Arrive back at the parking area.

From the bottom of Kent Falls, the three large sheet falls are easily visible as they pour from one pool to the next.

5 Wadsworth Big and Little Falls

Wadsworth Big Falls, which is almost roadside, is a high-volume single-drop block waterfall, and the mellow hike to the much taller Wadsworth Little Falls makes this two-for-one well worth the visit.

Start: Parking lot on Cherry Hill Road
Distance: 1.75 miles out and back (to both falls)
Hiking time: About 1 hour
Approximate elevation gain: 150 feet
Difficulty: Easy to moderate
Beauty: Excellent
County: Middlesex
Land status: Wadsworth Falls State Park

DeLorme map: Page 35, H-16
Other map: Wadsworth Falls State Park Map, www.ct.gov/deep/lib/deep/stateparks/maps/wadsworth.pdf
Trail contact: Connecticut State Parks and Forests (part of the Department of Energy and Environmental Protection); (860) 424-3000; www.ct.gov/deep/wadsworthfalls

Finding the trailhead: Take exit 16 off CT 9 and follow CT 66 West, turning right onto Washington Street from Main Street. Continue about 1.3 miles and turn left onto CT 157, which turns from West Street into Middlefield Street into Forest Street. After going 2.5 miles and passing the first entrance to Wadsworth Falls State Park, turn left onto Cherry Hill Road; there's a parking lot just up on the left. **GPS:** N41 31.573' / W72 41.813'

The Hike

Wadsworth Big Falls is a large 25-foot block waterfall with a large volume of water all year long. A giant pool sits below the falls, and at the far side of this pool there is a big rock overhang. Wadsworth Little Falls is on a seasonal stream, but it is much more secluded and significantly taller than its big brother.

From the parking area, head down the trail to Wadsworth Big Falls, which is just a few hundred feet away. There is a pool that you can wade in below the falls, and a little fenced-in pathway leads to the top of the falls. Walk through the open field above to return to the parking area.

For Wadsworth Little Falls, start at the parking area and follow the road south as it crosses the bridge. Continue along this road, crossing the railroad tracks, and look for a trailhead on the left about 75 yards past the tracks. As you enter the woods, there will be an info board on your right and a trail coming in from the right. Follow the wide, flat path straight ahead.

Stay on this trail for 0.5 mile and then turn left onto a short steep spur trail to the base of Wadsworth Little Falls. Return along the same trail.

Wadsworth Big and Little Falls

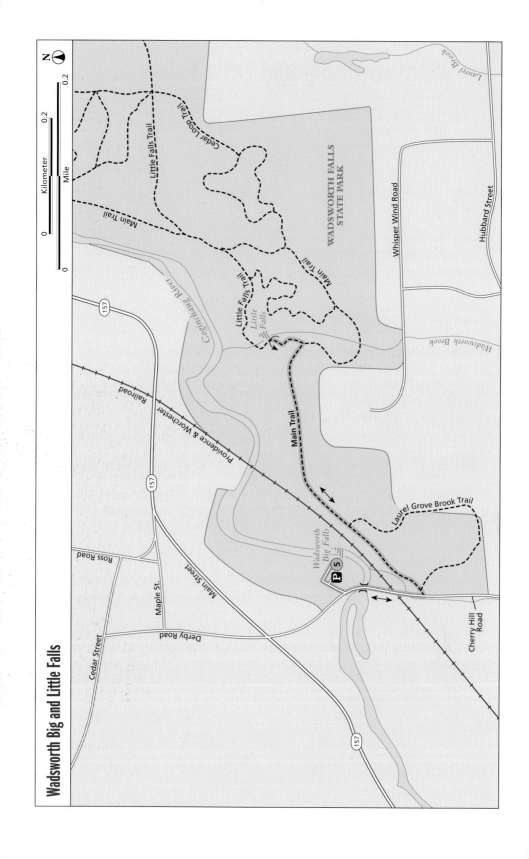

Miles and Directions

0.0 Start at the parking area and head down the path to Wadsworth Big Falls.

0.1 Reach Wadsworth Big Falls (N41 31.587'/W72 41.747'). Return to the parking on the path or through the field.

0.2 Reach the parking area. Head south over the bridge and railroad tracks along Cherry Hill Road.

0.4 Turn left onto the trail for Wadsworth Little Falls.

0.9 Turn left onto a steep spur trail down to Wadsworth Little Falls.

0.95 Reach the bottom of Wadsworth Little Falls (N41 31.675'/W72 41.345'). Return the way you came.

1.75 Arrive back at the parking area.

A man fishes below Wadsworth Big Falls.

PHOTOGRAPHY TIP: USING A LONG SHUTTER SPEED

When you see photographs in which flowing water looks like smooth white curves and lines, such as the photo of Wadsworth Big Falls below, they are due to a long shutter speed. Leaving the shutter open a little longer allows the light reflected off the water as it moves to create a streak. The longer the shutter speed, the smoother and more elongated the white lines become. The length of time the shutter needs to be open depends on multiple factors, including how close you are to the water and how fast the water is moving.

To get the effect, make sure to (1) use a tripod, (2) use a small aperture (the higher the number, the smaller the aperture), and (3) use the lowest ISO on your camera. Ideally, use a timer or remote release so that you don't shake the camera when touching the shutter button. If it is really bright, even with a small aperture the shutter speed may not be long enough. In that case you will need to use a neutral density filter. This is basically a darkening filter that you put over your lens to keep light out, requiring you to increase the length of time your shutter is open.

A good starting exposure time for reasonably fast-moving water is at least ½ second.

The many small ledges in Wadsworth Big Falls, when taken out of context, create a multitude of wispy shapes that catch the small pockets of sunlight filtered through the canopy.

6 Chapman Falls

This roadside falls inside 860-acre Devil's Hopyard State Park drops over 50 feet, making a great place for a picnic lunch and, in low water, a fun place to explore. The state park also offers hiking, fishing, and camping opportunities.

Start: Across road from parking lot near park entrance
Distance: 0.2 mile out and back
Hiking time: About 5 minutes
Approximate elevation gain: 75 feet
Difficulty: Easy
Beauty: Excellent
County: Middlesex
Land status: Devil's Hopyard State Park
DeLorme map: Page 37, J & K-13 (marked as Devil's Hopyard)

Other map: Devil's Hopyard State Park Map, www.ct.gov/deep/lib/deep/stateparks/maps/devilshopyard.pdf
Trail contact: Connecticut State Parks and Forests; (860) 424-3000; www.ct.gov/deep/devilshopyard
Special considerations: Devil's Hopyard State Park is open from April 1 to December 1. Dogs must be leashed.

Finding the trailhead: (From CT 9) Take exit 7 and follow signs for CT 82 East for 5.5 miles. After merging with CT 151, take an immediate left onto CT 434/Mt. Parnassus Road. Follow this for 6 miles and turn right onto Hopyard Road, following signs to "Devil's Hopyard State Park" where in 0.7 mile you will turn left onto Foxtown Road and park in the parking lot on the left.

(From I-395) Take exit 80 onto CT 82 West. Follow this for 13.5 miles; turn right onto Hopyard Road and follow signs to "Devil's Hopyard State Park." In 3.5 miles turn right onto Foxtown Road and park in the lot on the left.

The falls are clearly marked and are located near the entrance to the campground, across from the parking lot. **GPS:** N41 29.080'/W72 20.522'

The Hike

Chapman Falls is a beautiful 60-foot block style waterfall with three distinct drops. It is a very popular waterfall in a state park that has a lot of other recreational opportunities. The falls contain a number of potholes, which were formed as rocks fell into the depressions and were swirled around, carving the depressions deeper and deeper over many years.

The waterfall is just across the street from the parking area. You can look down from above and then take a nice graded path down to the bottom. On the other side of the falls from the path, you can clamber out on rocks above the falls.

There are a number of stories as to the origin of the name "Devil's Hopyard," but the most commonly cited revolves around Satan. As the tale goes, Satan was upset that he got his tail wet while heading down the river, so as he climbed up the falls, he stamped his hot hooves into the rock, leaving the pothole depressions.

Miles and Directions

0.0   Start from the parking area, cross the street, and take the obvious trail to the bottom of the falls.

0.1   Reach the bottom of the falls. Return the way you came.

0.2   Arrive back at the parking area.

In low water, Chapman Falls becomes a collection of smaller drops along the rocky ledges.

7 Bailey's Ravine

This hike takes you on a short loop through The Nature Conservancy's Ayers Gap Preserve. You'll travel through a beautiful forest, over a cool stream, and end at a small ravine where a few small falls cascade through a tight gap with steep walls.

Start: Parking on north side of CT 207 at "Bailey's Ravine at Ayers Gap—The Nature Conservancy" sign
Distance: 1.6-mile loop
Hiking time: About 1 hour
Approximate elevation gain: 300 feet
Difficulty: Moderate
Beauty: Good
County: New London
Land status: Protected preserve managed by The Nature Conservancy

DeLorme map: Page 38, A-1 (marked as "Ayers Gap")
Other maps: None
Trail contact: The Nature Conservancy; (203) 568-6270; www.nature.org/ourinitiatives/regions/northamerica/unitedstates/connecticut/placesweprotect/ayers-gap-preserve.xml; e-mail: ct@tnc.org
Special considerations: There is a small amount of road walking at the end of the loop.

Finding the trailhead: From exit 83 on I-395, follow CT 97 North for 3.1 miles into the town of Baltic. Turn left onto CT 207 and follow this west for 3.4 miles. The parking area is on the right, 0.1 mile after the second Ayer Road intersection. The trail begins near a sign for "Bailey's Ravine at Ayers Gap—The Nature Conservancy." **GPS:** N41 37.996' / W72 08.275'

The Hike

This serene walk in the woods ends with a beautiful cascade surrounded by moss-covered rocks. The only strenuous part of this hike is at the very beginning, and it is very short-lived.

Head up the trail that leaves directly from the parking area. This section is steep and requires scrambling over large rocks and roots. At the top of this climb, you will be rewarded with a nice outlook with views to the local hills. Continue to follow this trail as it winds through a beautiful hemlock forest. You will notice that there is not much of an understory, a characteristic of hemlock groves.

Continue climbing at a much more gradual pace for 0.5 mile then, as you descend, cross Bailey Brook. There is a nice little cascade here. After crossing the brook, you will climb for another 0.1 mile until you hit a junction. Turn right and follow this trail to the south as it levels off and then descends, passing near what appears to be a logging site before quickly tucking back into the woods as you near Bailey Brook again.

At 1.3 miles you reach a short spur down the brook and Ayers Falls. Suddenly the ravine gets rugged as a 6- to 8-foot plunge is quickly followed by a similarly sized

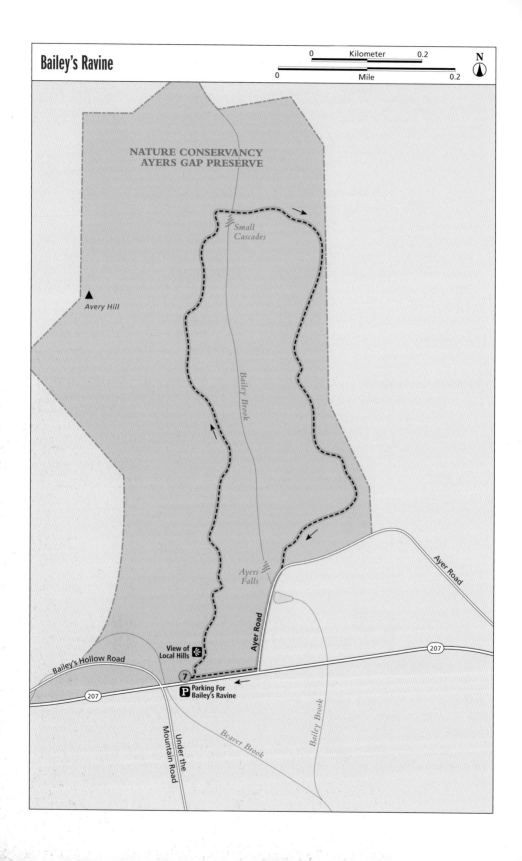

Bailey's Ravine

NATURE CONSERVANCY
AYERS GAP PRESERVE

Small
Cascades

▲
Avery Hill

Bailey Brook

Ayers
Falls

View of
Local Hills

Ayer Road

Ayer Road

207

Bailey's Hollow Road

7

P Parking For
Bailey's Ravine

207

Under the
Mountain Road

Beaver Brook

Bailey Brook

N

0   Kilometer   0.2

0   Mile   0.2

cascade. It pours over moss–covered rocks and lands in a little pool that is flanked by tall, smooth rock walls. Just below the falls are two plaques fixed on a rock, which you will see as you pop out onto Ayer Road. Head right on the road and in 0.1 mile turn right onto CT 207; walk along the road to the parking area, just ahead on the right.

Miles and Directions

0.0   Start clockwise on the white-blazed trail, directly up a steep hill from the parking area.

0.1   Reach a viewpoint. Continue along this trail.

0.7   Arrive at a small cascade and cross Bailey Brook.

0.8   At a trail junction, turn right and follow the trail to the south.

1.3   Reach Ayers Falls (N41 38.128' / W72 08.154').

1.4   Turn right onto Ayer Road; follow this to CT 207.

1.5   Turn right onto CT 207.

1.6   Arrive back at the parking area.

A small cascade flows down through the bottom of Bailey's Ravine.

8 Blackledge Falls

Blackledge Falls is a cool series of two to three waterfalls that usually only flow during periods of high water. These beautiful plunges, the highest of which is almost 30 feet, fall over a semicircular ledge.

Start: Far (narrow) end of parking lot on CT 94/Hebron Avenue
Distance: 0.7 mile out and back
Hiking time: About 30 minutes
Approximate elevation gain: 100 feet
Difficulty: Easy
Beauty: Very good
County: Hartford
Land status: Owned and managed by Town of Glastonbury

DeLorme map: Page 45, J-18 (unmarked)
Other map: Town of Glastonbury Blackledge Falls Trail System, www.glasct.org/Modules/ShowDocument.aspx?documentid=4777
Trail contact: Town of Glastonbury Parks and Recreation Department; (860) 652-7679; glasct.org/index.aspx?page=184
Special considerations: This hike is better in spring; by midsummer, low flow turns these falls into a trickle. Dogs must be leashed.

Finding the trailhead: From exit 8 off CT 2, which is just southeast of Hartford, take CT 94/Hebron Avenue east for 7.6 miles. Look for a parking area and "Blackledge Falls" sign on the left. Parking is down a very short drive; the trailhead is located at the far end of the lot. **GPS:** N41 41.844'/W72 27.341'

The Hike

The best time to visit these falls is after a period of rain, when three falls plunge over a semicircular vertical ledge. Regardless of flow, Blackledge Falls is a unique formation accessed by a short, pleasant hike.

Begin the hike on the unmarked trail that leaves from the northwest edge (the far narrow end) of the parking area. After 0.1 mile go left at the junction with the blue-and-white-blazed trail. At 0.3 mile you reach another trail junction. Stay left; do the same in a few hundred feet as the blue-blazed trail comes in from the right. Blackledge Falls is just a few hundred feet beyond this, down a short decline.

The middle falls is an almost 30-foot plunge, but after a dry spell you may just find a fine trickle. The dark wall of the ledge is covered in moss and shrouded by the forest canopy. Head back the way you came to return to the parking area.

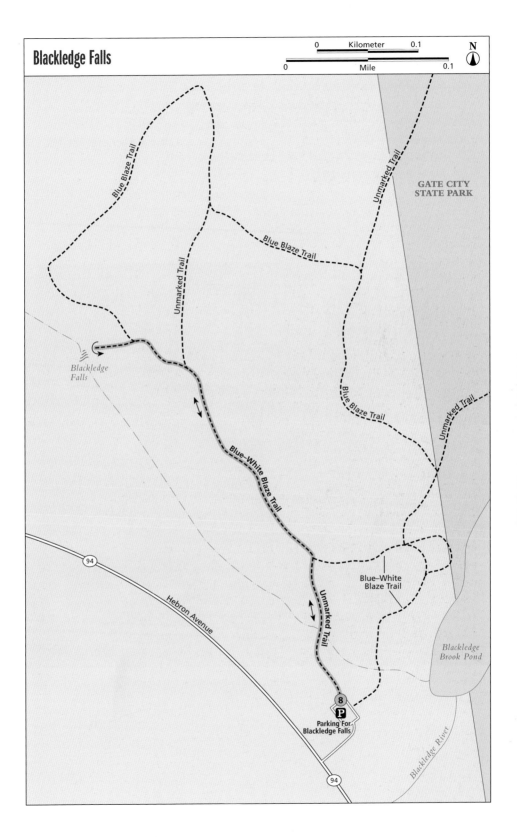

Blackledge Falls

0 Kilometer 0.1

0 Mile 0.1

N

GATE CITY
STATE PARK

Blue Blaze Trail

Unmarked Trail

Blue Blaze Trail

Blue Blaze Trail

Unmarked Trail

Blackledge
Falls

Blue–White Blaze Trail

94

Blue–White
Blaze Trail

Hebron Avenue

Unmarked Trail

Blackledge
Brook Pond

8
P
Parking For
Blackledge Falls

94

Blackledge River

Miles and Directions

0.0 Start on the unmarked trail that leaves from the far (narrow) end of the parking lot.

0.1 Go left at the junction with the blue-and-white-blazed trail.

0.3 Stay left as an unmarked trail comes in from the right.

0.35 Stay left as the blue-blazed trail comes in from the right, and arrive at Blackledge Falls just below (N41 42.043'/W72 27.524'). Return the way you came.

0.7 Arrive back at the parking lot.

Even in low water, the vertical wall of Blackledge Falls provides a unique geology.

9 Enders Falls

With five distinct waterfalls in less than half a mile from your car, don't be surprised if you end up spending more time here than you planned. These waterfalls are beautiful in any season but may be crowded on the weekend. Highly recommended!

Start: Parking lot at "Enders State Forest" sign on CT 219/Barkhamsted Road
Distance: 0.8 mile out and back (with spurs/excursions)
Hiking time: About 30 minutes (But plan for more!)
Approximate elevation gain: 150 feet
Difficulty: Easy
Beauty: Spectacular

County: Hartford
Land status: Enders State Forest
DeLorme map: Page 52, F-5 (unmarked)
Other maps: None
Trail contact: Connecticut State Parks and Forests; (860) 424-3000; www.ct.gov/deep/stateparks
Special considerations: The falls may be crowded on weekends.

Finding the trailhead: From the town of Granby on US 202/CT 10, follow US 20 West for 3.6 miles. Turn left onto CT 219/Barkhamsted Road and look for a parking lot and sign for "Enders State Forest" on the left in 1.3 miles. **GPS:** N41 57.296'/W72 52.727'

The Hike

If you are visiting waterfalls in Connecticut, Enders Falls should be at the top of your list. A truly stunning collection of five distinct falls, all of which are accessible in a 1.0-mile hike, make this a must-see destination.

The fourth waterfall (counting from upstream) is surrounded on all sides by rock walls.

From the parking area, head down the obvious trail. In a few hundred feet, just as the trail curves to the left, a short spur trail heads down to the river on your right. This will take you to the uppermost falls, a nice 6-foot cascade. Head back to the main trail and continue a few hundred yards to another spur trail on the right. Head down to the brook, where you will be at the top of the third waterfall. Cross the brook here and head up the other side a few yards to reach a great view of the second falls. Here the water plunges through a gap, falling over 25 feet as water behind the plunge crosses under it and cascades into the pool.

Head back downstream, bypassing where you crossed, to get a good view of the third waterfall, which drops about 20 feet. The water here pours over the lip of a flat ledge, lands on another ledge below that slants down to the right, and finally cascades into the big pool below. There is also a small cascade just a few feet below the pool.

Enders Falls

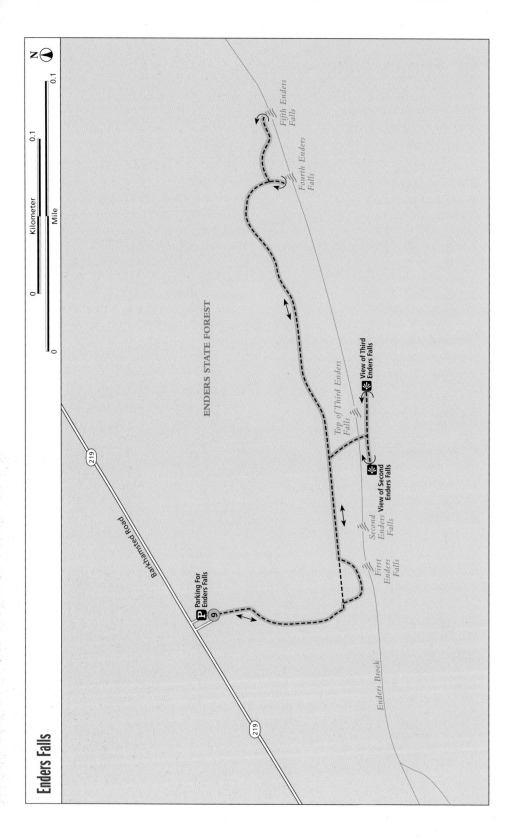

Kilometer
0   0.1   0.1

Mile

N

219

Barkhamsted Road

Parking For
Enders Falls
P
9

ENDERS STATE FOREST

First
Enders
Falls

Second
Enders
Falls

View of Second
Enders Falls

Top of Third Enders
Falls

View of Third
Enders Falls

Fourth Enders
Falls

Fifth Enders
Falls

Enders Brook

219

Cross the brook and head back up to the trail. From the main trail, head 0.1 mile farther and look for another short spur on your right to the fourth falls. This waterfall plunges off a vertical ledge, hits a moss-covered bench below, and cascades into a pool that is surrounded on all sides by rock walls.

Back on the trail, the spur for the fifth falls is just a few hundred feet below. It heads to the brook slightly downstream from these lowest falls and switchbacks up toward the bottom of the falls. This final set of falls is composed of a plunge through a narrow notch that lands on a ledge, spreads out, and plunges again to the pool below. Head back up the main trail to the parking area.

Miles and Directions

- **0.0** Start at the parking area and head down the trail.
- **0.1** Reach the spur trail on the right to the uppermost falls. Head down to the brook and then back up to the main trail.
- **0.15** From the main trail, a spur trail leads to the top of the third falls, where you can cross and get a great view of the second falls. Stay on this side of the brook to get a view from below of the third falls as well. Return to the main trail.
- **0.3** Head downstream to a spur to the fourth falls. Return to the main trail.
- **0.4** Reach the final spur to the fifth falls.
- **0.45** Arrive at the fifth (lowest) falls. Return along the main trail.
- **0.8** Arrive back at the parking area.

The second waterfall (counting from upstream) pours through a notch in the rock as smaller cascades flow behind it.

Rhode Island

Stepstone Falls shows that waterfalls don't have to be big to be beautiful.

10 Stepstone Falls

Stepstone Falls is a set of small falls, the largest only 3 feet tall, that flow over wide flat ledges, creating beautiful curtains that step down a short section of the Wood River.

Start: Parking on south side of Falls River Road near small bridge
Distance: 0.1 mile out and back
Hiking time: About 5 minutes
Approximate elevation gain: 20 feet
Difficulty: Easy
Beauty: Very good
County: Kent
Land status: Arcadia Management Area (protected recreational area managed by the State of Rhode Island Division of Parks & Recreation)
DeLorme map: Page 70, C-3 (marked)
Other maps: None
Trail contact: Forest Environment Headquarters; (401) 539-2356; www.riparks.com/Locations/LocationArcadia.html
Special considerations: The road may be closed in winter; call the trail contact to make sure you can get there.

Finding the trailhead: From I-95 take exit 5B and turn onto RI 102 North. Follow this for 3.8 miles; turn left onto Plain Meeting House Road and continue 3.9 miles. Cross Plain Road to go straight (a slight left) onto Liberty Hill Road, which intersects Hudson Pond Road. Go left and follow this for 1.1 miles before turning right onto Falls River Road. Parking is on the left in 0.6 mile, just after you cross a small bridge over Wood River. **GPS:** N41 36.755' / W71 45.639'

The drop isn't big, but the formation of the ledges over which Stepstone Falls flows are unlike any other waterfall in this book.

The Hike

From the parking area, follow the obvious trail down to the falls, which are only a few hundred feet away. *Note:* It is possible to make this into a short hike and overnight by following the River Trail beyond Stepstone Falls for 0.3 mile to a small overnight shelter and camping area called the Stepstone Falls Backpacking Area. The Ben Utter Trail continues farther downstream for another mile as well. Return back to the parking up the same trail.

Miles and Directions

0.0 Start at the parking area and head down along the brook to the falls.

0.05 Reach Stepstone Falls. Return the way you came.

0.1 Arrive back at the parking area.

MASSACHUSETTS

The upper view provides a bird's-eye look at Royalston Falls (hike 22).

11 Campbell Falls

This is a picturesque waterfall even in low flow. You'll park in Massachusetts, walk into Connecticut, and return to Massachusetts, all in about 5 minutes.

Start: Parking area on Campbell Falls Road next to "Campbells Falls" sign
Distance: 0.4 mile out and back
Hiking time: About 20 minutes
Approximate elevation gain: 100 feet
Difficulty: Easy to moderate
Beauty: Excellent
County: Berkshire
Land status: Campbell Falls State Park (Connecticut)

DeLorme map: Page 44, M-11 & M-12 (marked)
Other maps: None
Trail contact: Campbell Falls State Park Reserve; (860) 424-3200; www.ct.gov/deep/cwp/view.asp?a=2716&q=325308; e-mail, deep.stateparks@ct.gov

Finding the trailhead: From the intersection of US 44 and US 7 (Elm Street) in North Canaan, Connecticut, take US 44 East for 2.8 miles then turn left onto Canaan Valley Road. Take this into Massachusetts; at 3 miles turn right to stay on Canaan Valley Road. In about 0.1 mile the road splits. Stay straight/right onto Campbell Falls Road. Keep an eye out for parking just off the road on the right after 1.3 miles, where there should be a sign just after crossing over a small river.
GPS: N42 02.710' / W73 13.912'

The Hike

This waterfall could easily have been included in the Connecticut section instead; in fact, the trail contact is the Connecticut state park system. However, since the falls actually are in Massachusetts, they have been included here. Campbell falls is a beautiful 50-foot waterfall that is made up of plunges and cascades. The water pours into a tight notch, lands on some rocks, and cascades into a small pool before making a right turn and falling in a small cascade at the bottom.

If you're careful, you can get a nice view from the middle of the gorge below Campbell Falls.

From the parking area you will see a large sign with an arrow pointing to the falls. Head down the obvious trail, descending about 150 feet in 0.2 mile. You first head southwest, crossing the border into Connecticut, then turn northwest and cross back into Massachusetts. Return using the same trail.

Campbell Falls

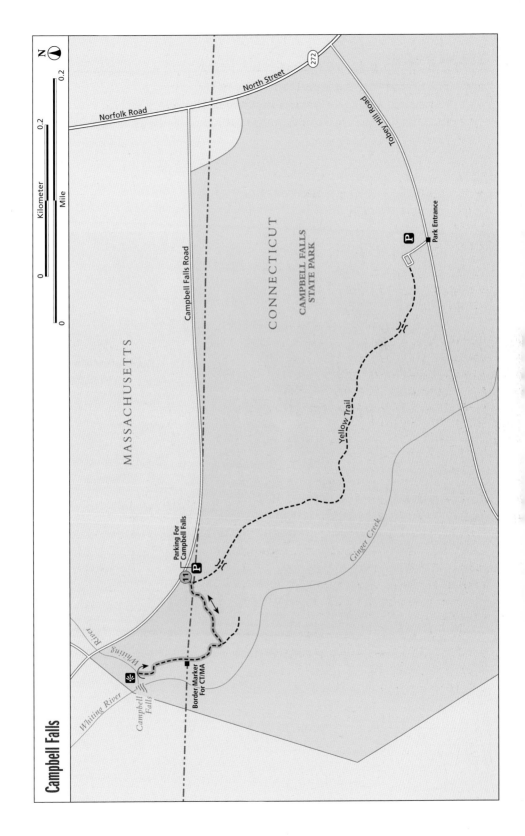

MASSACHUSETTS

CONNECTICUT

CAMPBELL FALLS
STATE PARK

Whiting River

Campbell Falls

Whiting River

Border Marker
For CT/MA

Parking For
Campbell Falls

Campbell Falls Road

Norfolk Road

North Street

272

Tobey Hill Road

Park Entrance

Yellow Trail

Ginger Creek

Kilometer

Mile

0   0.2   0.2

N

Miles and Directions

0.0 Start at the parking area and head down the obvious trail.

0.1 Pass a marker signifying the Massachusetts–Connecticut border.

0.2 Reach Campbell Falls (N42 02.740' / W73 13.994'). Return the way you came.

0.4 Arrive back at the parking area.

Campbell Falls is a beautiful waterfall that pours into a short but narrow gorge right on the Connecticut/Massachusetts line.

12 Race Brook Falls

Race Brook Falls is actually a series of falls that drop for hundreds of feet. The largest falls is at the bottom, but cascades and other falls extend well above the lowermost. The hike described here goes to the bottom and top of the falls, requiring some backtracking.

Start: Parking area on MA 41 South/South Undermountain Road, just north of the intersection with Salisbury Road
Distance: 2.8-mile lollipop with spur to lower falls (both upper and lower falls)
Hiking time: About 2 hours for both falls
Approximate elevation gain: 1,200 feet
Difficulty: Moderate to lower falls; more difficult to upper falls
Beauty: Spectacular
County: Berkshire
Land status: Mount Everett State Reservation
DeLorme map: Page 43, J-30 (marked)

Other map: Mount Everett State Reservation hiking trail map, www.mass.gov/eea/docs/dcr/parks/trails/mwashington.pdf
Trail contact: Mount Everett State Reservation; (413) 528-0330; www.mass.gov/eea/agencies/dcr/massparks/region-west/mt-everett-state-reservation-generic.html
Special considerations: Even though the top of the lower falls is only a scant distance from the base, you'll need to head back down to get back to the trail that leads to the upper falls. You can follow the trail farther up to the Appalachian Trail and to the summit of Mount Everett.

Finding the trailhead: From US 7 in Sheffield (6 miles south of Great Barrington, Massachusetts, and 10.8 miles north of North Canaan, Connecticut), head west on Berkshire School Road. Follow this for 2.8 miles then turn left onto MA 41 South/South Undermountain Road. The parking area is on the right in 1.3 miles, just before the intersection with Salisbury Road. **GPS:** N42 05.371'/W73 24.675'

The Hike

Before beginning this hike, please note that the trail network here is a little confusing. The route described here takes you to the bottom of the lowermost falls and then backtracks a bit to visit the upper falls. There is a way to visit the lower falls without backtracking as much, but the trail is hard to find and not well marked—as well as being steep—so the route provided here is recommended.

From the parking area, follow the Race Brook Trail into the woods to the left. You gradually climb until at 0.3 mile you reach a junction with a sign pointing right to the lower falls and left to the upper falls. The view from the bottom of the lower falls should not be missed, so take the right fork. The trail is fairly gradual, with a slightly steeper and rockier section before reaching the bottom of the falls at 0.8 mile. Of all the falls on Race Brook, this is the most spectacular, and the hike to this point would be a rewarding shorter day hike. The combined drop of this bottom set of falls is over 100 feet!

Race Brook Falls

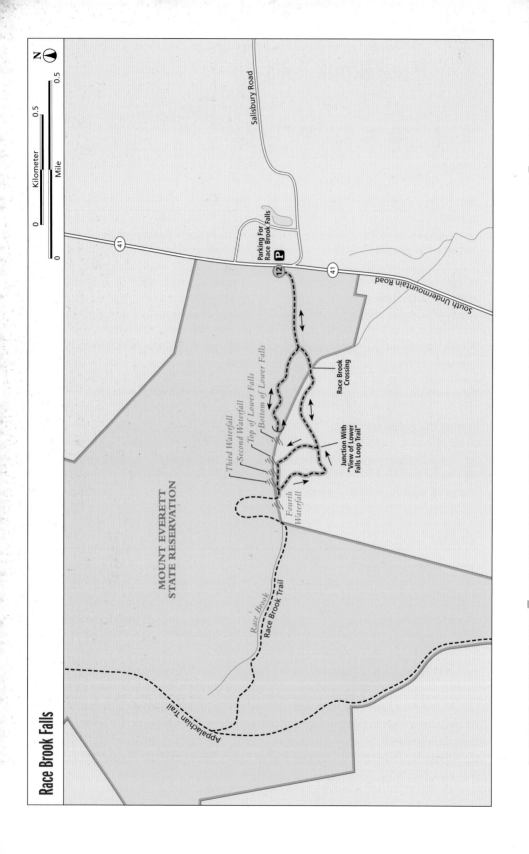

MOUNT EVERETT
STATE RESERVATION

Race Brook

Race Brook Trail

Appalachian Trail

Third Waterfall

Second Waterfall

Top of Lower Falls

Bottom of Lower Falls

Fourth Waterfall

Junction With
"View of Lower
Falls Loop Trail"

Race Brook
Crossing

Parking For
Race Brook Falls

Salisbury Road

South Undermountain Road

N

Kilometer

0   0.5
0   0.5
Mile

When the water is low, the mossy streambed reveals a bright green hue.

Return to the junction; this time take the other branch, now a right turn. In 0.1 mile you cross Race Brook, which can be difficult in high water. After a fairly strenuous 0.3 mile you reach a junction for the "View of Lower Falls Loop Trail." Go right here and in 0.2 mile reach the top of the lower falls and a magnificent view to the east.

From here the trail become less defined, but if you are climbing along the side of the brook, you are going in the right direction. The next set of falls is just above the top of the large lower falls and consists of a 30-foot horsetail that gracefully slides down the bedrock though a cushion of emerald-green moss. Keep on climbing along the very rough trail until you reach a third set of falls, with a 10- to 15-foot plunge just above another beautiful horsetail cascade. Don't be discouraged if you are doing a bunch of scrambling, as the climbing is very difficult here. There should be blue triangles on the trees here to guide you.

After only 0.25 mile from the top of the lower falls, although it will feel like much more, you pop out onto the maintained Race Brook Trail again, just as it crosses back over the brook. Lucky for you, the next waterfall is right here and extremely beautiful as well. Unlike the falls up to this point, this is a powerful steep fall that pours through a deeply carved channel in the rock, giving the brook a sense of power only implied by the lower falls.

If you headed right here, you would leave the brook then swing back around and reach another fall higher up the mountain. The trail eventually meets up with the Appalachian Trail in between the summits of Mount Race and Mount Everett. For the purpose of this hike, however, take the maintained Race Brook Trail back down the mountain all the way to the parking area.

Miles and Directions

0.0 Start at the parking area and follow the blue-blazed Race Brook Trail to the left.

0.3 Reach a junction. Turn right to reach the bottom of the lower falls.

0.7 Reach the bottom of the lower falls. Head back down the trail.

1.1 Arrive back at the junction; turn right to head farther up the Race Brook Trail.

1.2 Cross Race Brook.

1.5 Turn right at the sign for the "View of Lower Falls Loop Trail."

1.65 Reach the top of the lower falls and bottom of the second set of falls (N42 05.377'/W73 25.322'). Continue following a rough path along the brook.

1.75 Reach the third set of falls (N42 05.374'/W73 25.386').

1.8 Reach the Race Brook Trail and the fourth waterfall (N42 05.378'/W73 25.437'). Return to the parking area by descending on the well-maintained Race Brook Trail on the left.

2.8 Arrive back at the parking area.

13 Bash Bish Falls

With a truly dramatic 60-foot plunge, this is one of Massachusetts's most well known and most visited waterfalls. A short, somewhat steep hike leads you down to the falls, where below the main pool a number of dramatic smaller falls continue downstream. A great view is located just above the parking lot.

Start: Parking area near top of the hill on Falls Road

Distance: 0.8 mile out and back (with spur to "summit")

Hiking time: About 1 hour

Approximate elevation gain: 350 feet

Difficulty: Moderate to difficult

Beauty: Spectacular

County: Berkshire

Land status: Bash Bish Falls State Park

DeLorme map: Page 43, I-26

Other maps: None

Trail contact: Bash Bish Falls State Park; (413) 528-0330; www.mass.gov/eea/agencies/dcr/massparks/region-west/bash-bish-falls-state-park.html

Special considerations: Can be very crowded on weekends. The described trail is very steep and can be hazardous in the rain. Pets must be leashed.

Finding the trailhead: At the intersection of US 7, MA 23, and MA 41 in Great Barrington, head south for just under a mile before turning right onto MA 23 West. Follow this road for 7.1 miles to the border of New York; continue on what is now NY 23 for another 2.8 miles. Turn left onto NY 22, heading south, and continue 4 miles. Turn left onto NY 344 West; in 0.5 mile take another left onto NY 344 East. Stay on NY 344 for 1.4 miles to the border of Massachusetts, where the road becomes Falls Road. Parking for the falls is on the right in 0.4 mile. (There are multiple lots, but the lot for this hike is large and is near the top of the hill.) **GPS:** N42 06.907'/W73 29.506'

The Hike

Note: The hike described here is the shortest, but steepest, route to the falls. There is another access that follows the river upstream to the base of the falls. This is an easier trail and leaves from a trailhead about a mile from the entrance to Taconic State Park, just over the border in New York. See Options below. Now back to our scheduled program.

From the parking lot, enter the woods at a sign pointing to the "Falls Trail." The sign notes that all pets must be leashed and the park closes at dusk. The trail, marked with blue triangles, curves around and begins descending to the north as it traverses the side of the hill. At 0.1 mile the trail doglegs to the west and starts to descend more rapidly as it follows the fall line. Be very careful—there are lots of roots and rocks. A hiking pole or walking stick could be helpful on the descent. You will cross a couple of small streams. Be aware that the trail can get significantly slipperier after a rain.

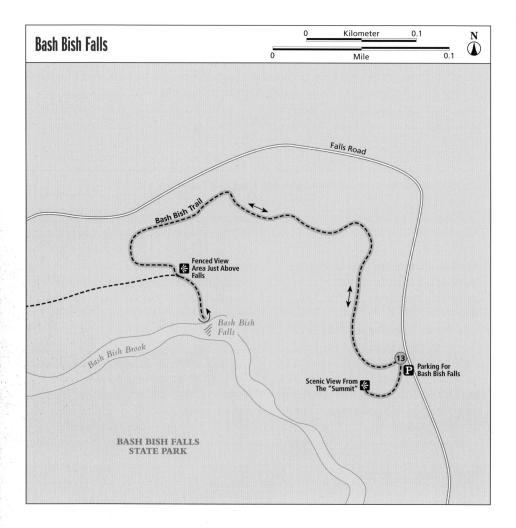

0   Kilometer   0.1

0   Mile   0.1

N

Falls Road

Bash Bish Trail

Fenced View
Area Just Above
Falls

Bash Bish
Falls

Bash Bish Brook

13

Parking For
Bash Bish Falls

Scenic View From
The "Summit"

BASH BISH FALLS
STATE PARK

At 0.2 mile you reach a flat area with fences, an informational sign, and some portable toilets. Continue down the nice stone stairway to the base of the falls. A giant boulder splits the falls in two. In low water these streams remain separate, but with enough flow, the back spray off the rocks appears to merge the two falls together.

Although the main falls are the primary attraction, wander downstream a bit and you'll be rewarded with a number of smaller cascades and falls down along Bash Bish Brook.

Like many other popular waterfalls, Bash Bish has seen its fair share of deaths (more than twenty-five in the last one hundred years). These have been due to a variety of reasons, but, understandably, swimming is prohibited. When you've soaked it all in, head back up the trail.

Before getting in your car and driving away, look for another trail to the left of the falls trail that heads up from the parking lot. A short climb will take you to a fantastic outcrop of rocks known as the "summit," with an incredible view over the

Massachusetts border into New York State. These rocks can be treacherous, which is why there is a fence.

There are multiple stories as to the provenance of the name Bash Bish—from the sound of the water hitting the rocks to the legend of a Mohican adulteress who was sentenced to a canoe ride over the falls.

Miles and Directions

0.0 Start from the parking area and follow the sign to the blue-blazed Falls Trail.

0.25 Reach the flat fenced-in viewing area. Follow steps down to the falls.

0.3 Reach the pool at the base of the falls (N42 06.906'/W73 29.610').

0.35 Head downstream to view additional cascades.

0.7 Return to the parking area. Take the trail to the left of the Falls Trail from the parking lot to visit the "summit" view above.

0.75 Reach the summit view. Return the way you came.

0.8 Arrive back at the parking area.

Options

For a little longer—but eas-ier—hike to the falls, park at a lot on the right about 0.9 mile past the intersection of NY 344 West and NY 344 East and about 0.5 mile before crossing over the bor-der back into Massachusetts.

From the parking lot, take a woods road upstream (east) along the brook. The trail will intersect a small road, and at 0.7 mile you will reach the bottom of Bash Bish Falls.

Although the big split drop with the large pool gets all the attention, the falls below are equally beautiful.

14 Wahconah Falls

Even in low water, the small cascades and larger 40-foot drop through a moss-covered rocky gorge are very picturesque. The picnic tables will inspire you to take your time and enjoy a lunch here.

Start: Parking area on Wahconah Falls Road, 0.4 mile east of MA 9 intersection
Distance: 0.4 mile out and back (includes short spur to top of falls)
Hiking time: About 10 minutes
Approximate elevation gain: 50 feet
Difficulty: Easy
Beauty: Excellent

County: Berkshire
Land status: Wahconah Falls State Park
DeLorme map: Page 33, A-18 (marked)
Other maps: None
Trail contact: Pittsfield State Forest; (413) 442-8992; www.mass.gov/eea/agencies/dcr/massparks/region-west/wahconah-falls-state-park-generic.html

Finding the trailhead: From the intersection of MA 9 and US 7 in Pittsfield, follow MA 9 East for 7.7 miles. Turn right onto Wahconah Falls Road. Parking is on the right in 0.4 mile. **GPS:** N42 29.359'/W73 06.898'

Waconah Falls widens before plunging into a wide pool.

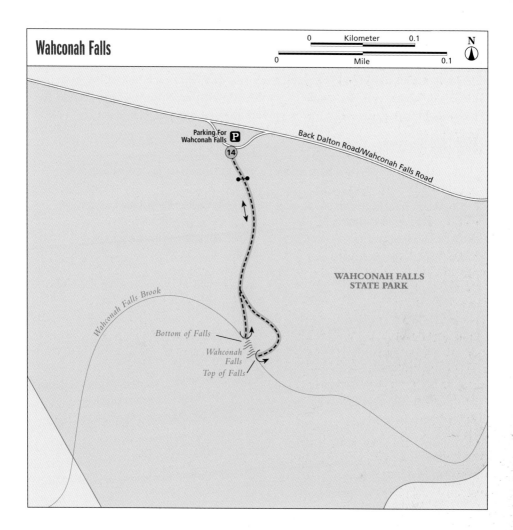

The Hike

This incredibly beautiful waterfall drops almost 40 feet into a large pool. The main drop hugs the left wall of the channel and spreads out in a horsetail formation near the bottom. This wall makes the falls echo and accounts for a fairly loud roar even if the water level isn't very high.

From the parking area, head down around the gate and follow the nice graded path to the base of the falls. You will pass some picnic tables and grills, making this an ideal spot for lunch. Giant slabs of rock litter the floor of the brook. A trail on the left skirts around the side of the falls and gives you a great view from above. There are a few 4- to 6-foot cascades and ledge falls just a short distance above the main falls.

With the easy exploration, nice pool for taking a dip, picnic facilities, and photogenic main falls, this is a great place for a family outing. Apparently Wahconah Falls is named for the daughter of Chief Miahcoma, who settled in the area. She was promised to a Mohawk chief but wanted to marry another young brave. It was decided that a canoe would be pushed over the falls, with each potential spouse on either side of the river. She would marry the man on whose side the canoe ended. As luck would have it, the canoe ended up with the one she wanted to marry.

Miles and Directions

0.0 Start from the parking area, go around the gate, and head down the obvious path to the falls.

0.1 Reach the bottom of the falls. To get to the top, head back up the trail and turn right onto a trail through the woods.

0.2 Reach the top of the falls (N42 29.270' / W73 06.893'). Return the way you came.

0.4 Arrive back at the parking area.

15 Windsor Jambs

The forested 80-foot-high gorge encompasses a number of decent size waterfalls. From above, you'll need to view most of the gorge from behind a metal fence, but at the bottom you can wade in when the water is low to get a unique perspective of the interesting geology.

Start: Directly below the parking area on Schoolhouse Road
Distance: 0.6 mile out and back
Hiking time: About 20 minutes
Approximate elevation gain: 150 feet
Difficulty: Easy to moderate
Beauty: Good (limited by fence)
County: Berkshire
Land status: Windsor State Forest
DeLorme map: Page 21, N-26 (marked)

Other maps: Windsor State Forest Map, www .mass.gov/eea/docs/dcr/parks/trails/wind sor.pdf
Trail contact: Windsor State Forest; (413) 339-5504; www.mass.gov/eea/agencies/dcr/ massparks/region-west/windsor-state-forest -generic.html
Special considerations: Stay behind the fence above the gorge.

Finding the trailhead: (From Northampton) From the intersection of US 5 and MA 9 in Northampton, take MA 9 West for 24.5 miles; turn right onto West Main Street in West Cummington. Go 0.3 mile; turn right onto Bush Road, which becomes West Street, then Windsor Avenue, then Windsor Bush Road. (Got that!?) From the turnoff from West Main Street, travel straight for 1.8 miles before turning left onto Schoolhouse Road. A parking lot is on the left in 0.9 mile.

(From Pittsfield) From the junction of US 7 and MA 9 in Pittsfield, follow MA 9 East for 14.8 miles. Make a sharp left onto High Street Hill/Hill Road; follow this for 1.5 miles, where you make a slight left onto River Road. In 0.2 mile stay right, leaving River Road to follow Windingo Road. In 0.7 mile turn right onto Windsor Jambs Road and then take the first right onto Schoolhouse Road. Parking is on the right in 0.1 mile. **GPS:** N42 31.391'/W72 59.547'

The Hike

This hike goes along the edge of the 80-foot chasm. This is a unique geological location, as the walls are near vertical in places. The schist bedrock has broken off into 90-degree rock slabs, a factor due to the structure of the rock.

The trail leaves directly from the parking area. Immediately you see a cool 8-foot cascade that is split in the middle by a big rock. As the brook heads down into the gorge, you parallel it from above, but your views are limited by the tree cover and, more importantly, a metal fence that prevents you from getting close to the edge of the cliff.

At 0.2 mile you get a view of the largest waterfall in the gorge, a 10- to 12-foot plunge. At 0.3 mile you reach the bottom of the gorge, where, if you don't mind getting your feet wet, you can walk up the streambed for a bit to get a view of the sheer

Windsor Jambs

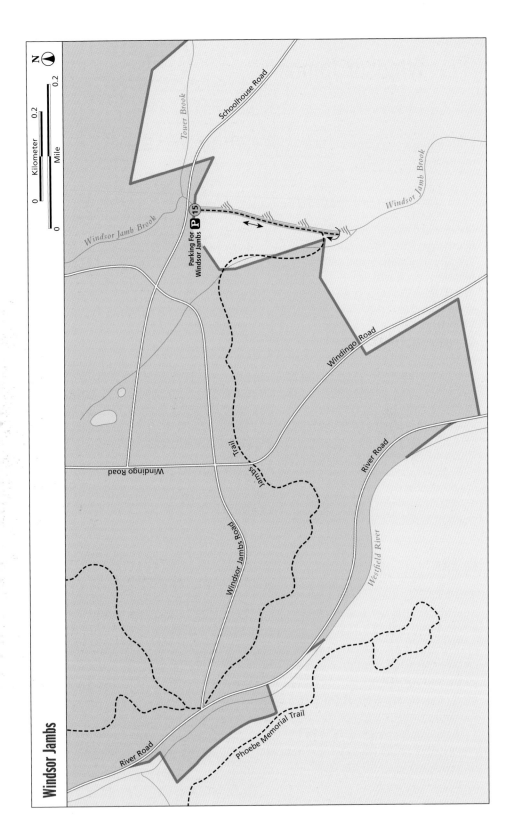

Parking For
Windsor Jambs

Tower Brook

Schoolhouse Road

Windsor Jamb Brook

Windsor Jamb Brook

Windingo Road

Windingo Road

Jambs Trail

Windsor Jambs Road

River Road

River Road

Westfield River

Phoebe Memorial Trail

N

Kilometer

0   0.2   0.2

0   0.2

Mile

rock walls. Return to the parking area on the same trail. A sign suggests that a donation to the Conservation Trust will help improve the park's programs and facilities.

Miles and Directions

0.0 Start hiking down the trail along the gorge, directly below the parking area. The first cascade is accessible just a few feet below.

0.2 Reach the view of the main falls.

0.3 Reach the bottom of the gorge (N42 31.239' / W72 59.563'). You can walk up the stream a little ways to get a good view of the rock walls. Return the way you came.

0.6 Arrive back at the parking area.

You can wade upstream from the bottom of the jambs to get a real feel of the sheer verticalness of the rock walls.

16 March Cataract Falls

High up on the side of Mount Greylock, Massachusetts's tallest mountain, this beautiful stepped falls is best seen early in the season or after some wet weather. In combination with a trip to the summit, this makes for a nice multifaceted outing.

Start: Gate at parking area on Sperry Road
Distance: 2.2 miles out and back
Hiking time: About 1.5 hours
Approximate elevation gain: 400 feet
Difficulty: Moderate
Beauty: Very good
County: Berkshire
Land status: Mount Greylock State Reservation
DeLorme map: Page 20, G-14 (not marked)
Other maps: Mount Greylock State Reservation hiking trail map: www.mass.gov/eea/
docs/dcr/parks/trails/mgry1.pdf; other guides and maps: www.mass.gov/eea/agencies/dcr/massparks/region-west/mount-greylock-maps-brochures-campground-maps-see-more.html
Trail contact: Mount Greylock State Reservation; (413) 499-4262; www.mass.gov/eea/agencies/dcr/massparks/region-west/mt-greylock-state-reservation-generic.html
Special considerations: You can reserve a campsite where the March Cataract Trail leaves Sperry Road. Sperry Road also leads to the beautiful Stony Ledge.

Finding the trailhead: (From Pittsfield) From the intersection of MA 9 and US 7 in Pittsfield, head north on US 7 for 6.6 miles. Turn right onto North Main Street and continue 0.7 mile before heading right onto Greylock Road/Rockwell Road. Stay on Rockwell Road for 6.6 miles as it passes a visitor center for Mount Greylock State Reservation and climbs into the mountains. Turn left onto the dirt Sperry Road; park just ahead on the right before the gate.

(From North Adams) From downtown North Adams, follow MA 2 West for 1.3 miles and turn left onto Notch Road. Follow this for 1.2 miles, taking the third left to stay on Notch Road. Continue 7 more miles before turning right onto Rockwell Road near the summit of Mount Greylock. In 1.6 miles turn right onto the dirt Sperry Road; park just ahead on the right before the gate. **GPS:** N42 37.521'/W73 11.388'

The Hike

March Cataract Falls is a beautiful waterfall on the western side of Mount Greylock, and the hike to it is fairly straightforward, with just a short section of moderately steep trail. Since Sperry Road is closed to vehicles, you will start at the gate and walk down along the road. You quickly pass a trail that crosses Sperry Road (Campground Trail on left, Hopper Trail on right) and then another cutoff to the Hopper Trail on the right.

At 0.5 mile you come to a ranger station, where the road splits. Take the right fork and go straight for 0.1 mile, passing some camping sites on your left. On your right you will see a post sticking out of the ground with vertical writing that says "To March Cataract Falls." Turn right off the road onto this hiking trail and climb gently for 0.25 mile before dropping steeply for another 0.25 mile to the falls.

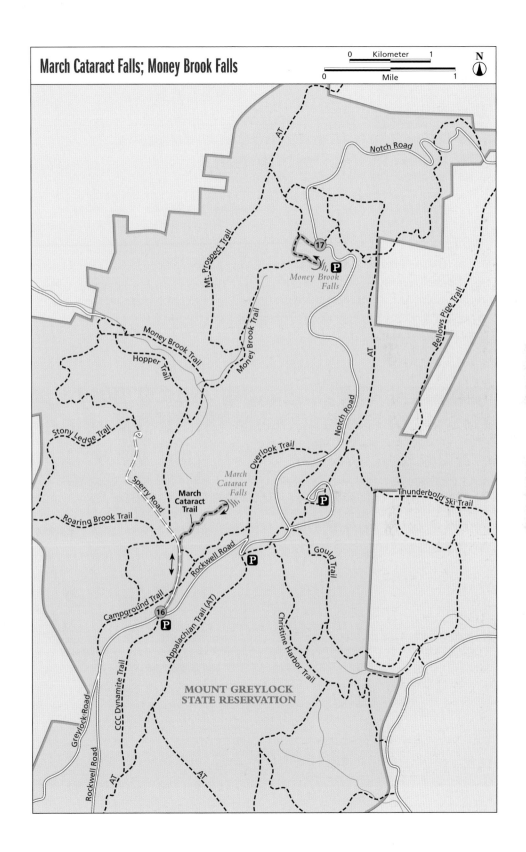

March Cataract Falls; Money Brook Falls

0 Kilometer 1
0 Mile 1

N

Notch Road

AT

Mt. Prospect Trail

Money Brook Trail

Money Brook Trail

Hopper Trail

17

Money Brook Falls

P

Bellows Pipe Trail

Stony Ledge Trail

Sperry Road

Overlook Trail

March Cataract Falls

Notch Road

AT

Roaring Brook Trail

March Cataract Trail

Thunderbolt Ski Trail

P

Rockwell Road

P

Gould Trail

Campground Trail

16

P

Appalachian Trail (AT)

Christine Harbor Trail

CCC Dynamite Trail

MOUNT GREYLOCK
STATE RESERVATION

Greylock Road

Rockwell Road

AT

AT

You can hike right up to the falls, which are most beautiful after a rain or in early summer. To get back to the vehicle, just reverse your steps.

Miles and Directions

0.0 Start from the parking area, go around the gate, and walk down Sperry Road.

0.5 Take the right fork in the road near the ranger station.

0.6 Turn right onto the March Cataract Falls Trail.

1.1 Reach March Cataract Falls (N42 38.194' / W73 10.801'). Return the way you came.

2.2 Arrive back at the parking area.

Options

If you take the left fork at the ranger station, you can stay on Sperry Road and follow signs to the Deer Hill Trail, which leads to Deer Hill Falls. If you stay on Sperry Road for 1.3 miles past the Ranger Station, you will reach Stony Ledge, an open rocky promontory with some of the best views in the park.

The late afternoon light reaches only one side of the valley, creating interesting angular shadows.

MOUNT GREYLOCK

At 3,491 feet in elevation, Mount Greylock is the highest peak in Massachusetts. An auto road climbs to the summit and is open from late May through the end of October. The Appalachian Trail goes over Mount Greylock as well. Geologically part of the Taconic Range, the mountain is now preserved as part of the 12,500-acre Mount Greylock State Reservation. A 93-foot-tall tower stands atop the mountain and affords a magnificent view. Supposedly, on a clear day five states are visible from the summit. Both March Cataract Falls and Money Brook Falls are on the mountain.

There are many viewpoints from the road up Mount Greylock.

17 Money Brook Falls

Money Brook Falls is on the north side of Mount Greylock, Massachusetts's highest mountain. Large falls above lead to a set of cascades that zigzag down the mountain and are accessed via a short, albeit somewhat steep trail.

See map on page 59.
Start: Parking area on Notch Road
Distance: 1.2 miles out and back
Hiking time: About 1 hour
Approximate elevation gain: 450 feet
Difficulty: Moderate
Beauty: Very good
County: Berkshire
Land status: Mount Greylock State Reservation
DeLorme map: Page 21, F-16 (not marked)

Other maps: Mount Greylock State Reservation hiking trail map: www.mass.gov/eea/docs/dcr/parks/trails/mgry1.pdf; other guides and maps: www.mass.gov/eea/agencies/dcr/massparks/region-west/mount-greylock-maps-brochures-campground-maps-see-more.html
Trail contact: Mount Greylock State Reservation; (413) 499-4262; www.mass.gov/eea/agencies/dcr/massparks/region-west/mt-greylock-state-reservation-generic.html

Finding the trailhead: (From North Adams) From downtown North Adams follow MA 2 West for 1.3 miles and turn left onto Notch Road. Follow this for 1.2 miles, taking the third left to stay on Notch Road. Continue another 3.8 miles and look for a small parking area on the right.

(From Pittsfield) From the intersection of MA 9 and US 7 in Pittsfield, head north on US 7 for 6.6 miles. Turn right onto North Main Street and follow this for 0.7 mile before heading right on Greylock Road/Rockwell Road. Stay on Rockwell Road for 7.8 miles as it passes a visitor center for Mount Greylock State Reservation and climbs near the summit. Near the summit, turn left onto Notch Road; follow this for 3.1 miles to a small parking area on the left.

GPS: N42 39.864'/W73 09.961'

The Hike

When you arrive at Money Brook Falls, you will find a steep rugged brook with small cascades seemingly popping out from under rocks. But if you look uphill you will see a set of beautiful horsetail falls and long unobscured cascades and step falls below.

From the parking area, follow the sign to the blue-blazed Money Brook Trail. This trail heads gently downhill to the east. At 0.2 mile you reach a signed junction. Head left on the Money Brook trail. Continue to head downhill as the trail gets steeper. At 0.4 mile the trail makes a left turn. At 0.5 mile you reach a junction with a sign pointing to the falls. Head left here and after descending 0.1 mile reach the bottom of the cascades.

This is where the trail ends, but if you are adventurous, you can try to rock-hop and bushwhack next to the brook to get a closer view of the upper falls. This may be

Uprooted trees and wide dark ledges are evidence of the waterfall's power in times of wet weather.

pretty difficult during high water, and you do get a nice view from the trail's end. To return to the parking area, retrace your steps.

Miles and Directions

0.0 Start from the parking area and follow the signs to the Money Brook Trail.

0.2 At the junction head left, continuing on the Money Brook Trail.

0.5 Reach another junction and again go left.

0.6 Reach the bottom of Money Brook Falls (N42 39.771'/W73 10.069'). Return the way you came.

1.2 Arrive back at the parking area.

18 Twin Cascade

Although it requires a bit of scrambling, the unique ability to stand where two water-falls come together make this an exceptional outing.

Start: Across the train tracks on the opposite (north) side from the parking area on River Road
Distance: 1.0 mile out and back
Hiking time: About 30 minutes
Approximate elevation gain: 150 feet
Difficulty: Difficult
Beauty: Excellent
County: Berkshire
Land status: N/A

DeLorme map: Page 21, E-25 & 26 (not marked)
Other maps: None
Trail contact: N/A
Special considerations: Do not walk on the train tracks! Stay off to the right near the woods. Getting above the dam below the falls is difficult; attempt only when conditions are dry. Be prepared to step in the water, so good boots/shoes are necessary.

Finding the trailhead: (From the east) From MA 2, 1.5 miles west of the intersection with MA 8A South in Charlemont, turn right onto Zoar Road and continue 2.5 miles before turning left onto River Road. Park on the left in a lot (before crossing the train tracks) in 4.5 miles. The trail begins across the tracks just to the right of the train tunnel entrance.

(From North Adams) Take MA 2 East for 6.7 miles and turn left onto Whitcomb Hill Road. This will curve to the right and go downhill. Turn left onto Whitcomb Hill; at the bottom, turn left onto River Road. Go 0.3 mile and park on the left in a lot before crossing the train tracks. The trail begins across the tracks, just to the right of the train tunnel entrance.
GPS: N42 40.473'/W72 59.778'

The Hike

From the parking area, walk across the train tracks and head to the left, staying to the right of the tracks. The tracks are on private property, not to mention extremely dangerous, so do not walk on them. Just before you get to the entrance of the tunnel, head up over a berm and then head left, walking along an old stone foundation. You will need to hop over a stone wall to continue following the brook upstream; this requires a 2- to 3-foot jump down off the wall.

From here the trail is obvious and climbs up through the woods, keeping the brook down to your right. The trail can be very muddy and slippery, and therefore dangerous. Follow this trail up the brook to an old dam. Unfortunately, there is no easy way to get to the falls above the dam, so you'll need to clamber over the dam to get the best view. Also be prepared to get your feet wet—you'll most likely need to walk through some water above the dam.

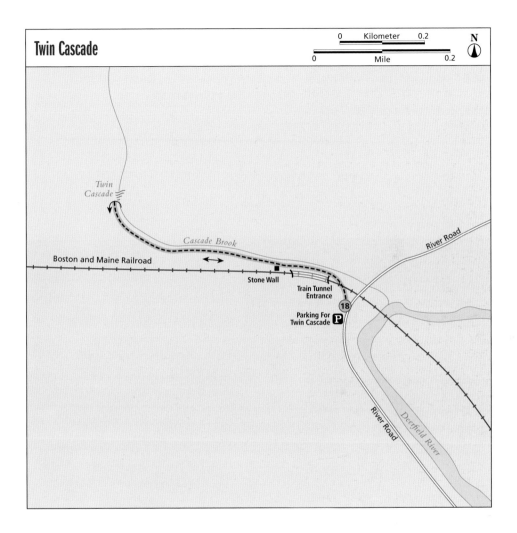

Twin Cascade

Twin Cascade

Boston and Maine Railroad

Cascade Brook

Stone Wall

Train Tunnel Entrance

Parking For Twin Cascade

18

River Road

River Road

Deerfield River

Kilometer 0 0.2

Mile 0 0.2

N

Once you are there, you will see why this is called Twin Cascade. On your right, Cascade Brook pours over large angled rocks that appear to be four giant steps, each about 15 feet in height. On your left, another stream pours out of a notch in the woods, tumbling down in a beautiful winding set of cascades for almost 100 feet right down to your boots.

Return to the parking area on the same trail.

Miles and Directions

0.0 Start from the parking area, cross the train tracks, and head left toward the tunnel entrance.

0.1 Just before reaching the tunnel entrance, head right over a berm.

0.15 Climb over an old stone wall and begin hiking up the trail on the left (south) side of the brook.

0.5 Reach an old dam. Carefully climb over the dam to the base of Twin Cascade (N42 40.605'/W73 00.182'). Return to the parking area on the same trail.

1.0 Arrive back at the parking area.

You will need a wide angle lens to capture both waterfalls coming from opposite directions.

19 Tannery and Parker Brook Falls

Tannery and Parker Brook Falls are both amazing, yet very different. The fact that they're literally hundreds of feet away from each other makes this a must-do trip if you're in the area.

Start: Parking area just off Tannery Road on short dirt road, 0.7 mile from Tannery Road junction with Black Brook Road
Distance: 0.6 mile out and back
Hiking time: About 20 minutes
Approximate elevation gain: 100 feet
Difficulty: Easy
Beauty: Excellent
County: Berkshire

Land status: Savoy Mountain State Forest
DeLorme map: Page 21, H-25 (not marked)
Other map: Savoy Mountain State Forest Trail Map: www.mass.gov/eea/docs/dcr/parks/trails/savoy1.pdf
Trail contact: Savoy Mountain State Forest; (413) 664-4800; mass.gov/eea/agencies/dcr/massparks/region-west/savoy-mt-state-forest-generic.html

Finding the trailhead: From I-91 in Greenfield, take MA 2 West for 23.7 miles (1.7 miles past the sign for "Savoy Town Line") and turn left onto Black Brook Road. (If traveling east on MA 2, this is a right just after the "Savoy Town Line" sign and 12 miles from downtown North Adams.) Follow Black Brook Road for 2.5 miles, making sure to fork right at 1.3 miles. Turn right onto Tannery Road; on the right in 0.7 mile is a small dirt road, with a parking area just beyond. **GPS:** N42 37.328'/W73 00.304'

The Hike

Tannery Falls is a beautiful 100-foot cascade that pours into a nice little pool; Parker Brook Falls is a unique slanted flume that is about 40 feet high. Shortly below these two falls, the separate brooks combine into Tannery Brook.

Start your hike by following the trail directly into the woods. Pass a small cascade on your right. Then the trail curves down along Ross Brook, where you encounter some beautiful small cascades and a cool channel that cuts through a steep mossy forest. Continue down the trail to a set of steps that lead to a great view at the top of Tannery Falls. Continue heading downhill; just before you get to the bottom of the descent, look for a waterfall on your right. That is Parker Brook Falls. At the bottom, head over to the left and you will be at the pool below Tannery Falls.

Return to the parking area the way you came in.

Note: On some maps Parker Brook is labeled as Tannery Brook, which is confusing, as Tannery Falls is actually on Ross Brook. There is also another waterfall accessible from the left side of the parking lot via a short trail.

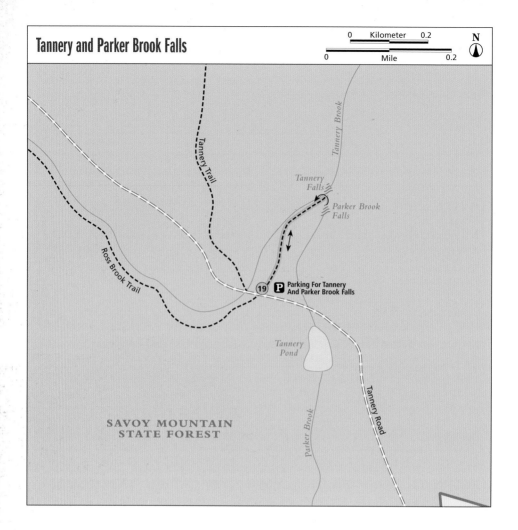

Tannery and Parker Brook Falls

Miles and Directions

0.0 Start from the parking area and head into the forest, following a trail with blue blazes.

0.2 Reach the top of Tannery Falls.

0.25 Reach Parker Brook Falls on your right (N42 37.420' / W73 00.198'). At the bottom of the stairs head to the left to get to Tannery Falls.

0.3 Arrive at the bottom of Tannery Falls (N42 37.442' / W73 00.217'). Return to the parking lot on the same trail.

0.6 Arrive back at the parking area.

Parker Brook Falls angles through a notch before meeting up with Tannery Brook.

Tannery Falls is a surprisingly large waterfall, and the curve of the rock attests to the power of this waterfall during high water.

20 Doane's Falls

Doane's Falls is one of the three sets of waterfalls along or near the Tully Trail in Royalston and is one of the most beautiful in the state. With over 200 feet of waterfalls, including wide cascades, narrow plunges, and stepped falls, there's a lot to see in a short distance.

Start: Parking area on Athol Road, just before junction with Doane Hill Road
Distance: 0.6 mile out and back
Hiking time: About 30 minutes
Approximate elevation gain: 150 feet
Difficulty: Easy
Beauty: Excellent
County: Worcester
Land status: Doane's Falls Reservation

DeLorme map: Page 24, F & G-13 (not marked)
Other map: The Trustees of Reservations Tully Trail Map: www.thetrustees.org/assets/documents/places-to-visit/trailmaps/Tully-Trail-Map.pdf
Trail contact: The Trustees of Reservations; (978) 248-9455; www.thetrustees.org/places-to-visit/central-ma/doanes-falls.html; e-mail: central@ttor.org

Finding the trailhead: From exit 17 on US 202 / MA 2, follow MA 32 north into Athol. After crossing over the river, MA 32 heads left; instead go right onto Chestnut Hill Avenue toward Royalston. Follow this for 4.1 miles (it will become Athol Road) until you reach a parking area on the left, just before the intersection with Doane Hill Road. **GPS:** N42 39.000' / W72 12.082'

The Hike

Doane's Falls consists of a long series of plunges and cascades of Lawrence Brook just above where it flows into Tully Lake. Doane's Falls is just off the Tully Trail, a 22-mile circular trail (map provided at web address above) that goes through Royalston and Orange and passes by three waterfalls, of which Doane's is one.

From the parking area the trail heads downhill along the brook. A fence blocks access to the falls for most of the way down, but there are a number of decent observation spots, including one about 0.1 mile down the trail where you can frame the falls in front of the stone arched bridge on Athol Road. (***Note:*** Swimming is prohibited. Stay on the trail.) Continue to head down the trail, where you will see various cascades and plunges, until you reach a flat area at the bottom, 200 vertical feet below the parking area.

The flat area is marked as "accessible" (from below) and provides some benches with a nice view to the lowest major fall, a 20-foot block fall. Here the trail merges with a dirt road that soon joins up with the Tully Trail and heads down to the campground and Tully Lake. Return the way you came.

Doane's Falls gets its name from Amos Doane, who operated a mill on Lawrence Brook in the nineteenth century.

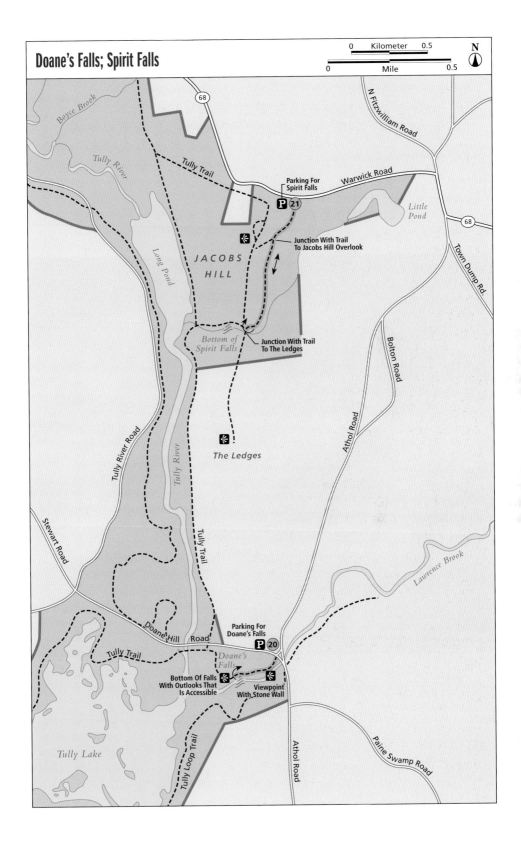

Doane's Falls; Spirit Falls

0   Kilometer   0.5

0   Mile   0.5

N

Boyce Brook

N Fitzwilliam Road

68

Tully River

Tully Trail

Parking For
Spirit Falls

P 21

Warwick Road

Little
Pond

68

JACOBS
HILL

Junction With Trail
To Jacobs Hill Overlook

Long Pond

Town Dump Rd.

Bottom of
Spirit Falls

Junction With Trail
To The Ledges

Bolton Road

Athol Road

The Ledges

Tully River Road

Tully River

Stewart Road

Tully Trail

Lawrence Brook

Doane Hill   Road

Parking For
Doane's Falls

P 20

Tully Trail

Doane's
Falls

Bottom Of Falls
With Outlooks That
Is Accessible

Viewpoint
With Stone Wall

Athol Road

Paine Swamp Road

Tully Loop Trail

Tully Lake

Miles and Directions

0.0 Start from the parking area and head down the trail that parallels the brook.

0.1 Reach a nice viewpoint next to a stone wall.

0.3 Reach a flat area with benches and view of a block fall (N42 38.943'/W72 12.268'). Return back up the same trail.

0.6 Arrive back at the parking area.

This photo of one of the lowermost falls shows that getting lower to the ground and closer to the waterfall creates depth in an image.

21 Spirit Falls

Spirit Falls is actually a set of cascades that parallel a trail down the side of a hillside. Along with Doane's and Royalston Falls, Spirit Falls is along the Tully Trail and makes a nice addition to an excursion if visiting the other two.

See map on page 71.
Start: Parking area on Warwick Road, 5.4 miles past "Royalston Town Line" sign and 0.6 miles east of the small Royalston town center
Distance: 1.6 miles out and back
Hiking time: About 1 hour
Approximate elevation gain: 350 feet
Difficulty: Moderate
Beauty: Good
County: Worcester

Land status: Jacobs Hill Reservation
DeLorme map: Page 24, E-12 (not marked)
Other map: The Trustees of Reservations Tully Trail Map: www.thetrustees.org/assets/documents/places-to-visit/trailmaps/Tully-Trail-Map.pdf
Trail contact: The Trustees of Reservations; (978) 248-9455; www.thetrustees.org/places-to-visit/central-ma/jacobs-hill.html; e-mail: central@ttor.org

Finding the trailhead: From exit 19 on MA 2, a few miles west of Gardner, turn right onto MA 2A East/US 202 North. In 2.5 miles turn left onto MA 68 West and follow this road for 9 miles to a parking area on the left for Jacobs Hill. (MA 68 will turn from South Royalston Road to Main Street to Warwick Road.) The parking area is 5.4 miles past the "Royalston Town Line" sign. **GPS:** N42 40.577'/W72 11.923'

The Hike

Another waterfall just off the Tully Trail, Sprit Falls is actually a series of steep cascades that drop almost 150 feet. From the trailhead, follow the only trail as it winds around the edge of a marsh. After about 0.25 mile and a slight climb, you will see a sign pointing right to the Jacobs Hill Overlook and left to Spirit Falls and the Ledges. Continue going straight/left and descend a bit, make a right turn, and then immediately reach another sign at 0.7 mile pointing left to the Ledges and straight to Spirit Falls. Continue straight.

Soon you will see the falls on your left. Continue climbing down a fairly steep trail to reach the bottom of the falls; then look up to get an idea of the size. Return the way you came in.

Miles and Directions

0.0 Start from the parking area and follow the trail down into the woods and along the edge of a marsh.
0.25 Reach a junction with a spur trail to Jacobs Hill Overlook. Stay straight/left to head to Spirit Falls.

0.7 Reach a junction with the trail to the Ledges. Continue straight to Spirit Falls. Descend for 200 feet to reach the bottom of the falls.

0.8 Arrive at the base of Spirit Falls (N42 40.140' / W72 12.311'). Return the way you came.

1.6 Arrive back at the parking area.

Option

If you have the time, you can take the cutoff to Jacobs Hill Overlook to get a beautiful view to the west. From there you can take the Tully Trail south to meet up with the trail to Spirit Falls.

Otis poses below Spirit Falls.

22 Royalston Falls

This beautiful 45-foot waterfall plunges into a rugged chasm and is one of three waterfalls on the 22-mile Tully Trail. Although this trail is easy and short (except for the optional descent into the chasm), the road to get here is extremely rugged and is only passable with a high-clearance four-wheel-drive vehicle.

Start: Small parking area on Falls Road, 3.2 miles from junction with MA 68/Warwick Road; the road is in poor condition and unless you have a big SUV, you may have to walk a portion of the road

Distance: 0.8 mile out and back (not including possible road walk)

Hiking time: About 30 minutes

Approximate elevation gain: 100 feet

Difficulty: Easy to moderate to edge of falls; difficult to bottom of falls

Beauty: Very good

County: Worcester

Land status: Royalston Falls Reservation

DeLorme map: Page 24, C-11 (not marked)

Other map: The Trustees of Reservations Tully Trail Map: www.thetrustees.org/assets/documents/places-to-visit/trailmaps/Tully-Trail-Map.pdf

Trail contact: The Trustees of Reservations; (978) 248-9455; www.thetrustees.org/places-to-visit/central-ma/doanes-falls.html; e-mail: central@ttor.org

Special considerations: Falls Road is extremely rugged. You must have a four-wheel-drive high-clearance vehicle to get to the trailhead. Otherwise you may need to park 0.5 mile down the road and walk up to the trailhead. Another trailhead accesses the falls from the west and leaves near the Newton Cemetery on the Athol-Richmond Road. This trail is about twice as long as the one described here. **Note:** You can climb down into the chasm below the falls, but this route is extremely muddy, slippery, and steep and should not be attempted if the water level is high.

Finding the trailhead: Reaching this trailhead requires driving on a rough road, appropriate for high-clearance vehicles only, or a bit of road walking. From exit 19 on MA 2, a few miles west of Gardner, turn right onto MA 2A East/US 202 North. In 2.5 miles turn left onto MA 68 West and follow this road for 9.9 miles before turning right onto Falls Road. (MA 68 will turn from South Royalston Road to Main Street to Warwick Road.) Falls Road is 1.3 miles west of Royalston. The trailhead is on the left in 3.2 miles, but after 2.3 miles the road gets rough. Park at 2.3 miles and walk to the trailhead, or travel as far as you are comfortable, depending on your vehicle. The trailhead is a small parking area after the road climbs a hill and makes a sharp right turn. There is a small sign saying "Connector Trail." **GPS:** N42 42.948'/W72 14.461'

The Hike

As mentioned, you may need to walk up the road to reach the trailhead, adding an additional 1.0 mile to your hike. These directions leave from the trailhead.

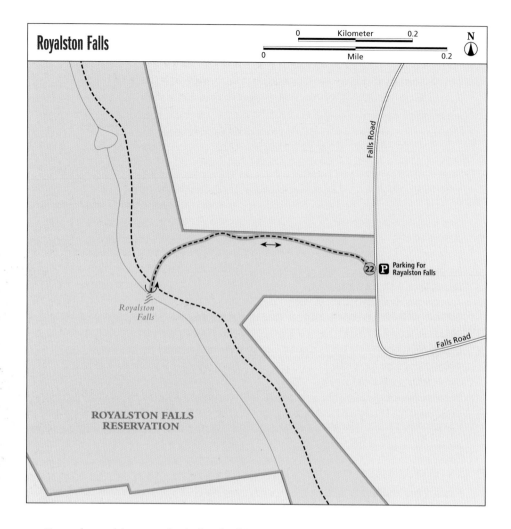

Royalston Falls

Falls Road

22 🅿 Parking For Rayalston Falls

Royalston Falls

Falls Road

ROYALSTON FALLS RESERVATION

From the parking area, look for the "Connector Trail" sign and follow this trail into the woods. The trail is mostly flat but starts heading downhill a short ways before reaching the falls. At 0.3 mile you reach a junction with a sign. The sign is oriented for hikers coming up the Tully Trail from the south and notes that a shelter is 0.3 mile north up the Tully Trail.

From here you get a fenced-off view of the falls, which pour off a ledge into a uniquely rounded gorge before flowing into a chasm filled with jagged rocks lined with thick moss and ferns.

If you are feeling adventurous—and the water level is not very high—you can scramble down one of the steep trails slightly downstream to the bottom of the gorge and work your way up along the bottom, clambering over rocks to get a cool perspective of the falls. Follow the same trail to get back to your vehicle.

Miles and Directions

0.0 Start from the trailhead and follow the marked trail into the woods.

0.3 Reach a trail junction and the fenced-off top of the falls (N42 42.906' / W72 14.749'). To see the falls from below, head down a steep trail to the bottom and work your way up the gorge.

0.4 Reach view at bottom of the falls. Return the way you came.

0.8 Arrive back at the parking area.

The chasm below Royalston Falls is rocky and narrow, providing an intimate view of the falls from below.

Vermont

The unique sculpted rock of Huntington Gorge speaks to the power and mystery of moving water (hike 41).

23 Jelly Mill Falls / Old Jelly Mill Falls

These small but beautiful falls cascade over slanted granite bedrock, with a number of nice shallow wading pools. This is a perfect family outing on a hot summer day.

Start: Parking area on Stickney Brook Road
Distance: 0.1 mile out and back (roadside)
Hiking time: About 5 minutes
Approximate elevation gain: 50 feet
Difficulty: Easy
Beauty: Very Good

County: Windham
Land status: N/A
DeLorme map: Page 22, F-6 (not marked)
Other maps: None
Trail contact: N/A

Finding the trailhead: From exit 2 on I-91, take VT 9 East toward Brattleboro for 0.5 mile; turn left onto Cedar Street. At the junction with Linden Street/VT 30 in 0.7 mile, turn left and follow VT 30 for 4.7 miles. Turn left onto Stickney Brook Road. Parking spots will be visible on the right in a few hundred feet. **GPS:** N42 54.880' / W72 36.820'

The Hike

How did Jelly Mill Falls get its name? Apparently there once was a mill here owned by John Taft. In addition to cutting wood, he also made cider and jelly. Hence the name.

There are no large drops here, but there are many 2- and 3-foot cascades and step falls, with one drop that reaches 8 feet. So why visit? The spot is very picturesque, and you can easily explore, as Stickney Brook pours over even granite bedrock.

On hot summer days, you may find a number of locals here wading in one of the many pools. If you are looking for a roadside falls that is beautiful and great for children, this should fit the bill.

From the parking on the road, head down to the brook and then follow it upstream, either along a dirt path or on the rocks if it's dry. Just note that wet granite can be very slippery, so be careful.

There are many interesting colors on the rocks at Jelly Mill Falls, and the water serves to make the colors much more bold than when dry.

Miles and Directions

0.0 Start from the parking area and take any of the informal paths down to the brook.

0.05 Reach the brook and explore. Retrace your steps to the parking area.

0.1 Arrive back at your car.

24 Pikes Falls

Pikes Falls is pretty small, with a number of short drops and cascades that flow over smooth bedrock. In the right conditions, you can slide down the lower cascade into an extremely large swim hole.

Start: Parking on the side of Pikes Falls Road just east of the junction with Day Road
Distance: 0.2-mile loop
Hiking time: About 15 minutes
Approximate elevation gain: 50 feet
Difficulty: Easy to lower pool; moderate scrambling to get to upper plunge and trail back to road
Beauty: Very Good

County: Windham
Land status: Green Mountain National Forest
DeLorme map: Page 26, J-1 (not marked)
Other maps: None
Trail contact: Green Mountain National Forest—Manchester Ranger Station; (802) 362-1251; www.fs.usda.gov/detail/green mountain/about-forest/offices

Finding the trailhead: (From the east) Take VT 30 to the town of Jamaica, which is 9.2 miles west of the intersection with VT 35 in Townshend. Turn left onto Pikes Falls Road and in 2.3 miles turn right to stay on Pikes Falls Road. There is parking on a wide shoulder on the left side of the road in 2.5 miles. If you cross a bridge and see Day Road on your left, you've gone about 0.1 mile too far.

(From the west) From the intersection of VT 11 and VT 30, just southwest of Bromley Mountain Ski Resort, follow VT 30 South for 7.3 miles and then turn right onto Stratton Mountain Access Road. Follow this straight for 1.3 miles then make a fairly sharp left onto Upper Taylor Hill Road. Follow this road for 3.6 miles as it becomes Pikes Falls Road. Parking is on the right side of the road, just after passing Day Road and a bridge over the brook.
GPS: N43 05.882' / W72 51.166'

The Hike

If you are just looking to visit beautiful waterfalls, you can probably skip this one. But if you like to play, this is one of the best.

From the parking area, head into the woods and go left down a dirt path. You soon reach a set of stairs that takes you to the base of the falls and the very large swimming hole, which at points is up to 10 feet deep. On a hot day, this is a perfect place for a dip. The lowest set of falls creates a natural waterslide. You can turn around here for an easy out-and-back hike.

If you like to climb around, follow the rocks up along the brook. The upper part of the falls has an interesting feature where the water falls into a pool and the next falls pour off at a 90-degree angle from the upper falls. Continue up and you'll find a trail on the right that leads back to the parking area.

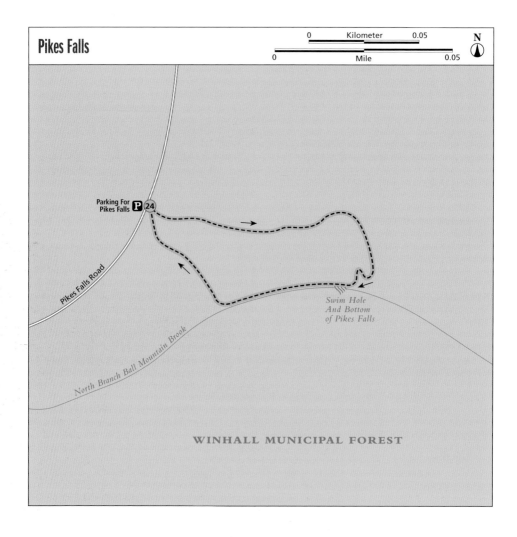

Pikes Falls

0   Kilometer   0.05

0   Mile   0.05

N

Parking For
Pikes Falls
P 24

Pikes Falls Road

North Branch Ball Mountain Brook

Swim Hole
And Bottom
of Pikes Falls

WINHALL MUNICIPAL FOREST

Miles and Directions

0.0 Start from the parking area, head into the woods, and take the trail to the left (clockwise).

0.1 Reach the pool at the bottom of the falls (N43 05.864' / W72 51.083'). To visit the upper falls, climb up along the rocks on the edge of the brook.

0.15 Reach the upper part of the falls. Return to the parking area on the trail to the right of the brook.

0.2 Arrive back at the parking area.

The upper part of Pikes Falls makes a sharp turn before eventually falling into the large pool below.

25 Lye Brook Falls

This incredibly beautiful waterfall drops over 150 feet down steep rocky steps and is one of Vermont's most well-known, and photographed, waterfalls. This is the longest Vermont hike in this book.

Start: Parking area at end of Lye Brook Falls Service Road
Distance: 4.6 miles out and back
Hiking time: About 2.5 hours
Approximate elevation gain: 900 feet
Difficulty: Moderate
Beauty: Spectacular
County: Bennington
Land status: Lye Brook Wilderness, Green Mountain National Forest
DeLorme map: Page 25, I-10 (not marked)
Other map: Green Mountain Club Manchester Area Hiking Trail Map with Stratton & Bromley
Trail contacts: Green Mountain Club; (802) 244-7037; www.greenmountainclub.org/news.php?id=258; e-mail: gmc@greenmountainclub.org
Green Mountain National Forest—Manchester Ranger Station; (802) 362-1251; www.fs.usda.gov/detail/greenmountain/about-forest/offices
Special considerations: Tropical Storm (previously Hurricane) Irene, which devastated much of Vermont in 2011, minimally altered the path of this falls, although you'll pass through the wide-open path of a giant mudslide on your way.

Finding the trailhead: From the junction of VT 11 and US 7 (exit 4 off of US 7) in Manchester, take VT 11 (Depot Street) east for 0.4 mile. Turn right onto East Manchester Road and follow this road for 1.1 miles. Turn left onto Glen Road just before going under US 7. Continue on Glen Road for 0.1 mile then turn right (actually stay straight) onto Lye Brook Falls Service Road. Parking is at the end of this road in 0.3 mile. **GPS: N43 09.537' / W73 02.477'**

The Hike

Easily one of the most photographed falls in Vermont, and the longest Vermont waterfall hike in this book, this should be on any waterfall lover's list.

Take the Lye Brook Trail from the parking area. It is fairly level for a little while then begins to climb, albeit at a relaxed pace. In a few tenths of a mile you see Lye Brook below as you stand atop a washout. At 0.4 mile you see a sign-in register. It's best to be safe and always sign in. Shortly thereafter, at around 0.5 mile, you see the sign for the Lye Brook Wilderness Area.

For much of the remainder of the hike, the graded trail goes in a straight line. That is because this used to be the site of railroad tracks used for logging. (Lye Brook Falls used to be called Trestle Falls, as a railroad trestle crossed the base of the falls.) Eventually the trail gets a little steeper and around 1.6 miles makes a turn to the left and then heads back around to the south. Along the way you cross a number of small streams.

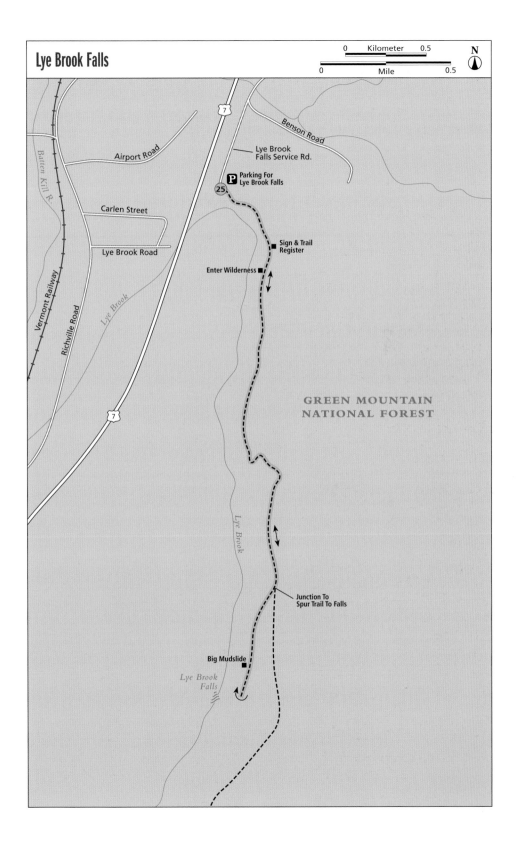

Lye Brook Falls

0 Kilometer 0.5
0 Mile 0.5

N

Benson Road

7

Airport Road

Lye Brook
Falls Service Rd.

P Parking For
Lye Brook Falls

25

Carlen Street

Sign & Trail
Register

Lye Brook Road

Enter Wilderness

Batten Kill R.

Vermont Railway

Richville Road

Lye Brook

7

Lye Brook

GREEN MOUNTAIN
NATIONAL FOREST

Junction To
Spur Trail To Falls

Big Mudslide

Lye Brook
Falls

At 1.8 miles you cross a somewhat wider stream; soon after, take a right at the fork for the spur trail to Lye Brook Falls. From here you actually start heading downhill. At 2.2 miles you pop out into a clearing. At first you may think this is a clear-cut, but it's the aftermath of a giant mudslide caused by the devastating Tropical Storm Irene, which ravaged Vermont's rivers in August 2011.

Upon reaching Lye Brook Falls at 2.3 miles, you can stand on a rocky outcrop to get a view of most of the waterfall. Depending on the season, the falls can look very different. The falls are mainly large step cascades at the top and horsetails at the bottom, but they can take on various forms under different water flows. You can head down to the bottom just a few feet below the outcrop and, if you're adventurous, follow the rough path partway up the side of the falls.

Miles and Directions

0.0 Start from the parking, head onto the Lye Brook Trail.

0.4 Reach the sign-in register and sign in for the trail.

0.5 Reach a sign and enter Lye Brook Wilderness Area.

1.8 Take the left fork onto the spur trail for Lye Brook Falls.

2.2 Cross a giant mudslide.

2.3 Reach Lye Brook Falls (N43 07.890' / W73 02.384'). Return the way you came.

4.6 Arrive back at the parking area.

The reward for a fairly long hike is a tall series of beautiful cascades ▶
that tumble down Lye Brook.

TROPICAL STORM IRENE IN VERMONT

From August 28 to August 29, 2011, Tropical Storm Irene (downgraded from a hurricane) pummeled all of Vermont, with some areas receiving more than 11 inches of rain on ground that was already saturated and rivers that were already running high. In many areas this created the largest or second-largest flooding in the state's recorded history. Roads and buildings were completely washed away, including the house of one of my closest friends.

Entire communities were destroyed; others were trapped by rising waters on all sides. At least three people in Vermont were killed, and many more were injured. Rivers created new paths, and mountains were ravaged by mudslides, including a large slide visible near Lye Brook Falls. Vermont is still recovering from the damage, which totaled hundreds of millions of dollars and created long-lasting impacts to Vermont's environment that the state is still grappling with today.

The aftermath of the mudslide caused by Tropical Storm Irene in 2011 is a reminder of the true destructive power that can be caused by too much water.

26 Hamilton Falls

This 125-foot waterfall undercuts slanted bedrock then splits before pouring into deep pools, which are often popular wading spots on hot summer days. This hike describes the route to the base of the falls, which affords the best view, but a note at the end of the hike description mentions how to get to the top of the falls.

Start: Parking area on Hamilton Falls Road
Distance: 0.7 mile out and back
Hiking time: About 15 minutes
Approximate elevation gain: 200 feet
Difficulty: Easy
Beauty: Excellent
County: Windham
Land status: Hamilton Falls Natural Area in Jamaica State Park
DeLorme map: Page 26, I-3 (marked)
Other map: Jamaica State Park Recreational

Trails Guide: www.vtstateparks.com/pdfs/jamaica_trails.pdf
Trail contacts: Jamaica State Park; (802) 874-4600; www.vtstateparks.com/htm/jamaica.htm
Vermont Department of Forests, Parks & Recreation—Lands Administration Division; (802) 272-4156; www.vtfpr.org/lands/vtna.cfm#hami
Special considerations: Note that there are trails to the top and bottom of the falls. These directions are for the bottom of the falls.

Finding the trailhead: From the junction of VT-35 and VT-30 in Townshend, follow VT-30 North for 4.5 miles then take a right onto Windham Hill Road and follow this for 4.3 miles. Turn left onto Burbee Pond Road then turn left onto West Windham Road in 0.9 mile when you have reached Burbee Pond. Take West Windham Road for 2.6 miles and then turn right onto Hamilton Falls Road. A sign on a tree for "Falls" is visible on the left, with parking ahead on the right. **GPS:** N43 08.201'/W72 45.786'

The Hike

Hamilton Falls is one of the biggest, most beautiful, and deadliest waterfalls in Vermont. According to one source, twelve people have died here. People swimming in the pool at the top of the falls have been washed down by the current. Climbing on the rocks is also dangerous, as the bedrock is tilted at a severe angle and is very slippery when wet.

To get to the bottom of Hamilton Falls, where it is safe to swim and where you will find the best view, head back up the road a few hundred yards and then turn right at a sign for "Falls" with an arrow pointing down the trail. Head down the Hamilton Falls Trail for 0.2 mile and then turn right at a sign for "Hamilton Falls." Head down this steeper trail for 0.1 mile to reach the base of the falls.

The falls is composed of three main tiers and totals 125 feet. The bottom section splits into two separate falls, which pour into fairly large pools, perfect for taking a dip

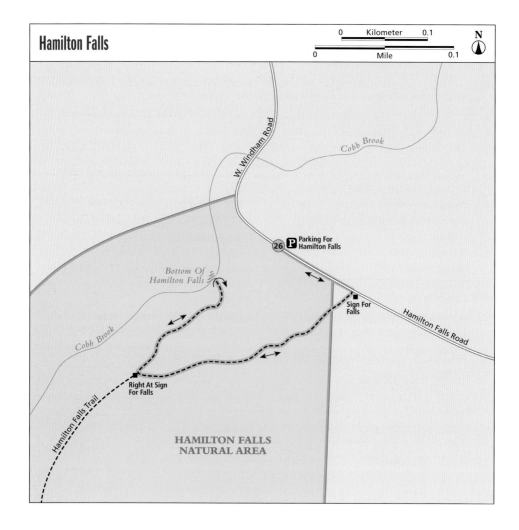

on a hot summer day. Here you can clearly see how the powerful flow of Cobb Brook has carved out the schist bedrock, which has been uplifted at a fairly steep angle.

Return the same way.

Note: From the parking area, if you head down the road in the opposite direction described in this hike, you will see a sign and a short path to the top of the falls. There is a ladder in the pool at the top, but this is an emergency escape ladder and should not be considered a suggestion to swim. Be safe; only swim at the bottom of the falls.

Miles and Directions

0.0   Start from the parking area and head back up Hamilton Falls Road.

0.05   Turn right at the "Falls" sign onto the Hamilton Falls Trail.

0.25   Turn right onto a steeper trail at a sign for "Hamilton Falls."

0.35   Reach the base of Hamilton Falls (N43 08.174' / W72 45.844'). Return the way you came.

0.7   Arrive back at the parking area.

Option

Going straight at the "Hamilton Falls" sign on the Hamilton Falls Trail leads you to the West River Trail in Jamaica State Park, where there are plenty of recreational opportunities, including biking, hiking, camping, and swimming.

A couple of boys swim in the cold pool below Hamilton Falls.

27 Buttermilk Falls (VT)

A short walk along Branch Brook takes you by three distinct falls and two nice deep swim holes.

Start: Pull-off on right side of Buttermilk Falls Road near sign for falls
Distance: 0.6-mile loop
Hiking time: About 20 minutes
Approximate elevation gain: 75 feet
Difficulty: Easy
Beauty: Very good

County: Windsor
Land status: Okemo State Forest
DeLorme map: Page 30, J-4 (marked)
Other maps: None
Trail contact: The Vermont River Conservancy; (802) 229-0820; www.vermontrivercon servancy.org/contact-us

Finding the trailhead: From the northern intersection of VT 100 and VT 103, about 1.7 miles north of downtown Ludlow, follow VT 103 North for 0.3 mile and turn right onto Buttermilk Falls Road. Continue 1.3 miles and park at a pull-off on the right near a sign for the falls. **GPS:** N43 26.121'/W72 43.607'

The Hike

Buttermilk Falls consists of three waterfalls spread over about a quarter mile along Branch Brook in Ludlow. From the parking area next to the "Buttermilk Falls Area" sign, head down and to the right to reach the lowest, and smallest, falls. Head back up along the river to the middle falls, which is a straight plunge. The pool below the middle falls is wide and somewhat deep and is a popular swimming spot.

Continue hiking up along the left (west) side of the river and in about 0.1 mile reach the pool below the upper falls. This pool is another wide deep pool that is excellent for swimming. You'll see the upper falls, which are primarily segmented horsetails. The right segment (looking upstream) is about 12 feet; the left is about 15 feet. There may also be a narrow plunge of about 10 feet near the informal hiking path.

Follow the path beyond this and you'll soon reach the end of the road and an old bridge. You can either take the road back to your vehicle or walk back down along the brook.

Buttermilk Falls

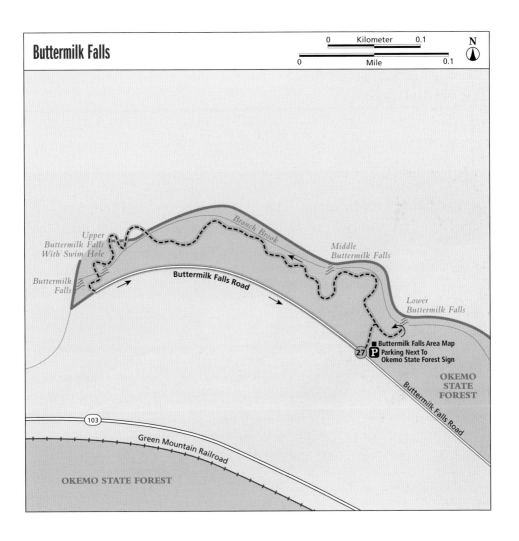

Upper
Buttermilk Falls
With Swim Hole

Branch Brook

Middle
Buttermilk Falls

Buttermilk
Falls

Buttermilk Falls Road

Lower
Buttermilk Falls

■ Buttermilk Falls Area Map
27 P Parking Next To
    Okemo State Forest Sign

OKEMO
STATE
FOREST

Buttermilk Falls Road

103

Green Mountain Railroad

OKEMO STATE FOREST

0   Kilometer   0.1
0   Mile   0.1

N

Miles and Directions

0.0 Start at the sign for Buttermilk Falls and head into the woods (counterclockwise). Head slightly downstream to the right to visit the lowest falls.

0.1 Arrive at the lowest falls (N43 26.136' / W72 43.564'). Head back up along the bank of the brook to the middle falls.

0.2 Reach the middle falls (N43 26.157' / W72 43.626'). Continue following a path upstream along the edge of the brook.

0.3 Follow the path a few more feet above the falls to the end of the old road, and take this back down to your vehicle.

0.6 Arrive back at your vehicle.

When the water level is low, two very distinct falls pour over the uppermost of the Buttermilk Falls.

28 Cascade Falls

You will first pass Little Cascade Falls before getting to 84-foot Cascade Falls, but getting to the bottom of the falls requires a short rough, steep descent.

Start: Parking lot on High Meadow Road, 0.4 mile from junction with Cascade Falls Road
Distance: 2.4 miles out and back
Hiking time: About 1.5 hours
Approximate elevation gain: 500 feet
Difficulty: Easy to moderate to top of falls; difficult to bottom of falls
Beauty: Excellent
County: Windsor
Land status: Mount Ascutney State Park

DeLorme map: Page 31, J-9 (not marked)
Other maps: Mount Ascutney State Park Recreational Guide: www.vtstateparks.com/pdfs/ascutney_rec_guide.pdf; Green Mountain Club Killington Area Hiking Trail Map with Ascutney & Okemo
Trail contact: Mount Ascutney State Park; (802) 674-2060; www.vtstateparks.com/htm/ascutney.htm

Finding the trailhead: From exit 8 off I-91, take VT 131 West for 3.1 miles. Turn right onto Cascade Falls Road and in a few hundred feet go left onto High Meadow Road; follow this for 0.4 mile to a parking lot for the Weathersfield Trail. **GPS:** N43 25.608'/W72 27.977'

The Hike

The Weathersfield Trail, located on the south side of Mount Ascutney, climbs all the way to the summit. However, you only need to follow this trail for 1.1 miles to reach Cascade Falls.

From the parking area, head into the woods, following the Weathersfield Trail. Gradually ascend, passing over some ledges that can be a bit slippery in wet weather. In 0.4 mile, and about 300 feet of climbing, you reach Little Cascade Falls. This waterfall drops about 45 feet, but unless you are there during the spring runoff or after a rain, it is not that impressive.

Continue for another 0.1 mile, cross over the stream, and climb up a ladder. From the ledge above the ladder, you can get a wonderful view to the south. The Weathersfield Trail continues to climb as it heads northwest, traversing the side of the mountain. You will get a few more good views. The trail levels off and then heads downhill slightly. At 1.1 miles you see a sign where the Weathersfield Trail heads to the right and continues climbing. Instead, head left down to the brook.

Reaching the brook, you are at the top of the waterfall. Mill Brook plunges precipitously off the ledge here, and you can get another fantastic view to the south. If you are comfortable on steep terrain, cross over the stream (upstream from the edge to prevent any nasty tumbles) and head down a very steep and eroded path along the right side of the stream. You'll get a great view of the falls from part of the way down.

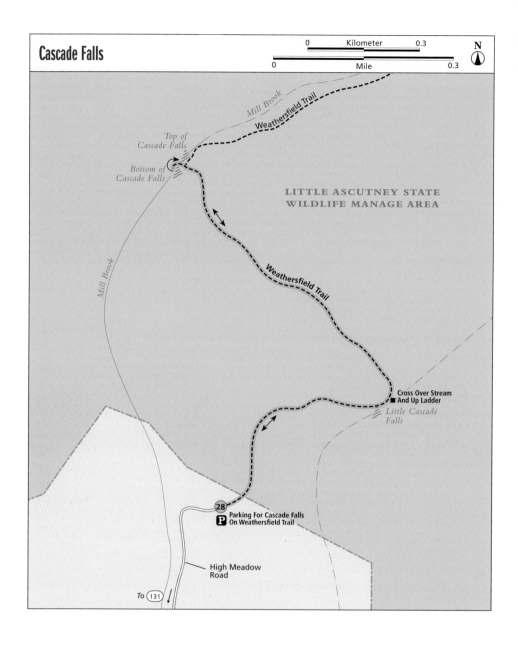

0   Kilometer   0.3

0   Mile   0.3

N

Mill Brook

Weathersfield Trail

Top of Cascade Falls

Bottom of Cascade Falls

LITTLE ASCUTNEY STATE
WILDLIFE MANAGE AREA

Weathersfield Trail

Mill Brook

Cross Over Stream
■ And Up Ladder

Little Cascade Falls

28
P Parking For Cascade Falls
On Weathersfield Trail

High Meadow Road

To 131

At the bottom, follow the stream back up to the base of the falls, where you can see the sheer rock wall stretching more than 80 feet straight up.

Head back the way you came, or make a day of it and continue to the summit of Mount Ascutney, where you can get unimpeded views in all directions from an observation tower.

Ice begins to coat the sides of the cliff on a cold October day.

Miles and Directions

0.0 Start from the parking area and head into the woods, following the Weathersfield Trail.

0.4 Reach Little Cascade Falls (N43 25.752'/W72 27.673'). Continue along the trail.

0.5 Cross over the brook and up a ladder, where you will get your first nice view.

1.1 Reach a junction. The Weathersfield Trail heads right; instead head left and in 100 feet reach the top of the waterfall. Cross over the stream, head down a steep path to the stream below the falls, then follow the stream up to the base of the falls.

1.2 Arrive at the bottom of Cascade Falls (N43 26.080'/W72 28.087'). Head back the same way.

2.4 Arrive back at the parking lot.

29 Hidden Falls

There is a good chance you'll have this little-known waterfall on Mount Ascutney's Bicentennial Trail all to yourself.

Start: Parking area at end of Coaching Lane
Distance: 1.8 miles out and back
Hiking time: About 1 hour
Approximate elevation gain: 400 feet
Difficulty: Easy to moderate
Beauty: Very good
County: Windsor
Land status: West Windsor Town Forest
DeLorme map: Page 31, I-9 (not marked)
Other map: Green Mountain Club Killington

Area Hiking Trail Map with Ascutney & Okemo (available for purchase online at greenmoun tainclub.org)
Trail contacts: West Windsor Town Clerk; (802) 484-7212; e-mail: west.windsor.townclerk@ valley.net
Sport Trails of the Ascutney Basin; stabvt.org
Special considerations: This trail is also used by mountain bikers.

Finding the trailhead: From exit 8 on I-91, head east on VT 131 for 0.4 mile. Turn left onto US 5 North and follow this for 1.2 miles. Turn left onto VT 44A/Back Mountain Road and follow this for 3 miles until it intersects VT 44. Take VT 44 West through the town of Brownsville and in 3.6 miles turn left onto Coaching Lane. Follow Coaching Lane for 0.6 mile then bear left, staying on Coaching Lane. Parking is at the end of the road in about 0.2 mile. **GPS:** N43 26.952' / W72 28.887'

The Hike

Hidden Falls is just off the yellow-blazed Bicentennial Trail, one of the lesser-used trails of Mount Ascutney. Be aware that there are popular mountain biking trails on this part of the mountain. This section of the trail is dual-use, so step out of the way if a mountain biker is coming by.

From the parking at the end of the road, follow the trail into the forest, where it turns to the left above a big field. The trail climbs through the forest, levels out for a while, and begins climbing again. There will be multiple trails coming from both sides, so make sure you follow the yellow blazes.

At 0.7 mile you cross a stream, and at 0.8 mile you hit a junction. There should be a sign at this junction. The Bicentennial Trail continues straight, but turn right onto the spur trail that leads to the falls, reaching them in 0.1 mile. (A spur trail to the left at the junction leads to some viewpoints, but these have grown in and are only worthwhile in winter when the leaves are off the trees.)

Hidden Falls; Gerry Falls

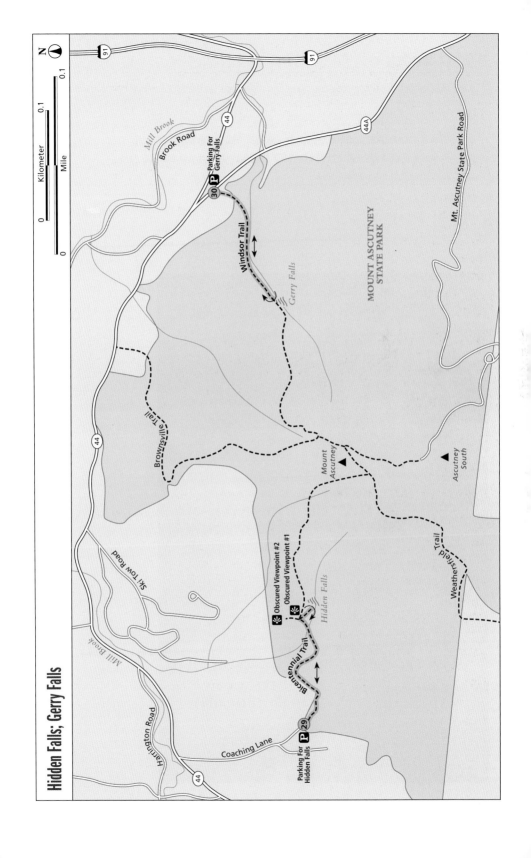

Miles and Directions

0.0 Start from the parking area and head into the woods on the Bicentennial Trail, marked by yellow blazes.

0.7 Cross a small stream.

0.8 Reach a trail junction. Head right onto the spur trail to the falls.

0.9 Reach Hidden Falls (N43 26.947' / W72 28.164'). Return the way you came.

1.8 Arrive back at the parking area.

Hidden Falls is a remarkably large waterfall tucked just a bit off the Bicentennial Trail.

30 Gerry Falls

Located partway up Mount Ascutney on the Windsor trail, Gerry Falls is a stair-stepped falls above a forested ravine.

See map on page 99.
Start: Parking for Windsor Trail on VT 44A/Back Mountain Road
Distance: 1.6 miles out and back
Hiking time: About 1 hour
Approximate elevation gain: 750 feet
Difficulty: Moderate
Beauty: Very good
County: Windsor
Land status: Mount Ascutney State Park

DeLorme map: Page 31, I-10 & 11 (not marked)
Other maps: Mount Ascutney State Park Recreational Guide: www.vtstateparks.com/pdfs/ascutney_rec_guide.pdf; Green Mountain Club Killington Area Hiking Trail Map with Ascutney & Okemo
Trail contact: Mount Ascutney State Park; (802) 674-2060; www.vtstateparks.com/htm/ascutney.htm

Finding the trailhead: From exit 8 on I-91, head east on VT 131 for 0.4 mile. Turn left onto US 5 North and follow this for 1.2 miles. Turn left onto VT 44A/Back Mountain Road and continue 2.8 miles. Turn left into the parking lot for the Windsor Trail. **GPS:** N43 27.419'/W72 25.326'

The Hike

From the parking lot, follow the Windsor Trail past a fence, through a field, and into the woods, where you begin to climb steadily. The river is on your left, deep down in a gorge.

Continue to climb and at 0.8 mile come to a sign for "Gerry Falls." Take the short spur out to the falls. The brook flows over large angular rock steps here, but the falls continue both above and below where the trail meets the brook. A sign here says, "In Memory of George Nelson Gerry—'The truth at the heart of nature, the light that is not of day, why seek it afar forever, when it cannot be lifted away' 1886–1931."

Return to your car the same way.

Miles and Directions

0.0 Start from the parking and follow the Windsor Trail through a field and up through the forest, with the brook on your left.

0.8 Reach the short spur trail to Gerry Falls. Continue 100 feet to the falls (N43 27.127'/W72 26.039'). Return to the parking area on same trail.

1.6 Arrive back at the parking area.

Option

For a bigger adventure, continue the 2.0 additional miles to the summit of Mount Ascutney, where there is a great viewing platform.

These small plunges are just a few of the many that comprise Gerry Falls.

31 Quechee Gorge

The gorge is one of the deepest in Vermont. With its unique geology, a waterfall at the northern end, an amazing view from a bridge, a visitor center, and a campground, this is a great outing for the whole family.

Start: Quechee State Park visitor center on US 4
Distance: 2.0 mile round-trip to see the whole gorge, waterfall, and view from the bridge
Hiking time: About 1 hour
Approximate elevation gain: 200 feet
Difficulty: Easy
Beauty: Excellent
County: Windsor
Land status: Quechee State Park
DeLorme map: Page 31, C-11 (marked)

Other map: Quechee Gorge State Park Trail System: www.vtstateparks.com/pdfs/quechee geo.pdf
Trail contact: Quechee State Park; (802) 295-2990; www.vtstateparks.com/htm/quechee .htm
Special considerations: You can also park in the parking lot near the shops, which is closer to the bridge but bypasses the walk through the woods.

Finding the trailhead: From exit 1 on I-89, take US 4 West for about 3 miles. Parking is at the Quechee Gorge State Park visitor center on the left. If you go over the bridge, you've gone too far. (You can also park closer to the gorge in the big lot on the right.) **GPS:** N43 38.214' / W72 24.352'

The Hike

Quechee Gorge is impressive in its sheer size. And, truthfully, the best view is right along the road from the edge of the bridge. This hike, however, provides other views along the gorge, as well as visiting the river at the bottom of the gorge and affording a good view of the waterfall at the top of the gorge. Between the hike and all the stores near the gorge, this makes a nice afternoon outing for everyone.

Starting at the visitor center, take the graded path behind the building. The trail traverses out and back at a very mild angle. At 0.2 mile you hit the Quechee Gorge Trail. Turn left and follow this for 0.5 mile to the bottom of the gorge. Along the way, much of the gorge is obscured by a fence, but you can get glimpses at certain points. When you reach the bottom of the gorge, head out into the river to see some small cascades and look back up toward the bridge.

When you are ready, head back up along the same trail, but continue past your original junction. Walk 0.8 mile, going under the bridge and following the trail upstream until you get a good view of Mill Pond Falls. The upper part of the falls is from a dam, but the lower portion is fairly impressive, with about a 30-foot drop.

From the bridge you can get a fantastic view to the south of the entire gorge.

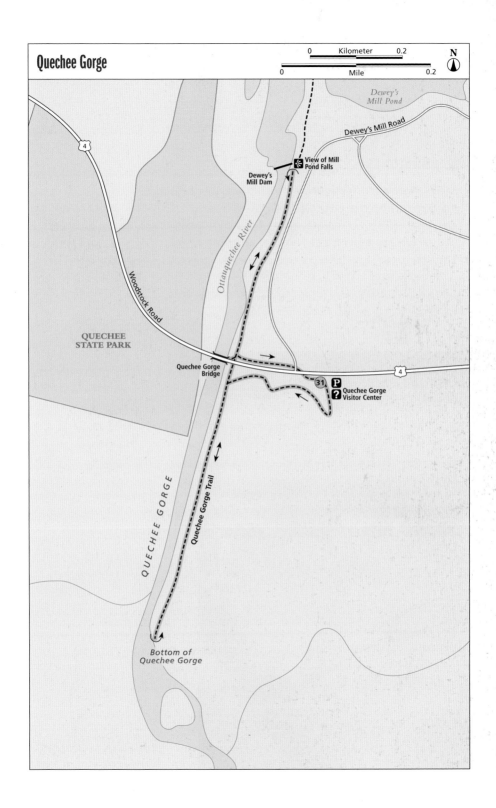

Quechee Gorge

Dewey's
Mill Pond

Dewey's Mill Road

View of Mill
Pond Falls

Dewey's
Mill Dam

Ottauquechee River

Woodstock Road

QUECHEE
STATE PARK

Quechee Gorge
Bridge

4

31

P
?

Quechee Gorge
Visitor Center

Quechee Gorge Trail

QUECHEE GORGE

Bottom of
Quechee Gorge

Interestingly, water from the falls and Mill Pond was used to make shoddy, which is reworked wool. Some of this shoddy was actually used in uniforms for the Red Sox and Yankees in the early part of the 1900s. Return along the same trail, but before heading to your car, walk across the bridge and take a look down. The bridge is a whopping 165 feet above the river. Walk back along the road to the visitor center.

If you're in the area and have time, you can stay at the Quechee Park campground.

Miles and Directions

0.0 Start at the visitor center and take the trail behind the building.

0.2 Reach the Quechee Gorge Trail. Turn left.

0.7 Reach the bottom of the gorge (N43 37.914' / W72 24.625'). Head out into the river to get a look upstream at the bridge. Head back along the trail.

1.5 After passing under the bridge and continuing along the path, reach the viewpoint of Mill Pond Falls (N43 38.450' / W72 24.398'). Turn around and head back along the trail.

1.8 Reach the bridge. Head out and take a look from both sides.

2.0 Arrive back at the visitor center parking lot.

Mill Pond Falls is comprised of both manmade and natural drops.

32 Thundering Falls / Thundering Brook Falls / Bakers Falls

With a 125-foot drop composed of multiple cascades flowing over steeply angled bedrock, this is a very impressive waterfall offering multiple viewing options, including a boardwalk that sits above the large lower falls.

Start: Parking on side of Thundering Brook Road, 1.3 miles from junction with US 4
Distance: 0.5-mile loop
Hiking time: About 20 minutes
Approximate elevation gain: 200 feet
Difficulty: Moderate
Beauty: Excellent
County: Rutland
Land status: Green Mountain National Forest
DeLorme map: Page 30, B-2 (not marked)

Other map: Thundering Falls Recreation Opportunity Guide: www.fs.usda.gov/Internet/ FSE_MEDIA/stelprdb5315878.pdf
Trail contact: Green Mountain National Forest— Rochester Ranger Station; (802) 767-4261; www.fs.usda.gov/detail/greenmountain/ about-forest/offices
Special considerations: There is a short road walk as part of this loop.

Finding the trailhead: From the intersection of US 4 and VT 100, just west of the Killington Access Road, take US 4 East for 0.5 mile. Turn left onto Thundering Brook Road and continue 1.3 miles; parking is on the left. The trail begins about 0.1 mile farther down the road on the left at signs for the Appalachian Trail. **GPS:** N43 40.784′/W72 47.301′

The Hike

Thundering Falls is just a short spur trail off the Appalachian Trail, which follows the Appalachian Mountains from Georgia to Maine. These falls, which are really steeply angled cascades, total 125 feet, with the lower falls counting for almost 90 feet of that. During the spring melt, these falls are truly "thundering" and are a sight to behold.

From the parking area, head down the road. Turn left onto the Appalachian Trail and follow this for 0.1 mile. Turn left off the Appalachian Trail at a signed junction to the falls. You will reach a viewing platform that sits high above the falls, providing a fantastic view. From the platform, follow the trail up along the side of the falls to reach the upper falls, a smaller version of the lower falls. Continue along this trail, passing the old dam and a nice pool below a small cascade, and arrive back at the parking area.

Thundering Falls/Thundering Brook Falls/Bakers Falls

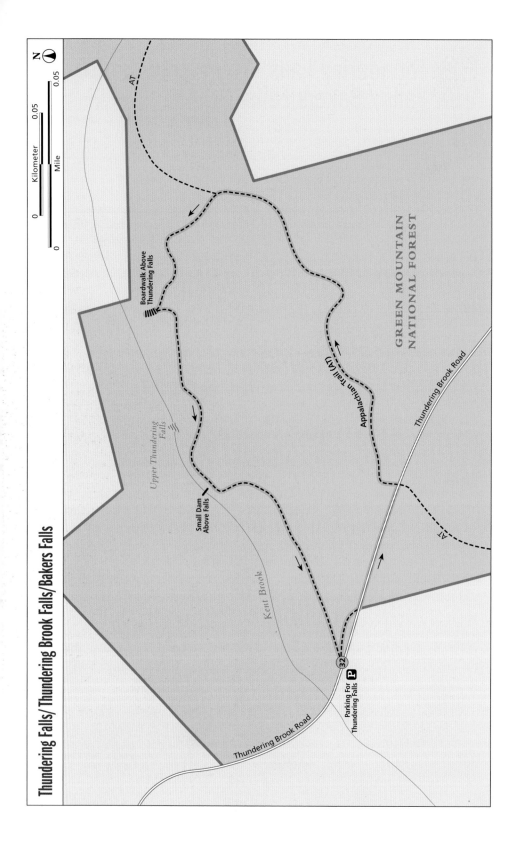

N

Kilometer
0   0.05   0.05

Mile
0   0.05

AT

Boardwalk Above
Thundering Falls

Upper Thundering
Falls

Small Dam
Above Falls

Kent Brook

Appalachian Trail (AT)

GREEN MOUNTAIN
NATIONAL FOREST

Thundering Brook Road

AT

Thundering Brook Road

Parking For
Thundering Falls

32

Miles and Directions

0.0 Start from the parking area and continue walking down the road.

0.05 Turn left onto the Appalachian Trail.

0.2 Turn left at a signed junction for Thundering Falls.

0.25 Reach the viewing platform above the falls (N43 40.840'/W72 47.169'). Continue following the steep trail up along the edge of the falls.

0.35 Reach the top of the upper falls.

0.4 Reach the dam above the falls.

0.5 Arrive back at the parking area.

The top part of Thundering Falls can be seen pouring into a small pool before continuing along even larger falls below and to the right of the photo.

33 Old City Falls

A hidden gem, Old City Falls in Strafford drops almost 50 feet and includes a main vertical plunge and two lower cascades. To get the best views, however, you'll have to be comfortable rock hopping in the stream and climbing a steep slope using trees as holds.

Start: Parking area on Old City Falls Road
Distance: 0.5 mile out and back
Hiking time: About 10 minutes
Approximate elevation gain: 125 feet
Difficulty: Easy to moderate to base; difficult to get best view of the upper falls
Beauty: Excellent
County: Orange
Land status: Old City Falls Nature Preserve (owned by Town of Strafford)

DeLorme map: Page 35, E-12 (not marked)
Other maps: None
Trail contact: Town of Strafford; (802) 765-4411
Special considerations: A view of the complete upper falls requires a steep scramble up the side of the hill, and even a decent view from the bottom requires you to get into the stream on rocks.

Finding the trailhead: (From I-91) From exit 13 off I-91, head east (toward Hanover, New Hampshire) on South Main Street / West Wheelock Street. At the bottom of the hill in 0.25 mile, head left at the light before the bridge onto River Road. Take this for 1.1 miles, where it meets up with US 5. Take US 5 North for 4.3 miles; turn left onto VT 132 West and continue 10.5 miles. In the town of South Strafford, stay straight onto the Justin Morrill Memorial Highway as VT 132 heads off to the left. Stay on this for 3.1 miles, veering right in the town of Strafford, and turn right onto Old City Falls Road. Follow this road up and to the left; in 0.8 mile turn left into the parking area for Old City Falls.

(From I-89) From exit 2 on I-89, take VT 132 East and follow this road for 6.2 miles. At the intersection head left onto the Justin Morrill Memorial Highway. Continue 3.1 miles, veering right in the town of Strafford, and turn right onto Old City Falls Road. Follow this road up and to the left; in 0.8 mile turn left into the parking area for Old City Falls. **GPS:** N43 52.939' / W72 22.207'

The Hike

This fall is beautiful, and runs all year long, but note that getting a good view of the falls requires some tricky rock hopping and scrambling. If you come in the off-season, you will need to park at the gate and walk 0.1 mile down the road. During summer you can pull into the parking area, which also has a nice shelter and picnic tables.

From the picnic area, head to the back edge of the field and into the woods on the only visible trail. It slopes downhill and then makes a sharp left turn as it descends, somewhat steeply, down to the river below. Once you reach the edge of the brook, follow the rough path to the base of the falls.

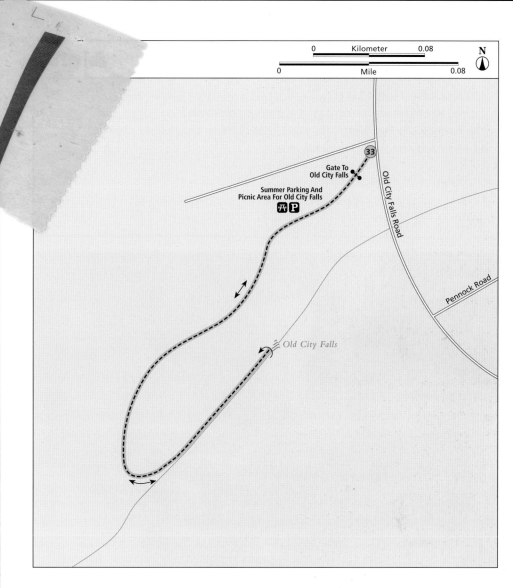

When you reach the end of the trail, you will notice that you still don't have a great view. From here you can rock hop to the middle of the stream to get a good view of the lower cascade and the top half of the upper falls. The lower cascade is about 20 feet long and curves along the sloping bedrock. To see the upper falls, a 25-foot plunge, you will need to climb along the edge using rocks and roots for support.

Over the years, climbers and severe storms have eroded the edge, making it even more difficult to climb up to the pool below the upper plunge. Please do so only if you are a very capable climber and conditions are dry.

The rock walls surrounding Old City Falls create an intimate setting; the brook below the falls is relaxing and beautiful. Return using the same trail you came down.

Miles and Directions

0.0   Start from the parking and picnic area and head down the trail into the woods. (***Note:*** Add 0.1 mile each way if parking at the front gate in the off-season.)

0.25   Reach Old City Falls (N43 52.864' / W72 22.247'). Return back along the same trail.

0.5   Arrive back at the picnic and parking area.

The upper part of Old City Falls is a plunge while the bottom is a cascade that gently slopes around a curve.

34 Glen Falls

Glen Falls is a narrow 25-foot plunge. With beautiful cascades both above and below, this short trip near Lake Morey is well worth the visit if you're in the area.

Start: Parking lot off Lake Morey Road, across from Vermont Fish and Wildlife boat launch
Distance: 0.6 mile out and back
Hiking time: About 20 minutes
Approximate elevation gain: 125 feet
Difficulty: Easy
Beauty: Very good
County: Orange

Land status: N/A
DeLorme map: Page 36, D-2 (not marked; Glen Falls Brook marked)
Other maps: None
Trail contact: Rivendell Trails Association; (603) 353-2170, ext. 209; www .crossrivendelltrail.org

Finding the trailhead: From exit 15 on I-91, follow signs to Lake Morey Road (right turn off ramp if coming from north; left turn if coming from south). At the intersection with Lake Morey Road, head straight (west) and follow this for 1.3 miles. A parking area is on the left, across from a Vermont Fish and Wildlife boat launch. The trail begins a few hundred feet back along the road on the west side, across from a tennis court at a private residence. **GPS:** N43 55.261' / W72 09.614'

The Hike

From the parking lot, head back to Lake Morey Road and turn right. In a few hundred feet you will see a tennis court on your left; the trailhead is across from this on the right. Shortly you see the first cascade, and in 0.2 mile from the parking area you reach the main plunge, which drops about 25 feet through a narrow cleft in the rock into a small circular pool. Hike for another few hundred feet above this main plunge to see some really nice cascades that wind down through the forest.

This trail is part of the Cross Rivendell Trail, a 36-mile hiking trail that goes from Vershire, Vermont, to the summit of Mount Cube in Orford, New Hampshire. Return to the parking area the way you came.

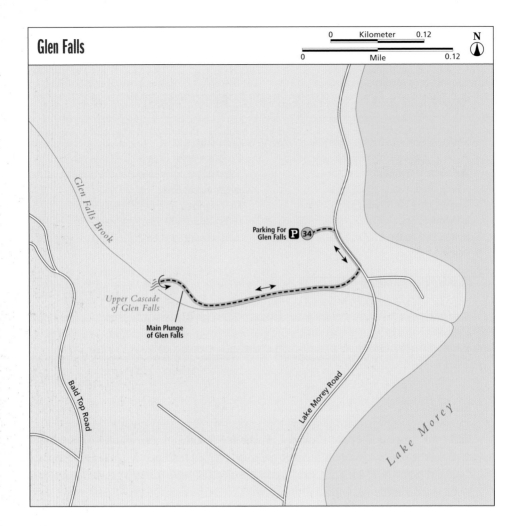

Miles and Directions

0.0 Start from the parking lot, get back on the road, and turn right.

0.05 Turn right onto a trail across the street from a tennis court.

0.2 Reach the main plunge of Glen Falls (N43 55.227' / W72 09.736'). Continue along the trail.

0.3 Reach the viewpoint of upper Glen Falls. Return the way you came.

0.6 Arrive back at the parking area.

The upper part of Glen Falls consists of a series of cascades and plunges that wind down around small cliffs.

35 Falls of Lana

One of the most beautiful waterfalls in Vermont, the Falls of Lana are composed of a number of steep drops and a rushing channel of water that makes a turn below the main drop. The falls can be accessed from both sides, and you can jump into a deep swimming hole below the first drop.

Start: Parking area on VT 53 just south of Branbury State Park
Distance: 1.5 miles out and back
Hiking time: About 45 minutes
Approximate elevation gain: 350 feet
Difficulty: Easy to first viewpoint; moderate to difficult to bottom of falls
Beauty: Excellent
County: Addison

Land status: Moosalamoo National Recreation Area, Green Mountain National Forest
DeLorme map: Page 33, E-10 (marked)
Other maps: None
Trail contact: Green Mountain National Forest—Middlebury Ranger Station; (802) 388-4362; www.fs.usda.gov/detail/greenmountain/about-forest/offices

Finding the trailhead: (From Middlebury) Travel 6.7 miles south on US 7 to VT 53 South. Continue 3.8 miles south; the parking lot is on the left, just past Branbury State Park.

(From Rutland) From the junction of US 7 and US 4 in Rutland, take US 7 North to Brandon. Turn right onto VT 73 and continue 3 miles to VT 53. Take VT 53 North for 5.25 miles to a parking area on the right. If you see Branbury State Park, you've gone too far.

(From the east) From the junction of VT 100 and VT 73 just south of Rochester, follow VT 73 for 14 miles then turn right onto VT 53. The parking area is on the right in 5.25 miles. If you see Branbury State Park, you've gone too far. **GPS:** N43 54.028'/W73 03.853'

The Hike

The Falls of Lana are truly spectacular. You could spend hours here viewing the falls from all the different angles and jumping into the deep pool about halfway down. Sucker Brook is a beautiful stream, which turns sharply before plunging off the ledge. The first two cascades, partway down the falls, fall into a deep pool, which has very little current and is deep enough to allow jumping off the surrounding rocks.

Below this pool the falls make a sharp left and pour down a narrow flume, bounded by a cliff on one side and a cool rock fin on the other. At the bottom, the falls take another right turn and cascade down the final stretch. The total drop is just over 100 feet.

From the parking area, follow the narrow trail that heads uphill and turn right on a dirt road. Follow this and at 0.3 mile come to a clearing where there is a large black pipe. You can get your first view of the falls by heading left and following a fence until you reach a nice viewpoint a few hundred feet down. Head back up and

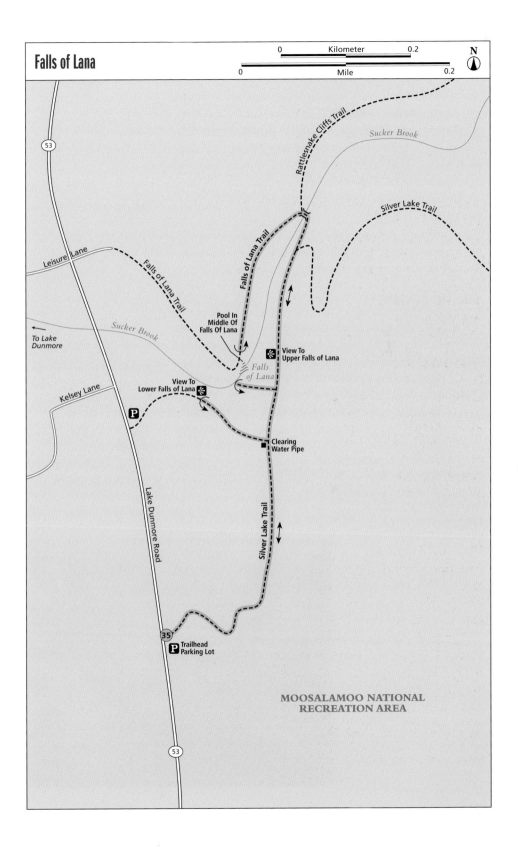

Falls of Lana

0 Kilometer 0.2

0 Mile 0.2

N

53

Rattlesnake Cliffs Trail

Sucker Brook

Silver Lake Trail

Falls of Lana Trail

Leisure Lane

Falls of Lana Trail

Sucker Brook

To Lake
Dunmore

Pool In
Middle Of
Falls Of Lana

View To Upper Falls of Lana

Falls
of Lana

View To
Lower Falls of Lana

Kelsey Lane

P

Clearing
Water Pipe

Lake Dunmore Road

Silver Lake Trail

35

Trailhead
P Parking Lot

MOOSALAMOO NATIONAL
RECREATION AREA

53

continue on the trail for a short distance; then head down a rough path to get a nice view of the upper falls. You can bushwhack down rough informal trails here to get to the pool and even to the bottom of the falls, but be prepared for treacherous footing.

To get to the other side of the falls, get back on the main trail and follow the stream for another 0.3 mile, passing the junction with the trail to Silver Lake. Reach a footbridge over Sucker Brook. Cross the bridge and take a trail on your left onto the Falls of Lana Trail, which leads to the pool at the base of the upper falls.

Apparently the Falls of Lana was named for US Army General John Wool, who explored the area in 1850. The Spanish word for wool is *llana*, hence the name of the falls.

If you have the time, make the trip to Rattlesnake Point by heading right after crossing the bridge. From the point you'll have amazing views out over Lake Dunmore. Retrace your steps to get back to the parking area.

Miles and Directions

- **0.0** Start at the parking area, following the trail up into the woods.
- **0.05** Head right on the gravel/dirt road then shortly turn left, continuing to follow the road.
- **0.3** Reach the water pipe. Head downhill along the fence for a few hundred feet to get the first view of the falls. Return to the trail and continue to follow it.
- **0.4** Turn left onto the informal trail, following the steep hill as far down as you feel comfortable. You will get a great view of the upper falls. If you're adventurous, you can get all the way to the bottom of the falls.
- **0.6** Cross over Sucker Brook on a bridge, then head left on the Falls of Lana Trail to reach the pool in the middle of the falls.
- **0.75** Reach the pool in middle of the falls (N43 54.262'/W73 03.770'). Return to the parking lot using the same trail.
- **1.5** Arrive back at the parking lot.

A swimmer readies herself to jump into a pool below the upper part of the Falls of Lana.

36 Bailey Falls

This little-known waterfall, just to the east of Middlebury Gap, is truly one of Vermont's finest. You'll need to make a short bushwhack to get there, but once you do, you'll be surprised at the size of the falls.

Start: Parking area at gate on south side of VT 125
Distance: 0.5 mile out and back
Hiking time: About 30 minutes
Approximate elevation gain: 50 feet
Difficulty: Moderate
Beauty: Spectacular
County: Addison
Land status: Green Mountain National Forest
DeLorme map: Page 33, D-13 (not marked)

Other maps: None
Trail contact: Green Mountain National Forest–Middlebury Ranger Station; (802) 388-4362; www.fs.usda.gov/detail/greenmountain/about-forest/offices
Special considerations: You will be walking on a ski trail for a short while, so be sure to respect the operation and stay out of the way of any machinery or vehicles.

Finding the trailhead: Parking for Bailey Falls is located on the south side of VT 125, 5.3 miles west of the junction with VT 100 in Hancock and 10.2 miles east of the junction with VT 116. Parking is on the east side of Middlebury Gap, 0.8 mile east of the high point and 1.5 miles east of the main entrance to the Middlebury Snow Bowl. Park in a dirt pull-off next to a gate; a dirt road heads to a pedestrian bridge across the stream to the base of a chairlift. **GPS:** N43 55.585' / W72 56.604'

The Hike

This is one of my favorite falls in Vermont, and it's just barely off the beaten path, literally! It's just 0.25 mile from the road, but you'll need to bushwhack through the forest and down an embankment to reach the falls.

Follow the sloping path behind where you parked and cross a small footbridge in sight of a ski lift tow, which is part of the Middlebury Snow Bowl. When you reach the edge of the ski trail, head left to stay along the edge of the woods. Continue for around 200 yards, and as the ski trail begins to ascend, head left into the woods.

You may be able to hear the falls from here. Head into the woods away from the ski trail, veering slightly uphill. Come over a rise and see the stream below. Use your judgment as to the best way down, as it depends on the season, conditions, and where you entered the woods. Hold onto trees and use a pole if you have one—the edge of Robbins Branch is steep and eroding in many places.

The falls consist of three drops that fan out above pools. However, there are many interesting cascades, and near the bottom the water courses through a narrow rock cleft. Be very careful if crossing the stream.

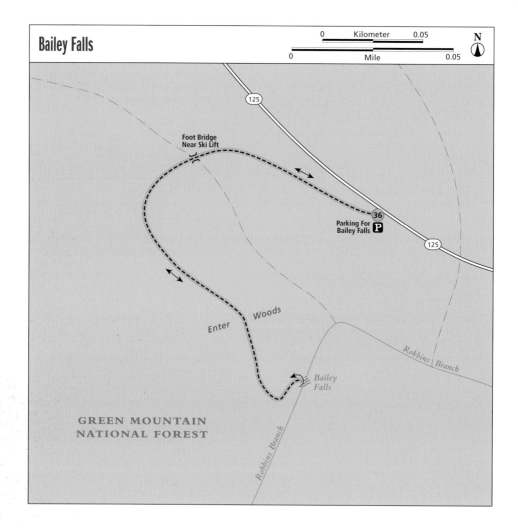

Miles and Directions

0.0 Start down the sloping path directly behind where you parked your car.

0.05 Cross a wooden footbridge and turn left when you hit the ski trail.

0.1 Head left into the woods as the ski trail starts to climb uphill. After crossing over a slight rise, carefully traverse down to Robbins Branch. **Note:** There is no trail, so take the path of least resistance through the woods.

0.25 Reach Bailey Falls (N43 55.540' / W72 56.634'). Head back the way you came.

0.5 Arrive back at your car.

BUSHWHACKING

Bushwhacking is the process of crossing terrain that has no trail. Sometimes it may be an easy walk along an open pine needle–coated forest floor; other times it may take hours just to move a mile or less due to dense shrubbery or understory. High-elevation spruce forests are notoriously difficult places to bushwhack.

When bushwhacking in New England forests, it is very easy to get disoriented. Make sure you pay close attention to your whereabouts. If possible, use a GPS unit or smart phone with topo maps pre-installed, and track your progress so that you can backtrack if needed.

Long pants, long sleeves, and glasses can protect your body and eyes from scratches. Use trees and rocks as hand- and footholds when the going gets steep, and always check to make sure that your hold is secure before putting your weight on it. Walk on rocks and avoid stepping on plants whenever possible, especially around sensitive areas along the banks of rivers and streams.

Finally, tell people where you are going, and travel with a companion whenever possible. Injury is more likely, and rescue more difficult, when you're traveling off-trail.

Bailey Falls consists of multiple sets of cascades.

37 Texas Falls

The trails and observation sites at this very popular, and highly photographed, falls and geologic formation allow for many interesting vantage points of this must-see destination.

Start: Parking area on Texas Falls Road, 0.5 mile from junction with VT 125
Distance: 0.45 mile out and back
Hiking time: About 15 minutes
Approximate elevation gain: 100 feet
Difficulty: Easy
Beauty: Spectacular
County: Addison
Land status: Green Mountain National Forest
DeLorme map: Page 33, D-14 (marked)
Other map: Texas Falls Area Trails: www

.fs.usda.gov/Internet/FSE_MEDIA/stel prdb5315875.pdf
Trail contact: Green Mountain National Forest—Middlebury Ranger Station; (802) 388-4362; www.fs.usda.gov/detail/greenmountain/about-forest/offices
Special considerations: The falls area will be busy on weekends and during foliage season. Hurricane Irene in 2011 severely affected the falls and closed down the area for a while, but everything is open again.

Finding the trailhead: (From the east) From the junction of VT 125 and VT 100 in Hancock, take VT 125 West for 3 miles and turn right onto Texas Falls Road. A fairly large parking area is on the left in 0.5 mile. To get to the trail, walk back down the road over the bridge and turn left at the sign.

(From the west) From the junction of US 7 and VT 125 in East Middlebury, take VT 125 East for 13 miles and turn left onto Texas Falls Road. A fairly large parking area is on the left in 0.5 mile. To get to the trail, walk back down the road over the bridge and turn left at the sign. **GPS:** N43 56.126'/W72 54.120'

The Hike

Texas Falls is very popular, so most of the access to the falls is fenced off and you are required to stay on the trails behind the fences. That's okay, though, because there are still a number of great views of the falls. Texas Falls comprises two nice plunges that flow through a narrow ravine, as well as two smaller falls. There is also a 1.2-mile nature trail that heads into the woods for a bit before returning to the falls; however, this hike just describes access to different views of the falls.

From the parking lot you can cross the street and get a glimpse of the falls. Walk across the bridge on the road and you will see a sign and a map for Texas Falls. Head left here and start across the bridge. From the bridge you can see the double plunge as the water pours into a narrow chasm. Cross the bridge and turn right onto the trail. Shortly you will see a spur trail on the right that descends down some really nice stone steps to the bottom of the chasm. From here you can look upstream and see the falls as well as a really interesting cave below the lower plunge.

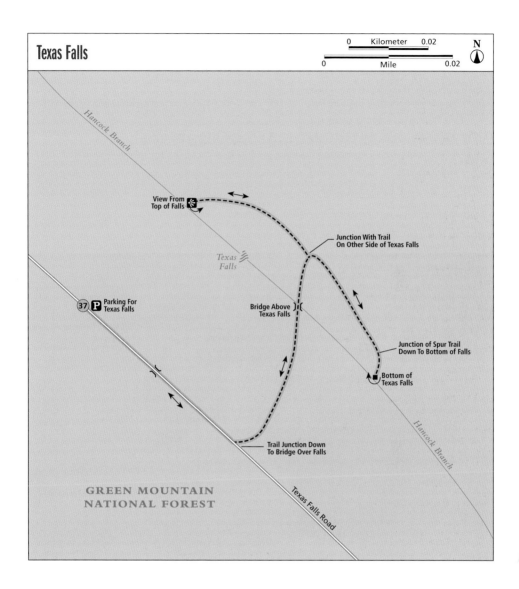

Texas Falls

0   Kilometer   0.02

0   Mile   0.02

N

Hancock Branch

View From
Top of Falls

Junction With Trail
On Other Side of Texas Falls

Texas
Falls

Parking For
Texas Falls

Bridge Above
Texas Falls

Junction of Spur Trail
Down To Bottom of Falls

Bottom of
Texas Falls

Trail Junction Down
To Bridge Over Falls

Hancock Branch

GREEN MOUNTAIN
NATIONAL FOREST

Texas Falls Road

Head back up the trail and turn left, heading upstream. Pass the bridge for a moment and go a little bit farther, where you can get to the top of the falls and look downstream. From here, head back over the bridge to the parking area. You can eat lunch at some nice picnic tables just up the road.

Miles and Directions

0.0 Start from the parking area; walk back down the road, and cross the bridge.

0.05 Turn left at the "Texas Falls" sign.

0.1 After crossing this second bridge, turn right.

0.15 Turn right onto the spur that leads to the bottom of the falls.

0.2 Reach the bottom of the falls (N43 56.110' / W72 54.072'). Turn around and head back up the trail the way you came.

0.25 Head left back up the trail at the intersection, continuing past the bridge.

0.3 Reach the top of the falls. Return to the parking area by crossing back over the bridge the way you came.

0.45 Arrive back at the parking area.

A cave is located just below the main drops of the falls.

38 Moss Glen Falls (Granville)

Vermont's famous Route 100 travels north–south through the middle of the state, border to border. This little gem of a waterfall is right off the road. A nice boardwalk to a viewpoint of the falls makes it accessible for most. Wander off the boardwalk to visit Little Moss Glen Falls as well.

Start: Roadside off VT 100 in Granville Gap
Distance: 0.2 mile out and back (with spur to little Moss Glen Falls)
Hiking time: About 10 minutes
Approximate elevation gain: 25 feet
Difficulty: Easy
Beauty: Very good
County: Addison
Land status: Granville Gulf State Reservation
DeLorme map: Page 34, A-1 (marked)

Other maps: None
Trail contact: Vermont Department of Forests, Parks and Recreation, Lands Administration Division; (802) 272-4156; vtfpr.org/lands/vtna.cfm#mgfg
Special considerations: Parking is roadside and is limited, so it may be difficult to find a spot on busy summer weekends or during fall foliage season. The boardwalk makes this wheelchair accessible.

Finding the trailhead: Parking for Moss Glen Falls in Granville Gap is located on the west side of VT 100, 13 miles south of the intersection with VT 17 in Irasville/Waitsfield and 6.9 miles north of the intersection with VT 125 in Hancock. **GPS:** N44 01.133' / W72 50.926'

The Hike

You will catch a glimpse of Moss Glen Falls as you drive along VT 100, but take an extra 10 minutes to visit in person. This 30-foot waterfall is very photogenic.

From the parking area, follow the short boardwalk to the end, where there is a larger viewing area. You can also go around and below the boardwalk to get a more intimate view of the falls. On your way back you'll see that the boardwalk crosses a small stream. Follow this stream for a few hundred feet up to a small pool below Little Moss Glen Falls, a narrow cascade that slides down a 45-degree rocky slab surrounded by moss.

Note: If you are using a tripod to photograph Moss Glen Falls, do not put it on the boardwalk—it will move when people are walking. Set your tripod on firm ground.

Miles and Directions

0.0 Start from the parking area and follow the boardwalk toward the falls.

0.1 Reach Moss Glen Falls (N44 01.081' / W72 51.005').

0.15 On your return to your car, head left upstream to visit Little Moss Glen Falls (N44 01.129' / W72 50.980').

0.2 Arrive back at the parking area.

Just off the road, Moss Glen Falls is accessible via a short boardwalk.

39 Abbey Pond Cascades

A series of cascades that drop almost 100 feet and are tucked under a think canopy, this gem of a waterfall is just a short hike in. Make sure to head to the bottom of the falls, below the bridge, to get the best view.

Start: Parking area at end of Abbey Pond Road, 0.4 mile from junction with VT 116
Distance: 0.75 mile out and back (to visit bottom and top of cascades)
Hiking time: About 30 minutes
Approximate elevation gain: 250 feet
Difficulty: Easy to moderate
Beauty: Excellent
County: Addison
Land status: Green Mountain National Forest

DeLorme map: Page 39, K-10 (Abbey Pond Trail marked)
Other map: Green Mountain National Forest Abbey Pond Trail Recreational Guide: www .fs.usda.gov/Internet/FSE_MEDIA/stel prdb5314969.pdf
Trail contact: Green Mountain National Forest—Middlebury Ranger Station; (802) 388-4362; www.fs.usda.gov/detail/ greenmountain/about-forest/offices

Finding the trailhead: Take VT 116 North at the junction with VT 125 in East Middlebury. (This junction is 0.5 mile east of the junction of US 7 and VT 125, which is 3.8 miles south of Middlebury on US 7.) Travel north on VT 116 for 4.3 miles; turn right onto Abbey Pond Road at a sign for the "Abbey Pond Trail." Parking is at the end of this road in 0.4 mile. **GPS:** N44 01.844' / W73 05.294'

The Hike

The Abbey Pond Trail leaves from the parking area and follows a wide gravel path into the woods. It narrows a bit as you climb, and in 0.25 mile you get to a wooden bridge. The cascades are both above and below you on the stream.

Informal trails on both sides lead both upstream to the falls in a narrower gorge and downstream, where the brook cascades down slanted rock. There is a gravel pit just below the bottom of the cascades, but it shouldn't detract too much from your enjoyment. The trail continues for another 1.8 miles to Abbey Pond, if you're so inclined.

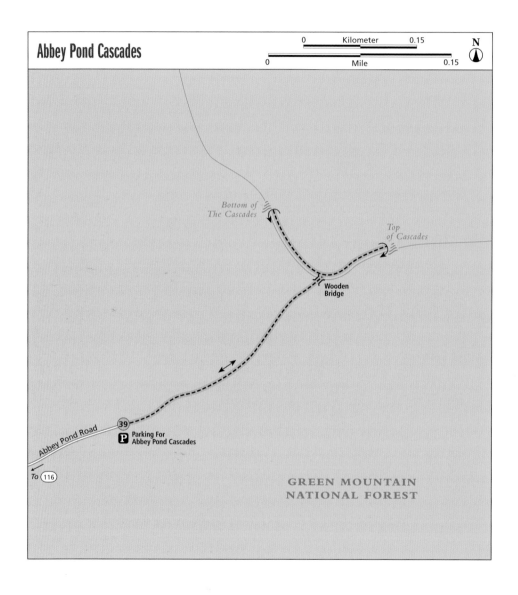

Abbey Pond Cascades

0   Kilometer   0.15

0   Mile   0.15

N

*Bottom of
The Cascades*

*Top
of Cascades*

**Wooden
Bridge**

Abbey Pond Road

39

P Parking For
Abbey Pond Cascades

To 116

GREEN MOUNTAIN
NATIONAL FOREST

Miles and Directions

0.0 Start hiking the Abbey Pond Trail, which leaves from the end of the parking lot.

0.25 Reach the wooden bridge and the Abbey Pond Cascades (N44 01.999' / W73 05.085').

0.5 After exploring the cascades above and below the bridge, use the informal trails on both sides of the stream to head back down the Abbey Pond Trail.

0.75 Arrive back at the parking area.

These dramatic falls are located just a few hundred feet above the bridge.

40 Bartlett Falls

This wide, beautiful waterfall pours over an overhanging rock down to a very large pool. The size of this pool (ideal for swimming) and the fact that you can (carefully) climb behind the waterfall during low flow make this one of the coolest locations in the state.

Start: Parking area on Lincoln Road, 0.2 mile from junction with VT 17
Distance: 0.1 mile out and back (basically roadside)
Hiking time: About 5 minutes
Approximate elevation gain: 25 feet
Difficulty: Easy
Beauty: Spectacular

County: Addison
Land status: Town of Bristol
DeLorme map: Page 39, H-19 (not marked)
Other maps: None
Trail contact: Town of Bristol; (802) 453-2410
Special considerations: This can be very crowded on a hot summer day.

Finding the trailhead: From the junction of US 7 and VT 17, 7.8 miles north of Middlebury, follow VT 17 East for 7 miles. Just after passing through Bristol, turn right onto Lincoln Road. Park on the side of the road in 0.2 mile. (**Note:** There are many small trails heading down to the falls. The main parking area on the immediate right after turning onto Lincoln Road is not the parking for the falls.) **GPS:** N44 07.640'/W73 02.792'

The Hike

This block type waterfall and the surrounding gorge are also referred to as New Haven River Gorge or Bristol Falls. This beautiful 15-foot waterfall plunges into a very wide and long pool, and you will likely see a lot of people here on hot summer days.

There are a lot of parking pull-offs along Lincoln Road, and it may take you a bit of time to find the real Bartlett Falls. That's okay, though; there are many smaller photogenic cascades and falls both above and below the main plunge. Above the falls, the sloping bedrock ledges can make for good waterslides in slow water.

Once you find the main falls, you'll see a great vantage point downstream that is higher than the falls. This affords a good view of the layers of bedrock, which are very distinct in their bench formations. There are spots deep enough to jump in and spots shallow enough for children to play in. If the current is low and you're comfortable climbing on wet rock, you can climb up onto the ledge to get behind the waterfall.

Bartlett Falls pours over a ledge that hangs out over the lower rock layers, allowing an opportunity to get behind the waterfall.

Miles and Directions

0.0 Start from a parking spot on the side of Lincoln Road and head toward the river.

0.05 Reach Bartlett Falls at the edge of the large pool, and follow paths down to water level (N44 07.636'/W73 02.815'). Return the way you came.

0.1 Arrive back at your vehicle.

41 Huntington Gorge

One of the most beautiful sections of river in Vermont, this unique gorge is infamous for the number of deaths that have occurred here, but it should not be missed on any waterfall tour of Vermont.

Start: Signed parking area on Dugway Road, 1.4 miles from junction with Huntington Road
Distance: 0.2-mile loop (almost roadside)
Hiking time: About 5 minutes
Approximate elevation gain: 50 feet
Difficulty: Easy to top; moderate to bottom
Beauty: Spectacular
County: Chittenden

Land status: Private land
DeLorme map: Page 45, K-12 (not marked)
Other maps: None
Trail contact: N/A
Special considerations: Do not jump from the gorge walls, and only swim in the bottom pool if the water, and current, is low.

Finding the trailhead: From exit 11 on I-89, follow US 2 South for 1.6 miles. In downtown Richmond turn right onto Bridge Street. In 0.6 mile turn right onto Huntington Road, and in 3.5 miles turn left onto Dugway Road. A signed parking area is on the right in 1.4 miles. **GPS:** N44 22.044' / W72 58.150'

The Hike

This truly stunning gorge is also the deadliest location in Vermont, with more than twenty known deaths here in the past sixty years, as noted on a sign next to the falls. The sign's list ends at 1994, but there continue to be deaths here every few years, the most recent (as of this writing) in 2012.

People die here for a number of reasons. Some people swimming above the falls have been swept down through the falls. Others have dived into the lower pool and hit rocks, because although the pool is deep, it's really two pools, with higher rock ledge in the middle that is unseen from above. And people who do go swimming can get caught in a whirlpool and dragged under. In the 1970s one part of the rock that had trapped people was dynamited, but that hasn't stopped the deaths from occurring.

This is not meant to turn you away from visiting but to make you aware that this is a dangerous place. Don't go into the water unless you know exactly what you're doing and are there with people who have been there before.

From the parking area you can take any path to the river. You can either walk down along the rocks or head down the road to take a somewhat steep path down to the bottom of the gorge.

In the 1800s this gorge was the site of a gristmill. In the early 1900s the property was sold to a power company, which diverted much of the water and used it for power generation. Since the 1950s the property has been privately owned and has been returned mostly to its natural state.

Miles and Directions

0.0 Start from the parking lot and head over to the rocks next to the top of falls.

0.05 Walk down along the edge of the gorge.

0.1 Reach the bottom of the gorge.

0.2 Arrive back at the parking lot.

The falls at the top of Huntington Gorge appear to drop right into the rock itself.

42 Honey Hollow Falls

These beautiful cascades fall 60 feet over a short distance and include long pools, angled cascades, and a lower falls that drops almost 30 feet, all tucked into an intimate brook shrouded by thick forest.

Start: Parking area near large boulders on Honey Hollow Road
Distance: 0.2-mile loop
Hiking time: About 10 minutes
Approximate elevation gain: 50 feet
Difficulty: Moderate to upper falls; difficult to bottom of lower falls

Beauty: Excellent
County: Chittenden
Land status: N/A
DeLorme map: Page 45, K-13 (not marked)
Other maps: None
Trail contact: N/A

Finding the trailhead: From exit 11 on I-89, follow US 2 South for 5.1 miles. Turn right onto Cochran Road, cross over the Winooski River, and take the first left onto Duxbury Road. Follow Duxbury Road for 1.8 miles and turn right onto Honey Hollow Road. Follow this road uphill for 0.5 mile to parking on the left. The parking area can be identified by a number of large boulders. **GPS:** N44 22.130' / W72 54.451'

The Hike

When you reach Honey Hollow falls, you may feel as though you've entered a different world—the unique nature and shaded intimacy of the place are really special. You will probably have the falls all to yourself as well.

The falls are just a few hundred feet below the road. Head right, along an informal path, to view the upper falls. You can get right down to the river here, and if you're into photography there will be some nice opportunities for you. The upper falls are really short, angled cascades that pour from one pool into the next.

You can also head downstream, but be careful; the footing can be treacherous. Near the bottom of these falls is the largest single drop of close to 30 feet. You can get a nice view from a rock along the edge just above the falls. If you're very adventurous, you can head down to the bottom of the falls near a shallow pool.

There are some well-used informal trails here, but they aren't maintained; use your discretion as to how much exploring you want to do. You can make about a 0.25-mile loop if you go from the top of the falls to the bottom.

Miles and Directions

0.0   Start from the parking area and head down to the river, going upstream to the right to see the uppermost falls.

0.05   Reach the uppermost falls. Head downstream to see the rest.

0.15   After bushwhacking, reach the bottom of the falls.

0.2   Arrive back at your vehicle.

Near the bottom of the falls, the largest plunge can be seen from a rock ledge.

43 Bolton Potholes

The potholes are nearly circular pools into which a number of waterfalls drop. The big pool at the bottom is an ideal swimming hole.

Start: Parking lot on Bolton Valley Access Road
Distance: 0.5 mile out and back
Hiking time: About 5 minutes
Approximate elevation gain: 50 feet
Difficulty: Easy
Beauty: Very good
County: Chittenden
Land status: N/A

DeLorme map: Page 45, K-14 (not marked)
Other maps: None
Trail contact: N/A
Special considerations: You will walk along a road that has a very narrow shoulder. The rocks here can be very slippery when wet and they slope into the water, so take the paths through the woods to move up and down next to the falls.

Finding the trailhead: (From the north) Take exit 11 off I-89 and turn right onto US 2 South for 8.1 miles. Turn left onto Bolton Valley Access Road and park in the lot a few hundred feet up on the right.

(From the south) Take exit 10 off I-89 and turn left onto VT 100. At the intersection in 0.5 mile, turn right and follow US 2 North for 6.6 miles. Turn right onto Bolton Valley Access Road and park in the lot a few hundred feet up on the right.

GPS: N44 22.419' / W72 52.709'

The Hike

These falls on Joiner Brook are just off the road and are a popular attraction in summer. The spot gets its name from the deep circular pools into which the falls pour. There are three main plunges in addition to a few small cascades above and a small plunge on the side. Each fall drops into a nice pool, with the middle one being almost perfectly circular, 10 feet deep (in the middle), and 25 feet in diameter.

The large pool at the bottom is a perfect wading pool; and with a pebble beach, it is a great place for children to experience swimming in a cold Vermont mountain stream. Some people jump into the potholes, but do so only when the weather is dry, as the footing on the slanted rock can be very treacherous when wet.

From the parking lot at the bottom of the road (the only legal place to park), walk up the road along an informal path on the right that leads behind a guardrail, then take any path that heads right to meet the river.

There used to be an old dam above the potholes, but no sign of that remains. Head back the way you came to return to the parking lot.

Next to the main falls and the potholes, smaller plunges drop into shallow pools before meeting up at the largest pool at the bottom.

Miles and Directions

0.0 Start from the parking area and head up the road on the right side.

0.1 Follow a path to the right of the guardrail.

0.2 Reach the top of Bolton Potholes (N44 22.495' / W72 52.562').

0.25 Reach the bottom swim hole. Return to the parking area along the same path.

0.5 Arrive back at the parking area.

44 Emerson Falls

Emerson Falls is just below a dam in St. Johnsbury where the water passes over wide rock ledge in many different cascades and streams. In low water you can walk all over the falls, climbing among the rocky ledges.

Start: Parking along Emerson Falls Road (hydro company lot on weekends)
Distance: 0.1 mile out and back (almost roadside)
Hiking time: About 5 minutes
Approximate elevation gain: 25 feet
Difficulty: Moderate
Beauty: Very good

County: Caledonia
Land status: Private land (Emerson Falls Hydro, Inc.)
DeLorme map: Page 48, I-5 (not marked)
Other maps: None
Trail contact: Emerson Falls Hydro, Inc.; e-mail: info@emersonfallshydro.com

Finding the trailhead: From I-91 take exit 21 and head east on US 2. Drive 0.8 mile and turn right onto North Danville Road then take another immediate right onto Emerson Falls Road. There is no specific parking area, so park on the side of the road. *Note:* On weekends you can park in the hydro company parking lot. **GPS:** N44 26.048' / W72 02.305'

The Hike

From where you parked along the road, either head directly into the woods and scramble down to the falls or head down the road to the hydro company parking lot and follow the rough path to the base of the falls. The falls are spread over a wide area, and depending on the flow, you can explore the rocks and individual streams and cascades to your heart's content.

Miles and Directions

0.0 Start from the road, or hydro company parking lot below (on weekends), and take a rough path down to the falls.

0.05 Explore the falls and climb on the rocks (N44 26.070'/W72 02.275'). Return to where you parked.

0.1 Arrive back at your car.

Hundreds of small steps and cascades create the wide and beautiful Emerson Falls.

45 Moss Glen Falls (Stowe)

One of the biggest and best waterfalls in the state, this waterfall drops 125 feet, starting with a narrow plunge that fans out toward the bottom as it drops into multiple pools. You can view this fall from a perch above and to the side or wade up to the bottom to get a unique perspective.

Start: Parking area on Moss Glen Falls Road 0.5 mile from intersection with VT 100
Distance: 0.6 mile out and back
Hiking time: About 20 minutes
Approximate elevation gain: 125 feet
Difficulty: Easy to viewpoint; moderate if wading to bottom of falls
Beauty: Spectacular
County: Lamoille
Land status: CC Putnam State Forest

DeLorme map: Page 46, G-6 (marked)
Other map: Green Mountain Club Mount Mansfield and the Worcester Range Hiking Trail Map
Trail contact: Vermont Department of Forests, Parks and Recreation Lands Administration Division, Worcester Range Management Unit; (802) 476-0174; www.vtfpr.org/lands/wstrrangemu.cfm

Finding the trailhead: From the intersection of VT 100 and VT 108 in Stowe, take VT 100 North for 3 miles. Turn right onto Randolph Road and in 0.4 mile turn right onto Moss Glen Falls Road. In 0.5 mile the road bends sharply to the right; instead go straight ahead into a parking area for the falls. **GPS:** N44 29.115' / W72 37.641'

The Hike

If you had to choose one Moss Glen Falls to visit, this is the one. This should be at or near the top of any waterfall lover's list, and the short hike and multiple viewpoints make it perfect for old and young alike.

From the parking area, follow the trail as it uses planks to cross over a marshy area. After 0.25 mile you enter the woods and begin climbing steeply. You hear the falls before you see them, and shortly you reach the edge of a steep cliff, where you get a magnificent view of the entire falls.

You can see the top of the falls, which is a multi-tiered plunge of 20 to 30 feet. Then the falls makes a turn and becomes a horsetail and then spreads wider before the largest drop, comprising three separate falls or a large sheet, depending on water flow. Below this the falls cascade in two separate drops into small pools before becoming a mild-mannered brook again.

Head back down to the base of the climb, but this time head toward the brook. If you are willing to get your feet wet, you can (carefully!) climb your way up to the base of the falls for an entirely different perspective. Here you are surrounded by moss-covered walls on both sides as the roar of the falls echoes around you.

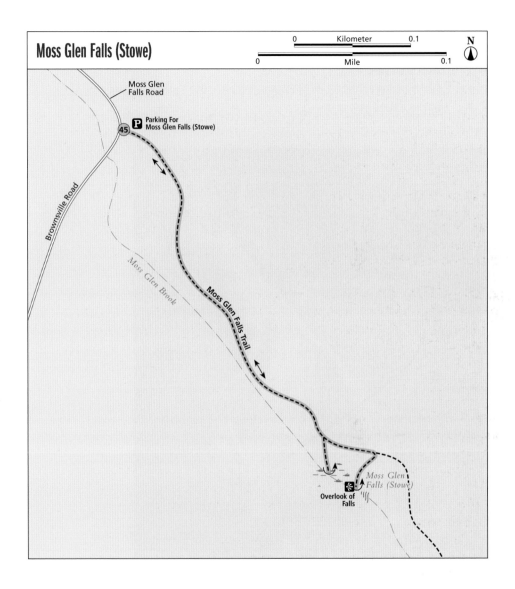

Moss Glen Falls (Stowe)

Moss Glen
Falls Road

P Parking For
Moss Glen Falls (Stowe)

45

Brownsville Road

Moss Glen Brook

Moss Glen Falls Trail

Moss Glen
Falls (Stowe)

Overlook of
Falls

0   Kilometer   0.1

0   Mile   0.1

N

Like many falls in Vermont, the source of this one had been dammed. Luckily there is almost no trace of this, and the waterfall is in its wild natural state. Return to the parking area along the same path.

Miles and Directions

0.0 Start from the parking area and follow the only path, crossing a marshy area on wooden planks to keep your feet dry.

0.25 Reach the edge of a cliff with a view to the falls. Return down the trail.

0.3 Reach the bottom of a steep section, then head toward the brook. Wade upstream to the bottom of the falls.

0.35 Reach the bottom of the falls (N44 28.946' / W72 37.491'). Return to parking area.

0.6 Arrive back at the parking area.

From the viewpoint on a cliff, the entirety of Moss Glen Falls becomes visible.

46 Bingham Falls

Bingham Falls, near the Stowe Mountain Resort, is a very popular waterfall due to the dramatic angle and clarity of the water. There are numerous other small falls above and below the main drop.

Start: Parking area on VT 108, 6.2 miles south of Jeffersonville and 6.2 miles north of Stowe
Distance: 0.6 mile out and back
Hiking time: About 20 minutes
Approximate elevation gain: 200 feet
Difficulty: Easy (some scrambling below falls)
Beauty: Excellent
County: Lamoille
Land status: Mount Mansfield State Forest

DeLorme map: Page 46, F-3 (marked)
Other maps: None
Trail contact: Vermont Department of Forests, Parks and Recreation, Lands Administration Division; (802) 272-4156; www.vtfpr.org/htm/gen_contact.cfm
Special considerations: This can be a very popular spot on weekends.

Finding the trailhead: (From the south) From the junction of VT 100 and VT 108 in Stowe, follow VT 108 North (Mountain Road) for 6.2 miles to parking on the right (east) side of the road. This is 0.4 mile north of the Toll Road. The trailhead is on the east side of the road.

(From the north) From the junction of VT 15 and VT 108 (Church Street) in Jeffersonville, follow VT 108 south through Smugglers' Notch for 11.4 miles to parking area on the left (east) side of the road. This is 1.1 miles south of both Spruce Peak Road on the left and the main entrance to Stowe Mountain Resort on the right. The trailhead is on the east side of the road.

GPS: N44 31.095' / W72 46.178'

The Hike

Bingham Falls is an extremely beautiful, and popular, waterfall very close to Stowe Mountain Resort. The falls consist of three main drops, the most photographed pouring over a ledge for 25 feet into a beautiful teal-colored pool, a popular swimming hole.

From the parking area, head down the main path on the east side of the road. You shortly pass some informational signs. When you reach the river in 0.2 mile, you can see the first and second falls. (If you head left here up a short path, you can get to the stream above the falls.) From the viewpoint of the first falls, head right and soon descend down some rock steps. Be careful—these, and the rocks near the pool, can be very slippery when wet. In just over 0.1 mile you reach the main falls, where you can go swimming (stay to the left side of the pool) and explore the small rapids and channeled rock below.

The rock here was originally sedimentary, formed more than a billion years ago. Heat and pressure changed these to metamorphic rocks, which can be seen in the exposed schist and gneiss. As schist is fairly soft, the water has been able to carve interesting notches into the rock.

Return to the parking area on the same trail.

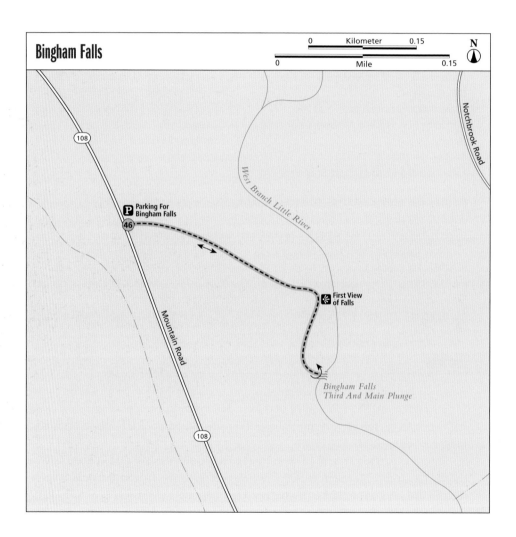

Bingham Falls

Miles and Directions

0.0 Start at the parking area and head down the main path into the woods.

0.2 Reach the first viewpoint of the upper falls. Head down to the right.

0.3 Reach a large pool and the main falls (N44 30.981' / W72 45.963'). Return the way you came.

0.6 Arrive back at your vehicle.

Bingham Falls drops into a beautiful aquamarine pool.

47 Hell Brook Cascades (Lower)

The Hell Brook Trail is one of the steepest trails up Mount Mansfield, Vermont's tallest mountain. There are numerous falls along the brook, but some nice dramatic ones can be found a short bushwhack off the trail not far from the trailhead.

Start: Across the road from Big Spring parking area on VT 108, 8.7 miles south of Jeffersonville and 8.9 miles north of Stowe
Distance: 0.4 mile out and back
Hiking time: About 10 minutes
Approximate elevation gain: 300 feet
Difficulty: Moderate
Beauty: Very Good
County: Lamoille
Land status: Mount Mansfield State Forest
DeLorme map: Page 46, E-2 (not marked)

Other map: Smugglers' Notch State Park Trail Map: www.vtstateparks.com/pdfs/smuggstrails.pdf
Trail contacts: Smugglers' Notch State Park; (802) 253-4014; www.vtstateparks.com/htm/smugglers.htm
Green Mountain Club; (802) 244-7037; e-mail: gmc@greenmountainclub.org
Special considerations: Many more cascades and falls can be found higher up the steep trail.

Finding the trailhead: (From the south) From the junction of VT 108 and VT 100 in the village of Stowe, follow VT 108 North for 8.9 miles. The Hell Brook Trailhead is on the left, across the street from the parking area for "Big Spring."

(From the north) From the junction of VT 15 and VT 108 in Jeffersonville, follow VT 108 South for 8.7 miles. The Hell Brook Trailhead is on the right, across the street from the parking area for "Big Spring." *Note:* In winter VT 108 is closed in this direction before reaching the trailhead. It will be necessary to walk from the road closure to the trailhead. **GPS:** N44 32.909'/W72 47.658'

The Hike

The Hell Brook Trail is a fun but very steep trail up Mount Mansfield, home of Stowe Mountain Resort and the tallest mountain in Vermont. The trail leaves from the Stowe side of Smugglers' Notch. Along the way it parallels and comes near Hell Brook a number of times. There are numerous falls along Hell Brook. This hike describes a short outing to reach the bottom set of falls.

Begin on the Hell Brook Trail, which is across the street from the signed "Big Spring" (where you can fill up with some nice cold springwater). Head up the trail for 0.1 mile. When you cross an old streambed, begin to bushwhack up it to the stream. In less than 0.1 mile farther, come across some nice cascades flowing through jumbled rock. During late summer and fall, Hell Brook may be reduced to a very low flow.

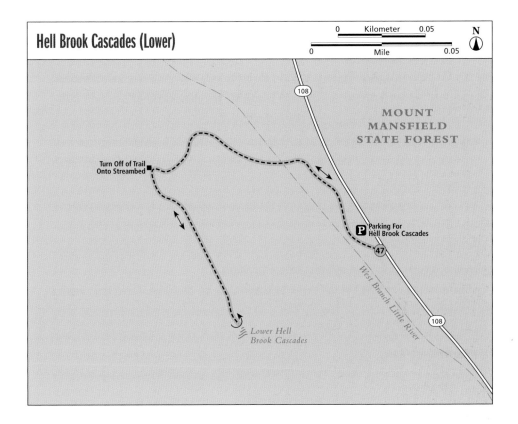

Hell Brook Cascades (Lower)

Miles and Directions

0.0 Start from the parking area and follow the Hell Brook Trail into the woods on the west side of VT 108.

0.1 At a streambed, turn off the trail and begin climbing up to and then along the stream.

0.2 Reach the lower falls (N44 32.879' / W72 47.710'). Return to the way you came.

0.4 Arrive back at the trailhead.

GREEN MOUNTAIN CLUB

The Green Mountain Club (GMC) is a Vermont-based nonprofit whose stated mission is to "Make the Vermont Mountains play a larger part in the life of the people by protecting and maintaining the Long Trail System and fostering, through education, the stewardship of Vermont's hiking trails and mountains." The Long Trail is the oldest long-distance hiking trail in the country. It travels 272 miles from the border of Massachusetts to the border of Quebec through the main spine of the Green Mountains. This beautiful and difficult hiking trail can be completed in about three weeks to a month.

In addition to maintaining the Long Trail, the Green Mountain Club is also responsible for maintaining 175 miles of side trails of the Long Trail, as well as seventy shelters and the Appalachian Trail through Vermont. The GMC also produces hiking maps for many locations throughout Vermont, as well as guidebooks and educational literature.

The volunteers and staff of the Green Mountain Club are dedicated. Caretakers steward the summits of many mountains, keeping people off the fragile alpine vegetation and answering questions of curious hikers. The GMC has a visitor center on VT 100 in Waterbury Center that is open seven days a week.

You can find out more about the Green Mountain Club, and join if you are interested, by visiting their website at www.greenmountainclub.org.

The Green Mountain Club maintains the Long Trail, which goes over the summit ridge of Mount Mansfield.

48 Sterling Falls Gorge

This beautiful series of falls, cascades, and pools are accompanied by a very educational self-guided tour. Although you can only reach a few of these falls, most are visible from the trail. The intimate setting and educational opportunity, along with the relative solitude you are likely to enjoy, make this a great trip with kids.

Start: Across the street and small bridge from the parking area on Sterling Gorge Road
Distance: 0.6 mile out and back
Hiking time: About 20 minutes
Approximate elevation gain: 125 feet
Difficulty: Easy to moderate
Beauty: Excellent

County: Lamoille
Land status: Sterling Falls Gorge Natural Area (owned by Town of Stowe)
DeLorme map: Page 46, E-4 (not marked)
Other maps: None
Trail contact: Town of Stowe; www.townofstowevt.org/contact/index.html

Finding the trailhead: From the junction of VT 108 and VT 100 in Stowe, take VT 108/Mountain Road north for 0.6 mile. Turn right onto Weeks Hill Road and in 1.3 miles turn right onto Percy Hill Road. Follow this road for 0.6 mile and stay left/straight as the road continues as West Hill Road. Continue 1.5 miles then stay left/straight as the road continues to Moren Loop. In 0.6 mile turn left onto Sterling Valley Road, and in 1.7 miles turn left onto Sterling Gorge Road. Park in a lot on the right in 0.1 mile. To get to the trail, follow the private road over a bridge and into the woods on the left. **GPS:** N44 32.355'/W72 43.188'

The Hike

This interesting gorge, with walls ranging in height from 11 to 50 feet, lies within a beautiful hemlock forest. In addition to being chock-full of interesting features, including six sets of cascades and three waterfalls, there is a very interesting and informative self-guided interpretive trail. One thing to note, however, is that for most of the hike, the brook itself is inaccessible and much of it is actually roped off. Therefore only some of the falls and cascades are visible. Nonetheless, there will be plenty to see and a lot of great information to be ingested.

From the parking area, continue over the bridge. The entrance to the gorge is on the left and is marked by a sign. The trail is very obvious as it works its way downstream along a ridge above the brook. There are many posts with informational text along the way. The information covers a wide range of subjects, from geology to ecology to history.

At the end of the trail and the bottom of the gorge, you will find a picnic table. A short spur just above this goes out to a small set of cascades and pools; it's labeled, appropriately enough, "Waterfall Trail." Return along the same trail.

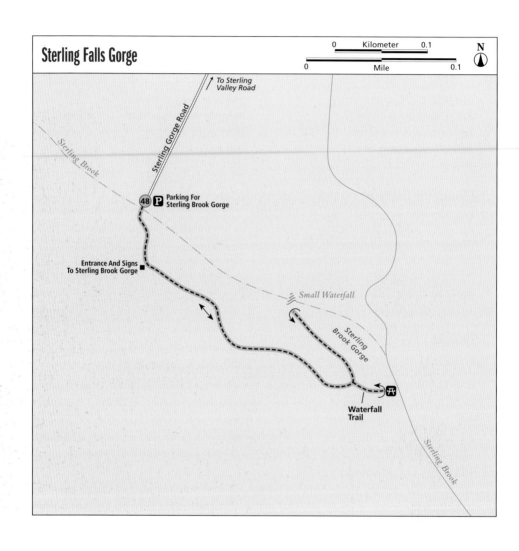

Sterling Falls Gorge

0   Kilometer   0.1

0   Mile   0.1

N

To Sterling
Valley Road

Sterling Gorge Road

Sterling Brook

48 **P** Parking For
Sterling Brook Gorge

Entrance And Signs
To Sterling Brook Gorge

Small Waterfall

Sterling
Brook Gorge

**Waterfall
Trail**

Sterling Brook

Miles and Directions

0.0 Start from the parking lot and cross a bridge.

0.05 Turn left into the entrance of Sterling Falls Gorge. Continue straight along this trail.

0.25 Reach a picnic table at the end of the gorge. Start back along the same trail.

0.3 Take the "Waterfall Trail" spur out to small cascades.

0.35 Reach the cascades (N44 32.291' / W72 43.054').

0.4 Return to main trail. Turn right to head back to the parking area.

0.6 Arrive back at the parking area.

Some of the falls are visible from the trail above the gorge.

49 Terrill Gorge

What makes this 5-foot-tall waterfall worth visiting? It's the unique way the waterfall pours through a cleft in the rock—and of course the giant swim hole right below it.

Start: Parking area on Stagecoach Road, 6.6 miles from junction with VT 100
Distance: 0.9 mile out and back
Hiking time: About 30 minutes
Approximate elevation gain: 100 feet
Difficulty: Easy, but includes a stream crossing; difficult at the very end due to a steep and slippery trail down to the pool (not necessary to see the falls)
Beauty: Very good
County: Lamoille

Land status: Owned by Vermont Department of Fish & Wildlife
DeLorme map: Page 46, D-6 (marked)
Other maps: None
Trail contact: The Vermont River Conservancy; (802) 229-0820; www.vermontriverconservancy.org/contact-us; e-mail: vrc@vermontriverconservancy.org
Special considerations: You will need to cross a river, so bring water shoes or be willing to go barefoot.

Finding the trailhead: From the junction of VT 108 and VT 100 in Stowe, follow VT 100 north for 1.7 miles. Turn left onto Stagecoach Road and continue 6.6 miles. Park in a small dirt parking area on the left, just before you reach a big field. **GPS:** N44 34.179'/W72 37.069'

The Hike

Although there are known falls above the lower falls described here, they are very inaccessible. The falls are actually at the lowest end of the gorge, and the walls get taller and narrower if you go beyond the lowest falls. These falls, which are 5 feet tall and 10 feet wide, are really composed of one short fall that is immediately succeeded by a cascade that pours into a large 30-foot-wide pool of deep green water. The interesting thing about the falls, however, is that it pours out of a notch surrounded by rock walls of approximately 15 to 20 feet high.

From the small parking area, follow the trail for 0.25 mile to Kenfield Brook. You will need to cross the brook, so sandals or Crocs are helpful if you don't want to go barefoot. The crossing is innocuous, however, and shouldn't prevent anybody from being able to do this hike.

Once across, head left and continue on the trail as it parallels the brook upstream. At 0.4 mile, just as the trail begins to steepen, you should see the falls over to the left. To get down to the pool, take a short but steep and eroded trail on your left. You will arrive at the large pool across from the falls. When you are ready, head back the way you came.

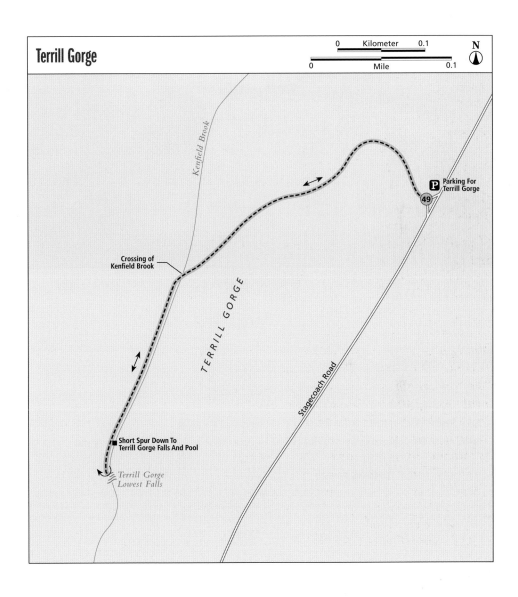

Terrill Gorge

0   Kilometer   0.1

0   Mile   0.1

N

Kenfield Brook

Parking For
Terrill Gorge

49

Crossing of
Kenfield Brook

TERRILL GORGE

Stagecoach Road

Short Spur Down To
Terrill Gorge Falls And Pool

Terrill Gorge
Lowest Falls

The notch made by the rock walls next to the falls at the bottom of the gorge prove that a waterfall does not need to be large in order to be beautiful.

Miles and Directions

0.0 Start from the small parking area and follow the trail downhill to the brook.

0.25 Cross the brook then head left along the trail.

0.4 Reach the spur trail down to the pool at the bottom of the gorge.

0.45 Reach the pool across from the falls (N44 34.013' / W72 37.321'). Return the way you came.

0.9 Arrive back at the parking area.

50 Jefferson Falls / Brewster River Gorge

From the bottom of the Brewster River Gorge, you may have a hard time viewing any falls through the huge jumble of boulders. But from the top you'll see a nice waterfall that funnels into a narrow gorge, where the river seemingly disappears into the rock.

Start: Parking area just beyond covered bridge on Canyon Road, 0.8 mile from intersection with VT 108
Distance: 1.5 miles out and back (includes short spur to bottom of falls)
Hiking time: About 45 minutes
Approximate elevation gain: 150 feet
Difficulty: Easy to moderate
Beauty: Very good

County: Lamoille
Land status: Conserved by the Vermont Land Trust
DeLorme map: Page 46, B-1 (not marked)
Other maps: None
Trail contact: Cambridge Conservation Commission; www.cambridgeconservation .com; e-mail: cambridgeconservation @gmail.com

Finding the trailhead: From the intersection of VT 108 and VT 15, follow the combined road south for 0.3 mile to the center of Jeffersonville; turn left, continuing to follow VT 108. Make a slight left onto Canyon Road in 0.8 mile; the large parking lot is straight ahead. To get to the trailhead, cross the covered bridge (on foot); the trailhead is just beyond the bridge on the right. **GPS:** N44 38.172' / W72 49.538'

The Hike

If you are only interested in big waterfalls, this may not be the place for you. But if you like seeing a unique geological feature and a river that seemingly drops down into the rock, definitely check this out.

From the large parking area, cross the covered bridge and turn right onto a trail with a sign marking it as the "Alden Bryan Brewster River Trail." Along this trail, which parallels the river, there are a number of nice spots to sit and relax. At 0.5 mile (from the parking area) take a short spur trail out to the bottom of the gorge. Unless there is a lot of water from rain or spring runoff, you may not see any falls at all. That is because the gorge is filled with piles of huge jumbled boulders that hide the path of the water. Nonetheless, it is an interesting scene and attests to the power of nature and erosion.

Head back to the main trail and climb for another 0.2 mile. Near the top you will see the largest fall, which pours into a pothole. Continue on and walk out onto the rocks above the falls. From here you can see some nice 4- to 8-foot cascades before the river narrows dramatically and pours through a deep cut in the rock then seemingly disappears over an edge. (***Note:*** If you have time, you can continue along on

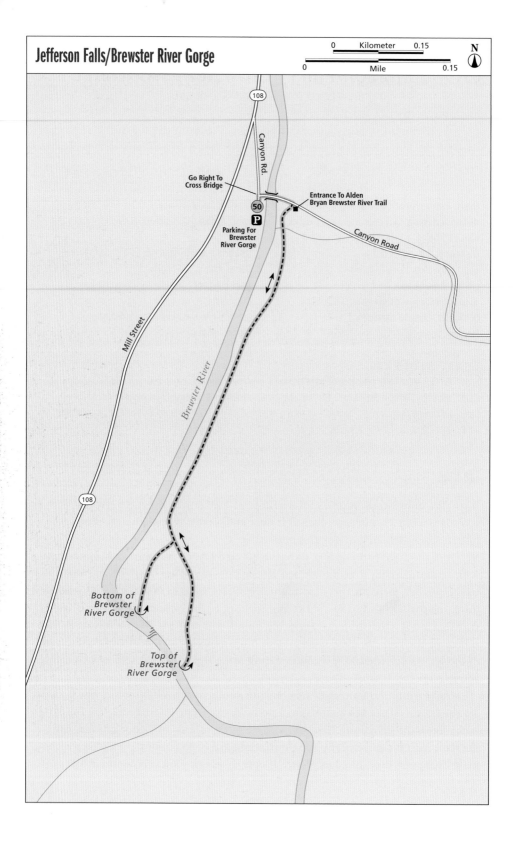

Jefferson Falls/Brewster River Gorge

0   Kilometer   0.15

0   Mile   0.15

N

108

Canyon Rd.

Go Right To
Cross Bridge

Entrance To Alden
Bryan Brewster River Trail

50

P

Parking For
Brewster
River Gorge

Canyon Road

Mill Street

Brewster River

108

Bottom of
Brewster
River Gorge

Top of
Brewster
River Gorge

the path along the Brewster River above the gorge, where there are more cascades and some nice spots for wading. However, a nearby note on a rock mentions a "nude area above falls," so be prepared, especially if you've got kids.) You can return the way you came.

Miles and Directions

0.0 Start from the parking area and head across the covered bridge.

0.1 Turn right onto the Alden Bryan Brewster River Trail.

0.5 Go right on a spur trail to the bottom of gorge.

0.6 Reach bottom of the gorge (N44 37.833' / W72 49.688').

0.7 Return to main trail and turn right.

0.85 Reach the top of the gorge (N44 37.833' / W72 49.688'). Return the way you came.

1.5 Arrive back at the parking area.

A scultped rock looks like a skull near the top of Jefferson Falls.

51 Jay Branch Gorge / Four Corners

Although the waterfall is small, it is pretty, and the swimming hole here is one of the most popular in the area.

Start: Dirt parking lot on VT 101, 1 mile north of the intersection with VT 242
Distance: 0.2 mile out and back (almost roadside)
Hiking time: About 5 minutes
Approximate elevation gain: 25 feet
Difficulty: Easy

Beauty: Good
County: Orleans
Land status: N/A
DeLorme map: Page 53, B-11 (not marked)
Other maps: None
Trail contact: N/A

Finding the trailhead: From the intersection of VT 100 and VT 101 in Troy, follow VT 101 North for 4.1 miles to a large dirt parking lot on the right. (This is 1 mile north of the intersection with VT 242.) **GPS:** N44 57.704' / W72 24.802'

The Hike

Only a few hundred feet from the road, this is one of the most popular swim holes in the area. It is very close to Jay Peak resort, which recently has expanded to include an indoor water park. But why play inside when you can have a great time outside?

There is only one real waterfall here, but it is very nice, pouring into a small pool that is immediately followed by a large pool. To get to the falls, head directly into the woods from the parking lot along an obvious trail. This will take you to the small cascades above the falls. From here, head up a rock to get a great view of the swim hole and falls from above. Keep on heading down along the side of the brook to access the pool.

Miles and Directions

0.0 Start from the parking area and head directly into the woods on an obvious path.

0.05 Reach the Jay Branch at a small cascade directly above the main plunge. Head right for a great viewpoint and the pool.

0.1 Arrive at the view above the pool and shortly thereafter the access to the pool. Return the way you came.

0.2 Arrive back at the parking area.

People have created numerous rock cairns above Jay Branch Gorge.

The Jay Branch pours over a rock wall into a large pool.

52 Big Falls

Just a couple miles from the Canadian border, you can get a cliff's-edge view above one of the most powerful waterfalls in the state.

Start: Parking area on River Road in Troy
Distance: 0.15 mile (almost roadside, but some exploring possible)
Hiking time: About 5 minutes
Approximate elevation gain: 50 feet
Difficulty: Easy to view; moderate to edge of falls
Beauty: Spectacular
County: Orleans

Land status: Big Falls of the Missisquoi Natural Area
DeLorme map: Page 53, A&B-11 (marked)
Other maps: None
Trail contact: Vermont Department of Forests, Parks and Recreation, Lands Administration Division; (802) 272-4156; www.vtfpr.org/htm/gen_contact.cfm
Special considerations: If the rocks are wet, do not get too close to the edge of the cliff.

Finding the trailhead: (From the east) From exit 26 off I-91, take US 5 North for 5.4 miles. Turn left onto VT 105 West and continue following signs for VT 105 for 12.5 miles until you almost get to North Troy. Turn left onto River Road shortly after passing a small road on the right to a cemetery. Parking for Big Falls is on the right in 1.4 miles.

(From the west) From the junction of US 7 and VT 105 in Saint Albans, take VT 105 East for 45.6 miles through Enosburg Falls, Richford, and North Troy. Turn right onto River Road not long after passing though North Troy. Parking for Big Falls is on the right in 1.4 miles. **GPS:** N44 58.396'/W72 23.133'

The Hike

Big Falls live up to its name, as even in times of low flow, the Missisquoi River still provides a significant amount of water. The total drop of the falls is 40 feet, and the narrow gorge that surrounds the falls has a cliff of almost 100 vertical feet.

After parking, head straight beyond the obvious boulders to an incredible vantage point above the falls. If the rock isn't wet, you can get right to the edge as you stand—or sit—more than 80 feet above the powerful waterfall. If you're brave, have someone take a photo of you sitting on the edge.

If you head down an informal path to the left after leaving your vehicle, you can climb down onto the rocks next to and above the falls, where you can feel the true power of the water as it pours over a ledge, splits around rocks into three distinct falls, and then comes together into a deep narrow flow in the narrowest part of the gorge.

If you head right after leaving your car, you can follow paths down to the stream below the falls. By wading out into the middle, you can get a direct view of the falls coming through the gorge as well as get a photo of the cliff you were previously standing on. Even though this is considered one of Vermont's most powerful falls, it has never been dammed, so you get a chance to see it in its original, natural state.

Miles and Directions

0.0   Start from your car and head straight to a flat area on a cliff above the falls.

0.05 Follow paths down to the right to reach the rocky shore of the stream below the falls. Wade out into the middle to get the best view.

0.1   Head left down another short path and over the big rocks to get a view right next to the waterfall. Return to the parking area.

0.15 Arrive back at your car.

A girl looks out over the edge of the clifftop viewpoint high above Big Falls.

New Hampshire

A little rock-hopping is needed to get across the stream, where you can see the rugged vertical rock walls across from Garfield Falls (hike 81).

53 Garwin Falls

Garwin Falls is a nice little waterfall in southern New Hampshire. Just a quick jaunt from the road, the falls drop more than 40 feet in three main plunges.

Start: Parking area on Isaac Frye Highway, 0.2 mile north of the junction with Sand Hill Road
Distance: 0.6 mile out and back (with very short spur to upper falls)
Hiking time: About 20 minutes
Approximate elevation gain: 125 feet
Difficulty: Easy

Beauty: Good
County: Hillsborough
Land status: N/A
DeLorme map: Page 21, F-9 (unmarked)
Other maps: None
Trail contact: N/A

Finding the trailhead: From the junction of NH 101 and NH 31 in Wilton, follow NH 31 north (marked as Island Street) for 0.3 mile to Main Street. NH 31 continues to the left; follow this for another 1.4 miles before turning left onto the Burton Highway as NH 31 splits off to the right. In 0.5 mile turn left onto Isaac Frye Highway; the parking area is the left (there may be a chain between two trees). The parking area is 0.2 mile north of the junction with Sand Hill Road. **GPS:** N42 50.803' / W71 46.287'

The Hike

Some waterfalls are special because they are so unexpected. Until you get to Garwin Falls, you could be excused for thinking you are on a wild goose chase. Once there, however, you will be impressed by the way the falls seem to pour out of the woods in two drops, landing on a ledge and then plunging once more to some smaller cascades and a large pool below.

From the parking area, head straight ahead down an old dirt road. At 0.1 mile a short spur to the left leads to a 4-foot cascade and a big pool. Continue down the old dirt road, past a small dam on the left, as the trail descends a bit more steeply before swinging to the left at the bottom of Garwin Falls. Return to the parking area along the same route.

Garwin Falls

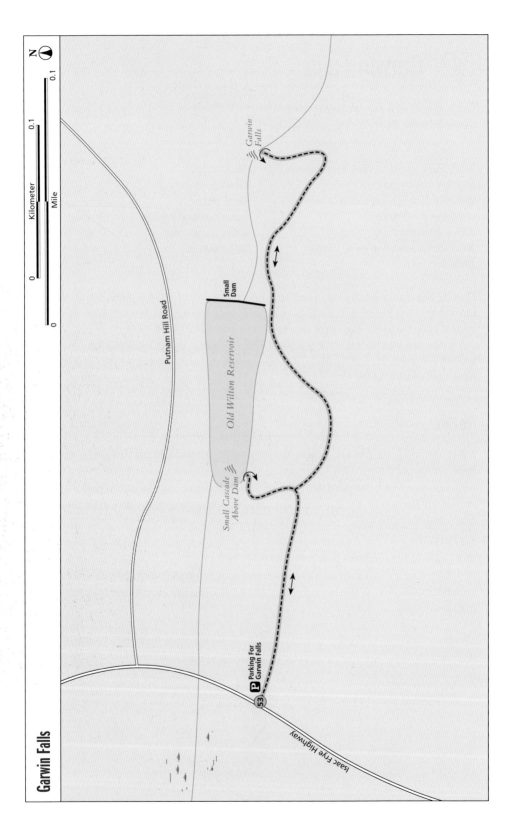

N

Kilometer
0   0.1   0.1

Mile
0   0.1

Putnam Hill Road

Old Wilton Reservoir

Small Dam

Small Cascade
Above Dam

Garwin
Falls

Parking For
Garwin Falls

53

Isaac Frye Highway

Miles and Directions

0.0 Start from the parking area and head straight down an old dirt road.

0.1 Reach a spur trail on the left, which leads to a small cascade.

0.15 Arrive at small cascade. Head back to trail.

0.2 Continue along the dirt road.

0.25 Head past a small dam on the left. Continue down the path below the dam to Garwin Falls.

0.35 Arrive at Garwin Falls (N42 50.801'/W71 46.027'). Return the way you came.

0.6 Arrive back at the parking area.

Water cascades over rocky ledges that create multiple parts of Garwin Falls.

54 Purgatory Falls

There are a number of different ways to view the falls along Purgatory Brook. This hike visits the Upper and Middle Falls along with providing a beautiful view of the surrounding hills while returning you to your vehicle via a loop.

Start: Pull-off near gate and information sign at end of Purgatory Road
Distance: 2.6-mile loop
Hiking time: About 2 hours
Approximate elevation gain: 700 feet
Difficulty: Moderate
Beauty: Excellent
County: Hillsborough
Land status: Purgatory Falls Brook Preserve and private land

DeLorme map: Page 21, E-11 (not marked)
Other map: Purgatory Falls Trails from Mont Vernon Town: www.montvernonnh.us/images/conservation/PurgatoryTrailSecond.png
Trail contact: Mont Vernon Conservation Commission, Town of Mont Vernon; (603) 673-6080; www.montvernonnh.us/index.php/boards-a-committees/conservation-commission

Finding the trailhead: From the junction of NH 13 and NH 101A in Milford, follow NH 13 north for 3.7 miles. Turn left onto Purgatory Road and park in one of the pull-offs near a gate and information sign at the end of the public road in 1.5 miles. **GPS:** N42 53.457' / W71 41.340'

The Hike

On this loop you will visit Upper Purgatory Falls, which comes out of a narrow rock cleft, makes a right turn, and becomes a beautiful cascade and plunge that drops into a pool with a large overhanging rock ceiling. You can get under this ceiling for a cave-like feel. Middle Purgatory Falls is a narrow horsetail that also falls about 25 feet and is completely encased by overhanging, moss-shrouded walls.

From the parking area, head past the gate and information booth on the south side of Purgatory Road. Follow this for 0.2 mile and pop out into an open field. The trail, which is marked by a sign and a red diamond, will be on your right when you reach the field. Before heading down this trail, head out above the field for a nice view of Pack Monadnock. Head down this trail for 0.6 mile until you reach the Purgatory Brook Trail, which is marked by yellow blazes.

Turn right and follow this upstream for 0.2 mile; look for a sign on your left marking a short steep spur trail to Middle Purgatory Falls. After returning to the trail from the falls, continue along the Purgatory Brook Trail, bypassing a trail junction coming in from your right. Pass a small cascade and shortly (0.3 mile from Middle Purgatory Falls) look for a short spur down to Upper Purgatory Falls.

After returning to the main trail from the falls, continue upstream, bypassing another trail junction on the right, until you come to what looks like a dirt road

Purgatory Falls

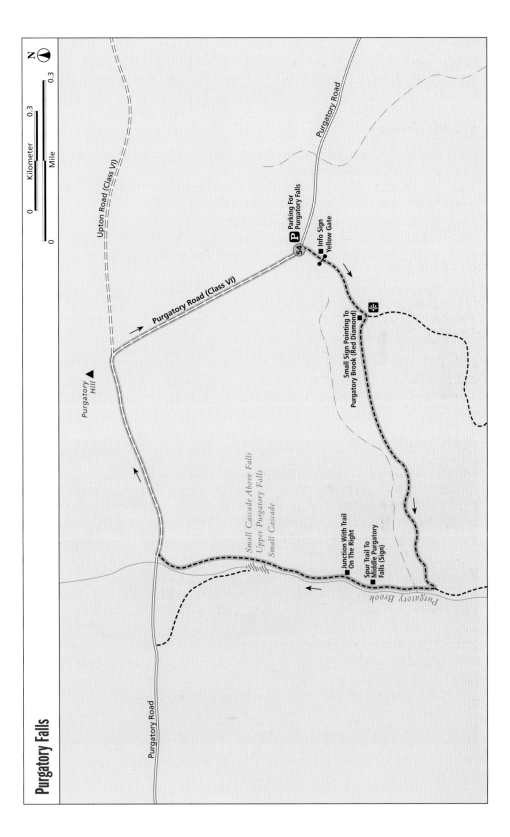

Purgatory Hill

Upton Road (Class VI)

Purgatory Road (Class VI)

Purgatory Road

Purgatory Road

Parking For Purgatory Falls

54

Info Sign
Yellow Gate

Small Sign Pointing To Purgatory Brook (Red Diamond)

Small Cascade Above Falls
Upper Purgatory Falls
Small Cascade

Junction With Trail On The Right

Spur Trail To Middle Purgatory Falls (Sign)

Purgatory Brook

N

0   Kilometer   0.3

0   Mile   0.3

heading up to your right. Follow this 0.4 mile uphill and turn right onto the private portion of Purgatory Road, which will lead you back to the parking area in another 0.5 mile.

Miles and Directions

0.0   Start from the parking area and head down the trail on the left (clockwise), passing a yellow gate and an information sign.

0.2   Reach an open field and a junction with the trail down to Purgatory Brook. Head out above the field to get a great view of Pack Monadnock Mountain.

0.8   Turn right onto Purgatory Brook Trail (yellow blazes).

1.0   Reach a signed spur to the left down to Middle Purgatory Falls (N42 53.031'/W71 42.536'). After visiting the falls, continue up along Purgatory Brook, passing a trail junction on the right.

1.4   Reach Upper Purgatory Falls (N42 53.229'/W71 42.498'). Continue up along the brook, passing a trail coming in from the left.

1.7   Turn right onto an old dirt road that heads uphill.

2.1   Turn right onto Purgatory Road.

2.6   Arrive back at the parking area.

Leaves and foam on the water and an overhanging cliff create a truly unique experience at the Upper Purgatory Falls.

55 Chesterfield Gorge

Although the falls are only moderately impressive, the gorge itself is unique and well worth a visit.

Start: Chesterfield Gorge State Wayside on NH 9

Distance: 0.8-mile lollipop

Hiking time: About 30 minutes

Approximate elevation gain: 100 feet

Difficulty: Easy

Beauty: Good

County: Cheshire

Land status: Chesterfield Gorge Natural Area

(state managed park)

DeLorme map: Page 19, D-9 (marked)

Other maps: None

Trail contact: Chesterfield Gorge Natural Area, managed by the New Hampshire Division of Parks and Recreation; (603) 363-8373; www.nhstateparks.org/explore/state-parks/chesterfield-gorge-natural-area.aspx

Special considerations: Pets must be leashed.

Finding the trailhead: Park at the Chesterfield Gorge State Wayside on NH 9, 9 miles east off exit 3 of I-91 and 5.7 miles west of the intersection with NH 12/NH 10. **GPS:** N42 54.875'/W72 24.295'

The Hike

This is a short, relaxing hike with a number of slides, cascades, and plunges visible from various points along the gorge.

Head down the path to the right of the information sign and in a few hundred yards make a sharp left at the "Gorge Trail" sign to stay to the left of the fence. Continue down along the Gorge Trail and at 0.25 mile cross a bridge on your right. After crossing the bridge, continue downstream for another 0.2 mile, where you cross back over the brook.

On your way back up the eastern side of the gorge, you will get a decent view of a the narrow stream cutting under a cliff then widening out into a two-tiered horsetail, which is probably the largest feature of the hike. Continue heading back upstream on the trail and soon return to the parking area.

Chesterfield Gorge

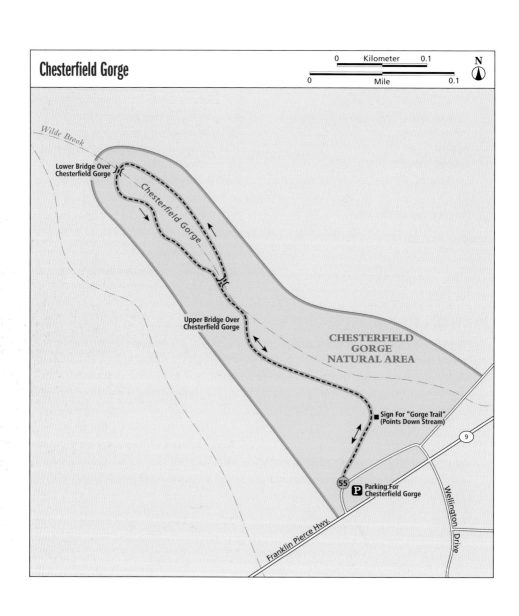

Wilde Brook

Lower Bridge Over
Chesterfield Gorge

Chesterfield Gorge

Upper Bridge Over
Chesterfield Gorge

CHESTERFIELD
GORGE
NATURAL AREA

Sign For "Gorge Trail"
(Points Down Stream)

9

55

Parking For
Chesterfield Gorge

Franklin Pierce Hwy.

Wellington Drive

0   Kilometer   0.1

0   Mile   0.1

N

Miles and Directions

0.0   Start from the information booth near the parking lot and head down the path to the right.

0.1   Make a sharp left turn at the "Gorge Trail" sign.

0.25 Cross the bridge over the brook and continue heading downstream.

0.4   Cross back over the brook on another bridge at the bottom of the gorge. Continue up along the side of the gorge and follow the trail back up to the parking area.

0.8   Arrive back at the parking lot.

Filtered light reaches the bottom of Chesterfield Gorge.

56 Beaver Brook Falls (Keene)

The journey down an abandoned paved road with a nice 10- to 12-foot waterfall at the end makes this an interesting little out-and-back.

Start: Gate on Washington Street Extension
Distance: 1.6 miles out and back
Hiking time: About 1 hour
Approximate elevation gain: 150 feet
Difficulty: Easy, but a little tricky to get down to the falls from the old road

Beauty: Good
County: Cheshire
Land status: City preserve (City of Keene)
DeLorme map: Page 19, B 12
Other maps: None
Trail contact: City of Keene; (603) 352-0133

Finding the trailhead: (From the west) Take exit 3 off I-91 and follow NH 9 East for 18.2 miles to the Washington Street exit. Go right onto Washington Street and follow this for 0.3 mile. Turn left onto Concord Road and make another immediate left onto Washington Street Extension. The trail (the old road) begins at a gate 0.25 mile down this road.

(From the east) Take exit 5 off I-89 and follow NH 9/Franklin Pierce Highway for 40.6 miles to the Washington Street exit near Keene. Go left onto Washington Street and follow this for 0.3 mile. Turn left onto Concord Road and make another immediate left onto Washington Street Extension. The trail (the old road) begins at a gate 0.25 mile down this road.

GPS: N42 57.300'/W72 16.098'

The Hike

Go straight ahead past the gate and follow the abandoned highway. Take the time to see how quickly nature is taking the land back over. The brook, which is located in a 26-acre preserve, is not easily visible for most of the way.

Follow the old road as it heads upstream. In 0.8 mile come to a post with a plaque on it; just beyond is the old parking area above the falls. Backtrack a short way and look for a path near the plaque that heads down to the brook. It's a little bit tricky and steep, so watch your footing. Return the way you came.

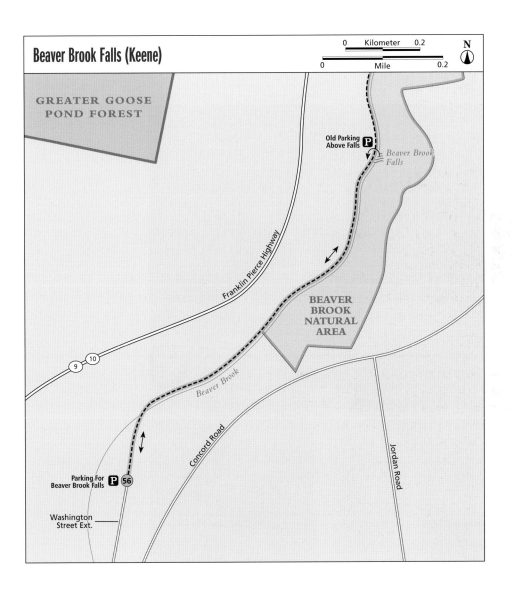

Beaver Brook Falls (Keene)

GREATER GOOSE
POND FOREST

Old Parking
Above Falls

Beaver Brook
Falls

Franklin Pierce Highway

BEAVER
BROOK
NATURAL
AREA

9 10

Beaver Brook

Concord Road

Jordan Road

Parking For
Beaver Brook Falls 56

Washington
Street Ext.

0   Kilometer   0.2
0   Mile   0.2

N

Miles and Directions

0.0 Start from the parking area and follow the old road straight ahead.

0.8 Arrive at a post with a plaque on it, just before an old parking turnout. Look for a short steep path that heads down to the falls (N42 57.752' / W72 15.597'). Return the way you came.

1.6 Arrive back at the parking area.

The tranquility of Beaver Brook Falls belies the fact that just a few decades earlier a parking area was right above the cliff.

57 Trues Ledges

The interesting geology and multi-tiered falls, as well as nice swim holes, make this excursion just off the West Lebanon "strip" a surprisingly worthwhile visit.

Start: Parking lot on Trues Brook Road, 0.7 mile from intersection with NH 12A
Distance: 0.25-mile loop
Hiking time: About 15 minutes
Approximate elevation gain: 50 feet
Difficulty: Easy
Beauty: Excellent
County: Grafton
Land status: Conserved land
DeLorme map: Page 33, B-11 (not marked)

Other maps: City of Lebanon Trues Ledges Natural Area map: http://council.lebnh.net/bcomm/conservation-commission/trues-ledges
Trail contact: City of Lebanon Conservation Commission; (603) 448-4220 (city clerk); http://council.lebnh.net/bcomm/conservation-commission
Special considerations: Park in the lot, not along the road.

Finding the trailhead: From exit 20 off I-89 in West Lebanon (the first exit off I-89 south of the intersection with I-91 in Vermont), take NH 12A south for 1.6 miles. Turn left onto Trues Brook Road; the parking lot is on the right in 0.7 mile. **GPS:** N43 36.369'/W72 18.906'

The Hike

Driving along this town road just a mile from Walmart and Home Depot, you'd be forgiven for thinking that you are in the wrong place. But just a short walk into the woods will take you to your first viewpoint. Here you stand atop an outlook above a rugged streambed. Water zigzags this way and that down multiple cascades and plunges, ranging from a few feet to more than 10.

The character of Trues Ledges changes dramatically depending on the amount of water flow. However, even in low water, this is a fun place to explore. You can walk down through the channel to get unique perspectives. Here at one of the lower drops, the water pours off a ledge from multiple angles and passes through a cleft between two rock walls.

From the parking area, head into the woods, following the trail in a counterclockwise direction. You will come to three distinct viewpoints, each unique and set above the floor of the brook. At the third viewpoint you can access the riverbed; slightly farther upstream there is another access to the water. At this last access there is a large swim hole below a decent-size falls just below the bridge on Trues Brook Road. On hot summer days this is a favorite spot of the locals. (I came here as a college student in the '90s, as it was only a few minutes from my school.)

Complete the loop by returning to the parking area along a short trail that parallels the road.

Trues Ledges

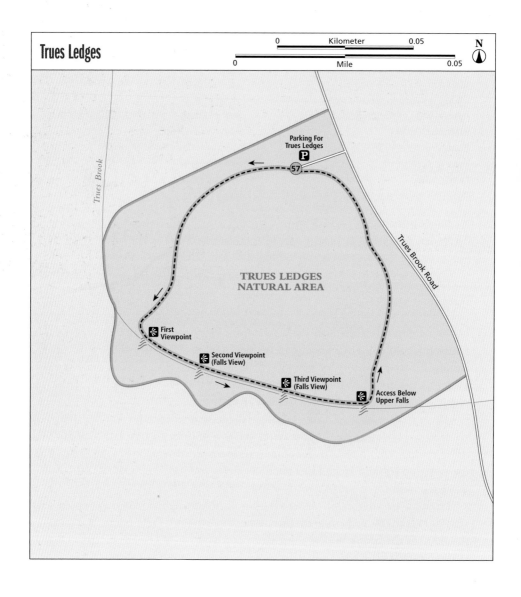

0   Kilometer   0.05

0   Mile   0.05

N

Parking For
Trues Ledges

P

57

Trues Brook

Trues Brook Road

TRUES LEDGES
NATURAL AREA

First
Viewpoint

Second Viewpoint
(Falls View)

Third Viewpoint
(Falls View)

Access Below
Upper Falls

The size of Trues Ledges only becomes apparent once you step out onto one of the viewpoints.

Miles and Directions

0.0 Start from the parking area and head into the woods, following the obvious trail to the right (counterclockwise).

0.05 Reach the first viewpoint.

0.1 Reach the second viewpoint.

0.15 Reach the third viewpoint and access to the brook just beyond (N43 36.325' / W72 18.911').

0.2 Reach the access to the pool and falls just below the bridge.

0.25 Arrive back at the parking area.

PHOTOGRAPHY TIP: THINK ABOUT YOUR COMPOSITION

When shooting waterfalls, it is easy to get into a pattern of setting up your tripod at the base of the falls, pointing your camera at the falls, and taking a picture. The problem with this is that your photo will look just like many other photos already taken. If you are looking for something unique, try mixing up your compositions. You could zoom in to a portion of the falls to create an abstract image.

You could pose a person to create something dynamic. One way to make your photo more interesting is to move farther downstream, with the main waterfall visible in the top of the image as the brook/stream gets larger in the foreground. One of my favorite techniques, as can be seen in the image for Trues Ledges, is to get right above the falls looking down. If the water is low, you can often wade up- or downstream and put your tripod right in the middle of the stream, giving the viewer the impression that he or she is right there.

Think about what is in your foreground. Something should draw the viewer toward and through the image. Is there a leaf on a rock below the falls, or a unique rock that can frame the falls?

A simple technique is to use the rule of thirds. This involves splitting your image into thirds—vertically, horizontally, or both. Then try to keep the horizons and subject matter in these zones. Photos with the subject matter dead center can be boring. Move the subject, such as a waterfall, up or down in the image. Finally, try moving your feet instead of just using your camera's zoom. You will be more thoughtful in your compositional process and will likely get better results.

When the water is low, you can put yourself in interesting spots along the streambed to get unique photos.

58 Profile Falls

This is a nice wide, angulating waterfall. The smaller falls above Profile Falls flow beneath a beautiful stone bridge, providing a great backdrop for photos.

Start: Parking lot on Mt. Hill Road, 0.1 mile from junction with Profile Falls Road
Distance: 0.4 mile out and back
Hiking time: About 10 minutes
Approximate elevation gain: 100 feet
Difficulty: Easy
Beauty: Excellent
County: Grafton

Land status: Profile Falls Recreation Area, maintained by US Army Corps of Engineers
DeLorme map: Page 35, C-10 (not marked)
Other maps: None
Trail contact: US Army Corps of Engineers, Franklin Falls Dam; (603) 934-2116; www .nae.usace.army.mil/Missions/Recreation/ FranklinFallsDam.aspx

Finding the trailhead: From exit 23 off I-93, take NH 104 West for 5.5 miles to Bristol. Turn left onto NH 3A (North Main Street) and follow this for 2 miles. Go left onto Profile Falls Road and after 0.2 mile make a sharp right onto Mt. Hill Road; the parking lot is on the right in 0.1 mile. **GPS:** N43 34.103' / W71 43.900'

The Hike

This waterfall is a cool angled horsetail, which at its tallest point is 30 feet high. In lower water the fall separates into multiple cascades that fan out along the ledge. Supposedly there is great fishing below this, and the view of the cascades above the falls is worthy of a short excursion.

From the parking area, take the flat trail to the falls. If you are willing to get your feet wet, you can head to the small island in the middle of the river for great head-on views. Climb an informal trail along the right edge of the falls to view a series of cascades topped by an arched stone bridge.

In addition to the falls, the Profile Falls Recreation Area provides hiking, biking, and picnicking opportunities.

Profile Falls

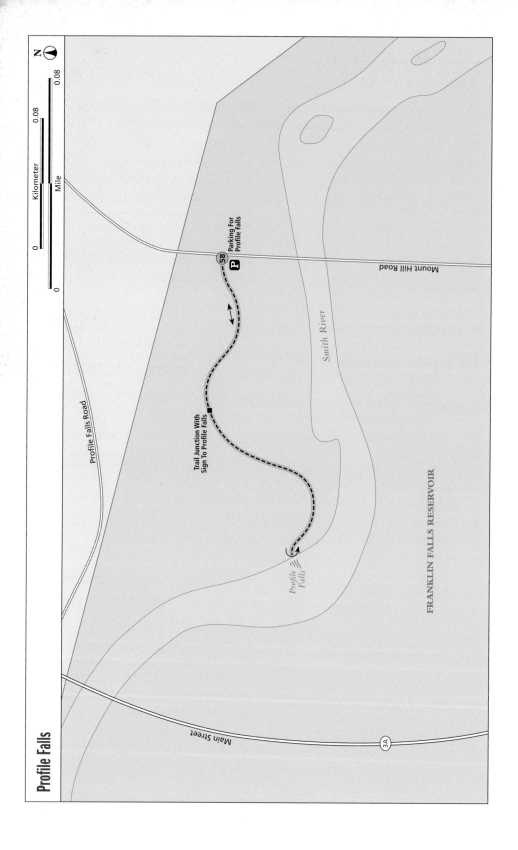

Profile Falls Road

Main Street

3A

Trail Junction With
Sign To Profile Falls

Profile
Falls

Smith River

58

Parking For
Profile Falls

Mount Hill Road

FRANKLIN FALLS RESERVOIR

N

Kilometer
0   0.08

Mile
0   0.08

A series of small cascades are framed by a stone arched bridge above Profile Falls.

Miles and Directions

0.0   Start from the parking area and follow the signed trail out to the falls.

0.15 Reach the pool below the falls. Climb up the rocks to the right of the falls for a view of the falls from above and the cascades above the falls.

0.2   Reach the top of Profile Falls (N43 34.076' / W71 44.042'). Return the way you came.

0.4   Arrive back at the parking area.

59 Livermore Falls

This unique cascade flows at an interesting angle and is flanked by a steep cliff. Industrial remains and a unique lenticular bridge can be seen nearby. A nice wide beach above the falls provides a great spot to take a dip on a hot summer day.

Start: Dirt pull-off on east side of US 3
Distance: 0.3 mile out and back
Hiking time: About 10 minutes
Approximate elevation gain: 100 feet
Difficulty: Easy
Beauty: Good

County: Grafton
Land status: Owned by the State of New Hampshire
DeLorme map: Page 39, G-12 (marked)
Other maps: None
Trail contact: N/A

Finding the trailhead: Parking for Livermore Falls is located 2.7 miles south of exit 27 off I-93 on US 3 and 1.2 miles north of the junction with NH 3A/NH-25. There are large dirt pull-offs on the east side of US 3. Look for a small sign and a path heading down under the power lines. **GPS:** N43 47.045'/W71 40.173'

The Hike

Although there are concrete structures, electric poles, train tracks, and an old bridge nearby, the area near the falls is, surprisingly, still very beautiful. The rapids here are very strong and cascade down wide slanted bedrock over a 25-foot drop. Many people jump off the cliff into the water, and a number of brave souls jump off the lenticular full-deck truss bridge. This should be done with extreme caution and at your own risk; more than a dozen confirmed deaths have occurred here, almost all from jumpers.

This area has historically been used for mills, and there was a dam here until the 1970s. There is a state forest on the east side of the river off NH 175, with a trail that leads down to the river and another beach, although there is no access to the falls from here.

From the parking off US 3, look for a gravel road that heads down and to the left. This quickly turns to dirt as it crosses a train track and a power line. Partway down on the right is a fenced-in view above the falls. Below this is the large beach area just upstream from the falls. The best view of the falls can be had by walking down the rocks below the beach. Return to the parking on the same path.

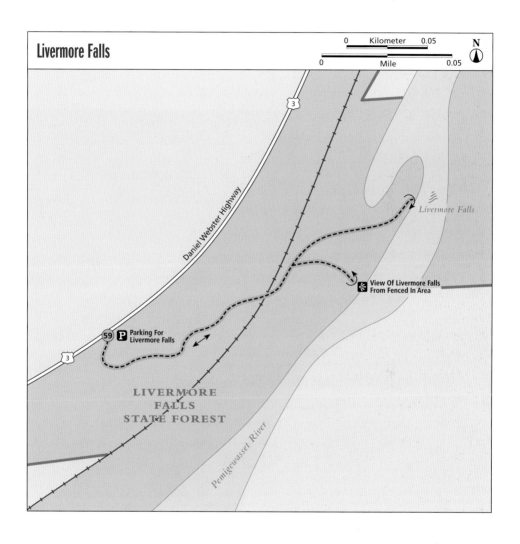

Livermore Falls

0 Kilometer 0.05

0 Mile 0.05

N

3

Daniel Webster Highway

Livermore Falls

View Of Livermore Falls
From Fenced In Area

59 P Parking For
Livermore Falls

3

LIVERMORE
FALLS
STATE FOREST

Pemigewasset River

Miles and Directions

0.0 Start from the parking on US 3; take the gravel road that heads down to the river and crosses over the train tracks.

0.1 Arrive at a fenced-in viewpoint above the falls.

0.15 Reach the beach at the top of the falls (N43 47.089' / W71 40.029'). Return the way you came.

0.3 Arrive back at the parking area.

The river is relatively calm before taking a left turn and skirting the cliffs along Livermore Falls.

60 Waterville Cascades

This gentle hike through the woods takes you along Cascade Brook. You will visit a number of beautiful cascades, falls, and pools, as well as the gently sloping, tranquil Norway Rapids.

Start: Large parking lot on Boulder Path Road, 0.4 mile from junction with NH 49
Distance: 4.4 miles out and back with spur
Hiking time: About 2 hours
Approximate elevation gain: 900 feet
Difficulty: Easy to moderate
County: Grafton
Land status: White Mountain National Forest
Beauty: Excellent
DeLorme map: Page 40, A-2 (not marked; Norway Rapids marked)

Other maps: AMC White Mountains Trail Map: Franconia Pemigewasset; Map Adventures White Mountains Hiking Trails
Trail contact: White Mountain National Forest—Pemigewasset Ranger District; (603) 536-6100; www.fs.usda.gov/detail/whitemountain/about-forest/offices
Special considerations: Some of the route uses multiuse trails and passes private property; be respectful and stay on the trail.

Finding the trailhead: Take exit 28 off I-93 and follow NH 49 East for 11.2 miles. Turn right onto Boulder Path Road and continue 0.4 mile to a large parking lot on the right, just before reaching Cascade Ridge Road. **GPS:** N43 57.609'/W71 30.528'

The Hike

Although this trail goes through a developed area, when you are standing by the Waterville Cascades you will feel as though you are in another world; the setting is beautiful and tranquil. From the large parking area, cross Cascade Ridge Road and begin your journey uphill on the Cascade Path, which is marked with a sign.

Continue up along the left side of the road as it veers away into the woods and at 0.25 mile reach a junction with the Boulder Path and Cascade Trail. Turn right onto the Cascade Trail. Cross a road shortly after and head directly up the ski trail. Turn left onto the Cascade Path and follow yellow arrows and signs to stay on the trail as you cross and intersect various dirt logging roads.

At 0.6 mile reach a junction with the Elephant Rock Trail. Stay left, following the sign toward the cascades. Continue along this path, eventually heading downhill and crossing a small bridge, keeping right as a rough dirt road comes in from the left. Shortly after this, at 1.3 miles, turn right toward the cascades as the Norway Rapids Trail comes in from the left. Continue upstream along Cascade Brook and at 1.6 miles reach the main drop of Waterville Cascades.

Waterville Cascades

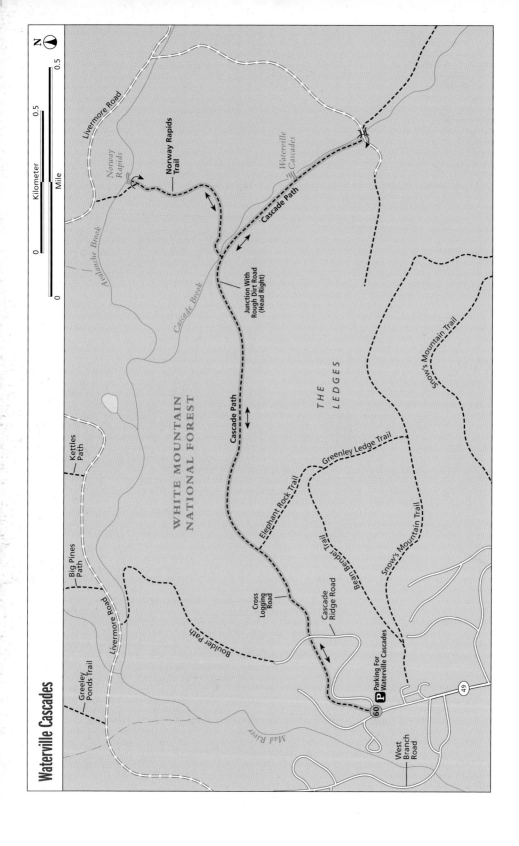

N

0   0.5   Kilometer   0.5
0   Mile

Greeley Ponds Trail

Livermore Road

Big Pines Path

Kettles Path

Boulder Path

Livermore Road

Norway Rapids

Avalanche Brook

Norway Rapids Trail

Cascade Brook

Waterville Cascades

Cascade Path

Junction With Rough Dirt Road (Head Right)

WHITE MOUNTAIN NATIONAL FOREST

Cascade Path

THE LEDGES

Cross Logging Road

Elephant Rock Trail

Greenley Ledge Trail

Bean Bender Trail

Snow's Mountain Trail

Snow's Mountain Trail

Cascade Ridge Road

Mad River

Parking For Waterville Cascades

60

West Branch Road

49

This is one of a number of beautiful falls along Cascade Brook.

Here the water pours over steep rock as a horsetail, briefly bounces off a small rock ledge, and then fans out in a pool below over a drop of about 20 feet. There are a number of nice observation spots here. You can continue up along Cascade Brook to visit more, smaller falls before popping out onto a road and a bridge above the brook. You can take a trail back down either side of the brook. Follow this all the way back to the intersection with the Norway Rapids Trail.

Head right at the Norway Rapids Trail and follow this for 0.4 mile to Norway Rapids, a set of whitewater that flows over rolling bedrock. Retrace your steps to the junction with the Cascade Trail and follow this back down to the parking area the same way you came.

Miles and Directions

0.0 Start from the parking lot, cross Cascade Ridge Road, and begin hiking up the Cascade Path.

0.25 Head right, following the Cascade Trail at the intersection with the Boulder Path. Cross the road and continue heading up the ski trail.

0.4 Turn left onto the signed Cascade Path.

0.6 At the junction with the Elephant Rock Trail, stay left. Follow this trail over a slight rise and head right as a dirt road comes in from the left.

1.3 At the junction with the Norway Rapids Trail, head right to the cascades.

1.6 Reach the main part of the Waterville Cascades (N43 57.795'/W71 29.157'). Continue upstream to see more cascades.

1.8 Reach a road and a bridge over Cascade Brook. Head back down the trail.

2.3 To head to Norway Rapids, turn right at the junction with the Norway Rapids Trail.

2.7 Arrive at the Norway Rapids (N43 58.106'/W71 29.162'). Turn around and head back down the same trail.

3.1 Reach the junction with the Cascade Trail. Return to the parking area by following this same trail back down the same way you came up.

4.4 Arrive back at the parking lot.

61 Beaver Brook Cascades (Moosilauke)

This very steep out-and-back climbs partway up Mount Moosilauke. The first 1.1 miles is flanked by tons of incredible cascades.

Start: Parking area on NH 112
Distance: 2.2 miles out and back
Hiking time: About 2 hours
Approximate elevation gain: 1,200 feet
Difficulty: Very difficult (steep)
Beauty: Excellent
County: Grafton
Land status: White Mountain National Forest
DeLorme map: Page 43, I-9 (marked as Beaver Brook Trail)
Other maps: AMC White Mountains Trail Map: Crawford Notch-Sandwich Range and

Moosilauke-Kinsmen; Map Adventures White Mountains Hiking Trails
Trail contact: White Mountain National Forest–Pemigewasset Ranger District; (603) 536-6100; www.fs.usda.gov/detail/whitemountain/about-forest/offices
Special considerations: This is an extremely steep trail with sections of steps and metal rungs bolted into rock. A White Mountain National Forest day-use or yearly parking pass is required. (You can pay at the trailhead.)

Finding the trailhead: (From the west) Take exit 17 off I-91 in Vermont and follow US 302 East for 6.8 miles, crossing into New Hampshire after the first 2.7 miles. Turn right onto NH 112 East and continue 14.4 miles to the trailhead parking on the right, just past parking for Beaver Brook Pond. If you start going downhill, you've gone too far.

(From the east) From the junction of US 3 and NH 112 in North Woodstock, take NH 112 West for 6.1 miles to the trailhead parking on the left, 0.4 mile past the parking for Lost River Gorge.
GPS: N44 02.419'/W71 47.560'

The Hike

The Beaver Brook Trail is part of the Appalachian Trail and one of the steepest trails in this book. Your reward for the nearly vertical climb is beautiful steep cascades and waterfalls all along trail. If you want to make a night of it, just a few tenths of a mile above the end of this hike is the Beaver Brook shelter, which affords great views over to the Franconia Range.

From the parking area, head into the woods, going south on the Appalachian Trail. A few hundred yards in you will pass a sign. The sign notes that this trail is maintained by the Dartmouth Outing Club (DOC), students from Dartmouth College who are passionate about the outdoors. (The DOC maintains the Appalachian Trail from Hanover to the Beaver Brook Trail.)

The trail starts off mellow enough, and at 0.4 mile in you reach the first set of cascades. From here the trail continues straight uphill, sometimes on wooden stairs that are bolted into bedrock. As you continue up the trail you have plenty of opportunities

Beaver Brook Cascades (Moosilauke); Lost River Gorge

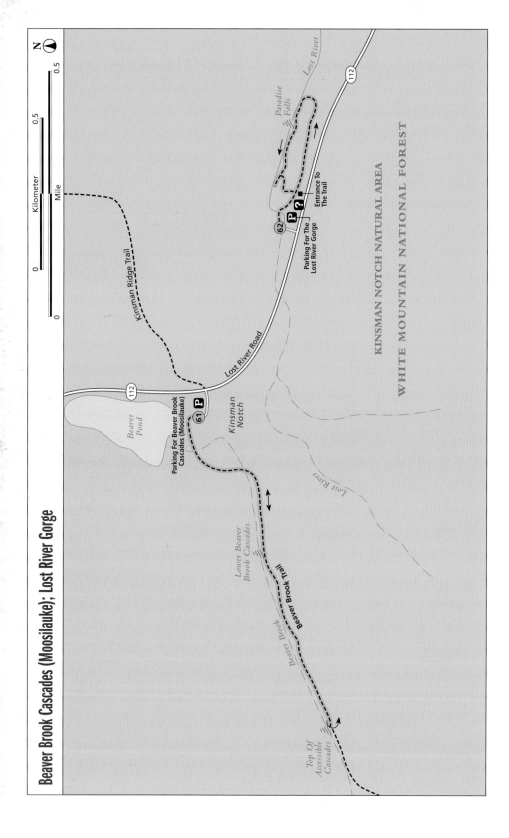

Before the trail and brook head back into the woods, you can get a great view across Kinsman Notch.

to check out the cascades. From the top of the cascades you are afforded fantastic views to the west.

At 1.1 mile reach the top of the most easily accessible cascades as the brook heads into the woods and the trail veers away. Head back the way you came.

Miles and Directions

0.0 Start at the end of the parking lot and head into the woods, going south on the Appalachian Trail.

0.4 Reach the first set of cascades.

1.1 Reach the last of the trailside cascades (N44 02.176'/W71 48.324'). Head back the way you came.

2.2 Arrive back at the parking area.

62 Lost River Gorge

Although there are some waterfalls here, the main reason to visit Lost River Gorge is to climb into any of the many caves, tunnels, and rock formations. A boardwalk takes you through the gorge, and the features are marked. This is a great place for children of all ages, and you could spend a half hour or half a day here. *Note:* There is an entry fee.

See map on page 190.
Start: Parking area on NH 112 at "Lost River Gorge" sign
Distance: 0.8-mile loop
Hiking time: About 30 minutes (much more time for exploring)
Approximate elevation gain: 200 feet
Difficulty: Easy, with some small and difficult features
Beauty: Spectacular
County: Grafton

Land status: Owned by the Society for the Protection of New Hampshire Forests; managed by the White Mountains Attractions Association
DeLorme map: Page 43, I-9 (marked)
Other map: Lost River Gorge Map: www.lostrivergorge.com/mapimages/mapbig.jpg
Trail contact: Lost River Gorge & Boulder Caves; (603) 745-8031; www.lostrivergorge.com
Special considerations: There is an entry fee for this attraction; check the website for current rates.

Finding the trailhead: (From the west) Take exit 17 off I-91 in Vermont and follow US 302 east for 6.8 miles, crossing into New Hampshire after the first 2.7 miles. Turn right onto NH 112 East and continue 14.8 miles to the large entrance on the left for Lost River Gorge.

(From the east) From the junction of US 3 and NH 112 in North Woodstock, take NH 112 west for 5.7 miles to parking on the right at "Lost River Gorge" sign. **GPS:** N44 02.263'/W71 47.100'

The Hike

This is one of just two New Hampshire hikes in this book that require a significant entry fee. However, it's also an excursion you won't likely forget, or regret. There are a few waterfalls of note here, but endless caves, tunnels, viewpoints, and interesting geological features make this a remarkable outing. There are too many features to list in this hike description, but know that there is something for everyone here.

A map is available when you buy your ticket, and children may actually have the upper hand here—there are numerous tight spaces to squeeze through, perfect for small bodies. If you are nervous about tight spaces, don't fear. The boardwalk through the gorge provides an easy route through otherwise inhospitable terrain.

The trail begins behind the visitor center. Head under the "Gorge and Caves" sign; soon the gravel trail gives way to a boardwalk with descending stairs. In 0.3 mile reach the first viewpoint of the gorge. Continue following the boardwalk as it winds its way up through the gorge, passing the Fenris the Wolf rock formation and the Cave of Odin before coming to Paradise Falls. This waterfall drops 35 feet in two plunges; the second is almost 30 feet. There are great views from the side of the falls, across the falls, and above the falls.

There are numerous other cascades and falls deep within the strewn boulders, but Paradise Falls is the only named falls. Continue along the path, visiting other features along the way, until you reach the final feature, Look Off Point, where you will get a view of the Hall of Ships below you and Mounts Tripyramid, Osceola, and Tecumseh in the distance.

Once out of the gorge, continue along the path to visit the informative Nature Garden before returning to the main entrance and the parking just below.

Miles and Directions

0.0 Start from the parking area and take the trail to the visitor center.

0.1 After purchasing your ticket, head down the trail behind the visitor center.

0.3 Arrive at the first viewpoint of the gorge, near the bottom. Follow the boardwalk as you visit numerous features along the way.

0.4 Reach Paradise Falls (N44 02.239' / W71 46.849').

0.6 Reach Look Off Point and the top of the gorge. Continue forward to loop around the Nature Garden.

0.7 Arrive back at the visitor center.

0.8 Arrive back at the parking area.

Paradise Falls can be found about halfway up the gorge.

A boardwalk heads down to the bottom of the Lost River Gorge.

63 Sabbaday Falls

Sabbaday Falls is a must-see destination along the Kancamagus Highway. It's a beautiful three-tiered waterfall with trail that's accessible for all.

Start: Well-marked parking area on the Kancamagus Highway/NH 112
Distance: 0.75-mile lollipop
Hiking time: About 30 minutes
Approximate elevation gain: 100 feet
Difficulty: Easy
Beauty: Spectacular
County: Grafton
Land status: White Mountain National Forest
DeLorme map: Page 44, K-4 (marked)
Other maps: None

Trail contact: White Mountain National Forest—Saco River Ranger District; (603) 536-6100; www.fs.usda.gov/detail/whitemountain/about-forest/offices
Special considerations: Parking can be very crowded, especially on weekends. A White Mountain National Forest day-use or yearly parking pass is required. (You can pay at the trailhead.) Swimming is prohibited. The top is wheelchair accessible; however, the incline is pretty steep without some serious pushing.

Finding the trailhead: The well-marked parking area for Sabbaday Falls is located on NH 112/Kancamagus Highway, 19.8 miles east of the intersection with I-93 in Lincoln and 15.5 miles west of the intersection with NH 16 in Conway. **GPS:** N43 59.852'/W71 23.590'

The Hike

The wooden boardwalk provides perfect views of all aspects of this waterfall, which is a truly stunning spectacle of nature. Sabbaday Falls has three distinct drops. The upper plunge falls about 10 feet into a gorgeous emerald green bowl before dropping another 25 feet or so into a narrow flume. Here the water makes a 90-degree turn as it is flanked by two enormous vertical walls. As it goes through the flume, it makes the final drop of about 12 feet down to another trough before flowing into the lowest pool.

From the parking area, take the wide flat path toward the falls. At 0.3 mile turn left at a junction, where you can get to the beautiful pool below the lowest falls. Wooden stairs and boardwalks head up and around the falls, providing viewing from every angle, including a bridge that crosses over the narrow gorge above the second drop. At the top of this path, meet up with the graded bath and turn right to return to the parking area.

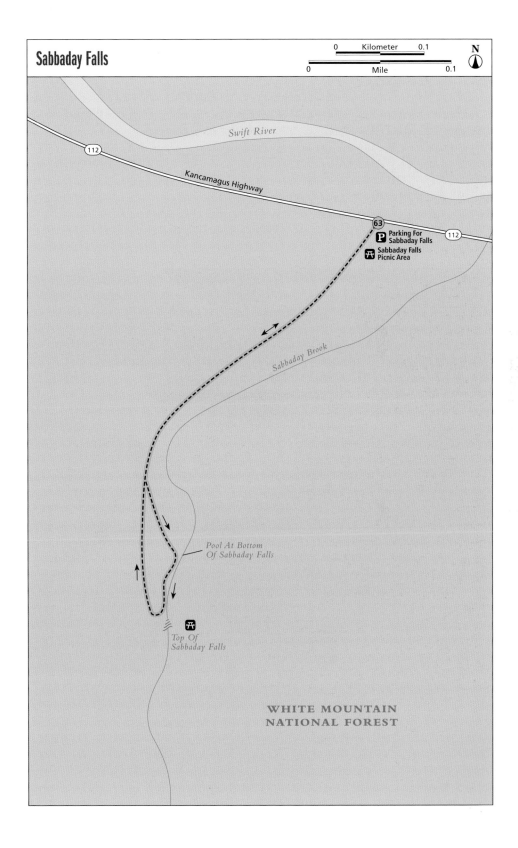

Sabbaday Falls

Swift River

112

Kancamagus Highway

112

63

P Parking For Sabbaday Falls

Ⓐ Sabbaday Falls Picnic Area

Sabbaday Brook

Pool At Bottom Of Sabbaday Falls

Ⓐ

Top Of Sabbaday Falls

WHITE MOUNTAIN NATIONAL FOREST

0   Kilometer   0.1

0   Mile   0.1

N

Miles and Directions

0.0 Start from the parking area and take the path that leads directly toward the falls.

0.3 Turn left at the junction for access to the lowest pool and a view of the bottom plunge from below. From here follow the path with stairs and a wooden boardwalk up and around to the top of the falls.

0.4 Reach the top of Sabbaday Falls (N43 59.613' / W71 23.762'). Take the wide graded path back down to the parking area.

0.75 Arrive back at the parking area.

Near the top of Sabbaday Falls, a small waterfall pours into a beautiful aquamarine pool.

KANCAMAGUS HIGHWAY

The Kancamagus Highway is a 35-mile scenic drive along NH 112. Often referred to as the "Kanc," the road passes a number of beautiful outlooks over the White Mountains. Along the way there are six campgrounds and many waterfalls, including Sabbaday, Champney, and Lower Falls. (The last two are roadside and worth checking out.) This is a particularly nice road to travel during fall foliage season.

A highly recommended driving route that goes by a number of the waterfall hikes in this book is to take the Kancamagus Highway east to NH-16 North to US 302, which goes through Crawford Notch. At Twin Mountain take US 3 South back to Lincoln, where you started the loop, as it is just off I-93.

Kancamagus means "the Fearless One" and was the name of the grandson of Passaconaway, who united seventeen Indian tribes in central New England in the 1600s. The highway opened in 1959.

There are many views from the Kancamagus highway including this view of Osceola and East Osceola in late April.

64 Flume Gorge / Flume Pool Loop

A walk through the flume gorge, one of the most popular attractions in the White Mountains, shouldn't be missed. In a short loop you'll see a deep mysterious chasm, cool waterfalls, covered bridges, interesting pools, and glacial erratic rocks. This is a great adventure for family members of all ages. As there's an entrance fee, it's worth taking your time and appreciating the scenery.

Start: Visitor center on US 3
Distance: 2.1-mile lollipop
Hiking time: About 1 hour minimum
Approximate elevation gain: 400 feet
Difficulty: Easy
Beauty: Spectacular
County: Grafton
Land status: Franconia Notch State Park
DeLorme map: Page 43, G-11 & 12 (marked)
Other map: New Hampshire State Park Map of Flume and Pool Areas in Franconia Notch State

Park: www.nhstateparks.org/uploads/pdf/ FlumeMap_web.pdf
Trail contact: Flume Gorge and Visitor Center; (603) 745-8391; www.nhstateparks.org/ explore/state-parks/flume-gorge.aspx
Special considerations: This can be very crowded on weekends, so it's a good idea to arrive early. There is an entry fee for this attraction; check the website for current rates. Pets are not permitted.

Finding the trailhead: Take exit 34A (from both the north and the south) off I-93. The sign for "The Flume" and "Franconia Notch State Park" will be visible soon after you get on US 3. The trail begins behind the visitor center. **GPS:** N44 05.834' / W71 40.776'

The Hike

Why pay for a waterfall hike when there are so many free options? No other hike, especially one as short as this, has as many interesting features, and the Flume Gorge is a geological treasure, unlike anything else in New Hampshire. If you can, try to visit on a weekday, as weekends can get very crowded. If you do go on a weekend, get there when it opens, before the hordes have arrived. You won't regret it.

There is no need to point out every feature along the Flume-Pool Loop. Part of the fun is discovering what is here, so this text will just describe the route and some key features. Know that you can spend an entire day here checking out all the features.

The trail begins behind the visitor center, where you get a great view of the Franconia Range. Continue along the sidewalk, which becomes a gravel trail. Pass a huge glacial boulder then turn right at a sign with an arrow pointing toward The Flume at 0.2 mile. Walk through a covered bridge over the Pemigewasset River then pass the Boulder Cabin, where there's a shuttle for people who don't want to walk there. Soon after, at 0.55 mile, get to Table Rock, a long, wide water slide.

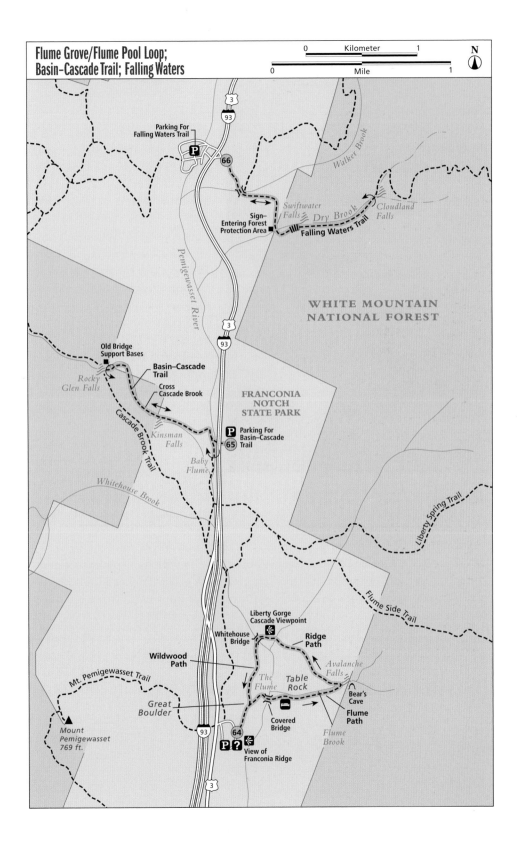

Flume Grove/Flume Pool Loop; Basin–Cascade Trail; Falling Waters

0   Kilometer   1

0   Mile   1

N

Parking For
Falling Waters Trail

P

66

Walker Brook

Pemigewasset River

Sign–
Entering Forest
Protection Area

Swiftwater
Falls

Dry Brook

Cloudland
Falls

Falling Waters Trail

WHITE MOUNTAIN
NATIONAL FOREST

Old Bridge
Support Bases

Basin–Cascade
Trail

Cross
Cascade Brook

Rocky
Glen Falls

Cascade Brook Trail

Kinsman
Falls

P

65

Parking For
Basin–Cascade
Trail

FRANCONIA
NOTCH
STATE PARK

Baby
Flume

Whitehouse Brook

Liberty Spring Trail

Flume Side Trail

Liberty Gorge
Cascade Viewpoint

Whitehouse
Bridge

Ridge
Path

Wildwood
Path

Avalanche
Falls

Mt. Pemigewasset Trail

The
Flume

Table
Rock

Great
Boulder

Bear's
Cave

Flume
Path

Covered
Bridge

Flume
Brook

P

64

View of
Franconia Ridge

Mount
Pemigewasset
769 ft.

A covered bridge crosses the Pemige-wasset River above the Pool.

Beyond Table Rock you enter the Flume Gorge on a boardwalk. Vertical walls enclose a narrow gorge, a truly dramatic sight. At the end of the Flume Gorge is Avalanche Falls, which plunges 45 feet to Flume Brook, where the water makes a 90-degree turn and flows down through the gorge. The boardwalk takes you up and around to the top of the falls.

Above Avalanche Falls the path splits. Head right along the Ridge Path (check out the Rim Path to the left if you are so inclined). At the next intersection continue to the right along the Ridge Path. At around 1.4 miles cross over the brook above Liberty Gorge. There are some nice cascades both above and below the bridge. Shortly after, take the spur trail to the view of Liberty Gorge Cascade, a stunning 70-foot horsetail that pours out of the woods.

Continue along the path and soon reach a great view of The Pool, a long deep pool flanked by huge rock walls. The path then takes you through another covered bridge. On the other side is a spur trail to a great view of The Pool and the covered bridge above it. Head back to the trail and follow it all the way back to the visitor center.

Miles and Directions

0.0 Start the loop from behind the visitor center.

0.2 After the large glacial boulder, turn right toward The Flume.

0.3 Cross the covered bridge.

0.5 Reach the Boulder Cabin and the end of the shuttle route.

0.55 Reach Table Rock.

0.6 Enter the Flume Gorge.

0.8 Reach Avalanche Falls (N44 06.030' / W71 40.131').

0.85 Turn right onto the Ridge Path.

1.4 Take the left spur to a view of Liberty Gorge Cascade (N44 06.242' / W71 40.576').

1.6 Cross the covered bridge above The Pool.

1.65 Reach the spur down to a better view of The Pool. Follow the path south toward the start.

1.9 Pass the glacial boulder, heading straight back toward the visitor center.

2.1 Arrive back at the visitor center.

A boardwalk creates an easy path through the Flume Gorge which is an incredibly impressive geologic feature.

65 Basin-Cascade Trail Falls

A fairly quick out-and-back, the hike up along the Basin-Cascade Trail visits the Basin, Kinsman Falls, Rocky Glen Falls, and the nearby Baby Flume. All are unique and worthy of a visit in this stunning Franconia Notch location.

See map on page 201.
Start: The Basin parking area off I-93
Distance: 2.7 miles out and back (including Baby Flume)
Hiking time: About 1.5 hours
Approximate elevation gain: 600 feet
Difficulty: Moderate
Beauty: Excellent
County: Grafton
Land status: Franconia Notch State Park (parking and the Basin); White Mountain National Forest (Basin-Cascade Trail)
DeLorme map: Page 43, F-11 & G-11 (Basin marked)
Other maps: Franconia Notch State Park Hiking Trails Map: www.nhstateparks.org/uploads/

pdf/FranconiaHikingMapAllWeb_2010.pdf; AMC White Mountains Trail Map: Franconia Pemigewasset; Map Adventures White Mountains Hiking Trails
Trail contacts: Franconia Notch State Park; (603) 745-8391; www.nhstateparks.org/explore/state-parks/franconia-notch-state-park.aspx
White Mountain National Forest—Pemigewasset Ranger District; (603) 536-6100; www.fs.usda.gov/detail/whitemountain/about-forest/offices
Special considerations: This is a very popular place, and parking can be difficult on weekends. This is a great spot for the whole family.

Finding the trailhead: (From the south) On I-93, north of Lincoln, take the exit for "The Basin," 2.1 miles north of exit 34a. The trail begins on the paved recreational trail that goes under I-93.

(From the north) On I-93 take the exit for "The Basin," 1.3 miles south of the Lafayette Campground. The trail begins on the paved recreational trail heading south. **GPS:** N44 07.203'/W71 40.873'

The Hike

The upper portion of this hike is rocky, rooty, and involves a stream crossing, but it is not too difficult and is well worth the effort. *Note:* These directions are from the northbound side of I-93. From the parking area on the southbound side, follow the path to The Basin and then continue these directions from there.

From the parking area on the east side of the highway, walk through a tunnel under the highway. This paved trail curves around to the right and immediately heads left onto a dirt trail with a sign to The Basin. Follow the path along the river and soon come to The Basin. This is a small waterfall that falls at a right angle into a 12-foot-deep pool that has been carved out over the millennia by swirling rocks. Take the trail up from The Basin and back around to the left to meet up with the Basin-Cascade Trail.

From this junction, hike up the trail as it begins to parallel Cascade Brook. In 0.4 mile reach a short steep spur trail down Kinsman Falls. This 15-foot plunge shoots through a small notch in between rock walls as it pours into a large pool, ideal for swimming on a hot day. Return to the trail. Note that even though there are just two named falls along this trail, there are many more unnamed but very beautiful falls and cascades all along the route.

In 0.1 mile past Kinsman Falls, you need to cross Cascade Brook. From there the trail becomes a bit rootier and rockier, so watch your step. Continue upstream along the Basin-Cascade Trail and in less than 0.5 mile reach Rocky Glen Falls. Rocky Glen Falls is actually composed of two falls. The lowermost is a dramatic 20-foot plunge between two sheer rock walls. You will need to scramble slightly off-trail to the right, over some boulders, to get the best view.

The upper plunge is accessed by continuing along the trail above the lower falls. When you curve back around, head through some small trees to the river's edge. If you go a little farther upstream, you will hit the bases of an old bridge and can work your way down to the top of the upper part of the falls, a 15-foot plunge into a big round pool.

Return back down the trail. At the bottom of the Basin-Cascade Trail, you can bypass The Basin to head back to the parking area. Just before turning onto the paved walkway, turn right, following signs to the Baby Flume, where the Pemigewasset River pours through vertical walls in a multitiered cascade. This is about a 0.15-mile spur off the main trail.

The Basin is an interesting geologic feature. The hole was rounded out by the swirling and scraping of rocks constantly churning around the pool over thousands of years.

Miles and Directions

0.0 Start from the parking area and take the path under the highway.

0.1 Turn left onto the trail to The Basin; then make an immediate right, following signs to "The Basin." Head up the path along the river.

0.2 Reach The Basin. Continue on the trail up and around to the left to the junction with the Basin-Cascade Trail.

0.25 Turn right up the Basin-Cascade Trail.

0.65 Reach the short spur trail to Kinsman Falls and head down to the river to view the falls (N44 07.307'/W71 41.366'). Continue heading upstream on the Basin-Cascade Trail.

0.8 Cross Cascade Brook. Continue along the trail.

1.25 Reach the bottom (just off-trail to the right) of the lower part of Rocky Glen Falls (N44 07.544'/W71 41.688'). Continue on-trail to top of falls.

1.3 Reach the top of Rocky Glen Falls by making a short bushwhack to the river's edge. Return back down the trail.

2.2 At the base of the Basin-Cascade Trail, head straight/right back to the parking area.

2.25 Just before reaching the paved path back to the parking area, bear right (actually straight) down along the river to the Baby Flume.

2.4 Reach the Baby Flume (N44 07.129'/W71 40.960'). Turn around and head back to the parking area.

2.7 Arrive back at the parking area.

66 Falling Waters

The Falling Waters Trail is a direct route to the Franconia Ridge and one side of a popular loop that traverses the ridge. In addition to a number of beautiful unnamed cascades and falls, Stairs, Swiftwater, and Cloudland Falls are all found along the bottom half of the trail and are required visits for any waterfall aficionado.

See map on page 201.
Start: Falling Waters parking area/Lafayette Campground exit off I-93
Distance: 3.0 miles out and back
Hiking time: About 2 hours
Approximate elevation gain: 900 feet
Difficulty: Moderate to difficult
Beauty: Excellent
County: Grafton
Land status: White Mountain National Forest

DeLorme map: Page 43, F-12
Other maps: AMC White Mountains Trail Map: Franconia Pemigewasset; Map Adventures White Mountains Hiking Trails
Trail contact: White Mountain National Forest—Pemigewasset Ranger District; (603) 536-6100; www.fs.usda.gov/detail/whitemountain/about-forest/offices
Special considerations: The parking lot can get very full on weekends.

Finding the trailhead: (From the south) Take I-93 north to the exit for the Lafayette Campground. This exit also has a sign for a trailhead and is where the Appalachian Trail crosses the highway. It is 1.5 miles north of the exit for "The Basin," 3.8 miles north of exit 34A.

(From the north) Take I-93 south to the exit for the Lafayette Campground, 2.3 miles south of exit 34B. Go under the highway, following the Appalachian Trail, to get to the trailhead. **GPS:** N44 08.524'/W71 40.878'

The Hike

If you are just hiking this trail to visit the falls, you will climb almost 1,000 vertical feet, although that is much less than hikers who are doing the loop over Franconia Ridge will encounter. If you have the time, this is one of the best hikes in all of New England. Franconia Ridge is a truly stunning ridgeline, with a steep drop on both sides well above tree line. Nonetheless, the hike to these three falls is a great hike in its own right.

Begin the hike by taking the paved path that leaves from the center of the parking lot and climbs into the woods. Continue along the Falling Waters Trail as it crosses over Walker Brook in 0.25 mile and then begins to head uphill in earnest. In a few tenths of a mile, the trail heads downhill slightly until you reach a sign saying you are entering a forest protection area. Soon after, cross another stream and then begin heading uphill again.

At 0.9 mile reach Stairs Falls. This is a fairly small but beautiful waterfall where the water bounces down granite ledges that wrap around the pool in a semicircle.

The best view of this waterfall is slightly off the trail. The next waterfall, Swiftwater Falls, is at 1.0 mile; the trail crosses right below the falls then goes around the side. Two cascades join above the final plunge as the water pours onto slanted granite that has a beautiful reddish hue.

At 1.4 miles reach the bottom of Cloudland Falls. This is without a doubt the largest and most dramatic of the three. At 80 feet in height, the water bounces from ledge to ledge in a steep horsetail formation. In low water there are separate streams; in high water these streams come together, turning the waterfall into a large fan. The trail is rocky and steep above here, but the short jaunt to the rim of the falls is well worth it; you can stand right next to the edge to get a great view. From here you can head back down the trail to the parking area.

Miles and Directions

0.0   Start from the middle of the parking area on the paved Falling Waters Trail. It quickly becomes a dirt trail.

0.25 Cross a wooden bridge over Walker Brook.

0.9   Reach Stairs Falls (N44 08.199'/W71 40.399'). Continue up the trail.

1.0   Reach Swiftwater Falls (N44 08.206'/W71 40.351'). The trail crosses the brook below the falls then continues uphill.

1.4   Arrive at the bottom of Cloudland Falls (N44 08.329'/W71 39.874'). The trail continues steeply up the left side.

1.5   Reach the top of Cloudland Falls. Return back down the trail to the parking area.

3.0   Arrive back at the parking area.

APPALACHIAN MOUNTAIN CLUB

Those hardy folks who do the highly recommended hike up the Falling Waters Trail, along Franconia Ridge, and down the Bridle Path, will pass the Greenleaf Hut, operated by the Appalachian Mountain Club (AMC). The AMC runs a number of huts all over the White Mountains; most require a hike to get to. Each hut is staffed by energetic crews who serve family-style meals every morning and night throughout summer and early fall.

In addition to running these mountain huts, trail crews from the AMC and thousands of volunteers maintain many trails all over the region. The organization also runs camps and educational programs and publishes many books and maps of the trails, all of which are highly recommended. According to their website, the AMC's mission is to "promote the protection, enjoyment and understanding of the mountains, forests, waters and trails of the Appalachian Region." Also according to their site, the "AMC is the nation's oldest outdoor recreation and conservation organization."

You can find out more about everything the AMC does, and become a member, at their website: www.outdoors.org.

The largest of the named falls along the Falling Waters Trail, Cloudland Falls is truly dramatic. Continue up the trail on the left to get a great view from the top of the falls.

67 Bridal Veil Falls

This 5.0-mile round-trip hike to one of the most famous waterfalls in the White Mountains, is rewarded with a plunge and set of cascades of unique character in a beautiful setting.

Start: Parking before "No Parking" sign on Coppermine Road
Distance: 5.2 miles out and back
Hiking time: About 2.5 hours
Approximate elevation gain: 1,100 feet
Difficulty: Moderate to view; difficult to base of falls
Beauty: Excellent
County: Grafton
Land status: White Mountain National Forest
DeLorme map: Page 43, E-10 (marked)
Other maps: AMC White Mountains Trail

Map: Crawford Notch–Sandwich Range and Moosilauke-Kinsman; Map Adventures White Mountains Hiking Trails
Trail contact: White Mountain National Forest–Pemigewasset Ranger District; (603) 536-6100; www.fs.usda.gov/detail/whitemountain/about-forest/offices
Special considerations: Parking may be tight on weekends. A shelter near the falls makes for an excellent overnight trip. Getting close to the falls requires some scrambling over steep rocks and roots.

Finding the trailhead: Parking for Bridal Veil Falls is located on Coppermine Road, which is off NH 116, 3.5 miles south of the junction with I-91 and 7.7 miles north of the intersection with NH 112. Park on the left a few hundred feet up the road before a sign marking "No Parking Beyond this Point." **GPS:** N44 10.859' / W71 45.353'

The Hike

The hike to the falls is not very interesting. Unlike other falls, you will not be on the banks of a stream, but once you arrive at the area near the waterfall, you will want to spend a lot of time there. Bridal Veil Falls is a beautiful 30-foot plunge that spreads out as it lands on angled rock, cascading into a narrow pool. Below this, the water slides a few hundred feet down slanted bedrock before landing in a nice pool. There is a shelter just below this pool as well, where you can stay the night if you choose.

From the parking area, follow Coppermine Road (on foot) for 0.4 mile. The Coppermine Trail heads off to the left where a brown sign with a hiker on it is visible a few yards away. Take this trail as it makes a consistent climb up the valley. At 2.3 miles a sign notes that you are entering a forest protection area that is within 0.25 mile of Coppermine Shelter. In another 0.1 mile cross Coppermine Brook on a bridge and at 2.5 miles reach the shelter. Continue past the shelter and reach the large pool below the water slide; Bridal Veil Falls is visible.

Things get a little trickier from here. Follow the left side of the stream as you work your way over boulders and around big roots to get to the base of the waterfall. Be

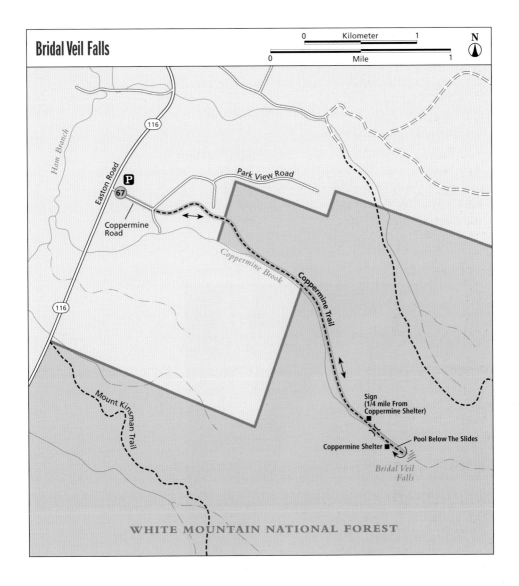

careful here, as the smooth rock surface can be very slippery. The boulders near the pool below the slides can be a great place to enjoy lunch—and a good place to stop for those who don't want to make the scramble to the base of the falls. When you're ready to leave, return down the trail to the parking area.

Miles and Directions

0.0 Start from the parking area and walk down Coppermine Road.

0.4 Turn left onto the Coppermine Trail, which is marked by a brown sign with a picture of a hiker.

2.3 Pass a sign saying you are entering a forest protection area.

2.4 Cross over Coppermine Brook.

2.5 Reach Coppermine Shelter. Continue on a trail past the shelter.

2.55 Reach the base of the slides below Bridal Veil Falls. Continue to the base of the falls by scrambling up the left side of the stream.

2.6 Reach Bridal Veil Falls (N44 09.626' / W71 43.447'). Return the way you came.

5.2 Arrive back at the parking area.

The upper part of the falls shows why Bridal Veil Falls has its name.

68 Diana's Baths

Although Diana's Baths is close to North Conway and is very popular, the abundance of interesting cascades, falls, and pools—all accessible via an easy path—make this a rewarding outing that's recommended for families.

Start: Parking lot on West Side Road
Distance: 1.2 miles out and back
Hiking time: About 45 minutes
Approximate elevation gain: 100 feet
Difficulty: Easy
Beauty: Excellent
County: Carroll
Land status: White Mountain National Forest
DeLorme map: Page 45, H-9 (unmarked)
Other maps: AMC White Mountains Trail Map: North Country-Mahoosuc; Map Adventures

White Mountains Hiking Trails
Trail contact: White Mountain National Forest–Saco Ranger District; (603) 536-6100; www.fs.usda.gov/detail/whitemountain/about-forest/offices
Special considerations: The parking lot can be packed on busy weekends. A White Mountain National Forest day-use or yearly parking pass is required. (You can pay at the trailhead.) The trail to the view of the falls is wheelchair accessible.

Finding the trailhead: From the junction of US 302 and NH 16 in Conway, drive 2.8 miles north through North Conway and turn left at a traffic light onto River Road. Follow River Road, which becomes West Side Road, for 2.3 miles to a large parking lot on the left. **GPS:** N44 04.470' / W71 09.837'

The Hike

North Conway is the center for tourism in the White Mountains, and Diana's Baths, just outside of town, is a popular location for families—and rightfully so. You will find plunges, slides, cascades, and pools as Lucy Brook drops 75 feet over a short distance. Although this is an impressive area when the water levels are high, it is possibly more fun in late summer, when most of the rocks are dry and exploration is possible.

In addition to being a great place to bring children, the path to view Diana's Baths is wheelchair accessible, so it is perfect for young and old alike. This area was privately owned and used as a sawmill in the second half of the nineteenth century. It later became a tourist attraction and a boardinghouse was set up. You will see remains of a concrete foundation as well—for a short while a small power generation plant was set up here. Almost everything was torn down after the government bought the property in the 1960s.

From the end of the parking lot, take the Moat Mountain Trail for 0.6 mile to the falls. There are a number of access points from the trail and some nice cascades above the main falls. Beyond Diana's Baths, the Moat Mountain Trail becomes rugged and climbs high up into the mountains, but for this excursion return along the same trail.

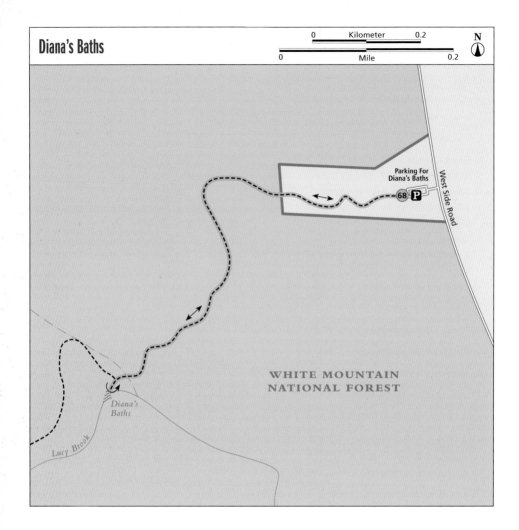

Miles and Directions

0.0 Start from the end of the parking area and take the Moat Mountain Trail into the woods as it winds its way to the falls.

0.6 Arrive at Diana's Baths (N44 04.269' / W71 10.250'). Return the way you came.

1.2 Arrive back at the parking lot.

This is one of the many unique waterfalls you'll find at Diana's Baths.

69 Nancy Cascades

A huge 300-foot cascade of water awaits you, but you have to earn it by climbing a very steep trail. The view from the cascades above the main falls is worth the extra effort. This is one of New Hampshire's finest waterfall hikes, and above the cascades you will cross through one of New Hampshire's few remaining old-growth forests.

Start: Trailhead on west side of US 302
Distance: 5.8 miles out and back
Hiking time: About 3 hours
Approximate elevation gain: 1,800 feet
Difficulty: Difficult
Beauty: Spectacular
County: Grafton and Carroll
Land status: White Mountain National Forest
DeLorme map: Page 44, G-4 (Nancy Brook marked)

Other maps: AMC White Mountains Trail Map: Crawford Notch–Sandwich Range and Moosilauke-Kinsmen; Map Adventures White Mountains Hiking Trails
Trail contact: White Mountain National Forest–Saco River Ranger District; (603) 536-6100; www.fs.usda.gov/detail/whitemountain/about-forest/offices

Finding the trailhead: The trailhead is located on the west side of US 302, 11.3 miles west of the intersection with NH 16 in Glen and 17.8 miles east of the intersection with US 3 in Twin Mountain. **GPS:** N44 06.222'/W71 21.168'

The Hike

The first part of this hike along the Nancy Pond Trail is pretty easy as is traverses the hillside to Nancy Brook. The second half of this hike is much steeper, but your reward is a beautiful 80-foot horsetail that fans out above a dark, tree-shrouded pool. The cascades above this are equally impressive and afford views out to Mount Crawford and the other peaks in the Desolation Wilderness.

From the parking area, head up Nancy Pond Trail, which starts as a dirt road then narrows to a typical trail. At 0.3 mile cross Halfway Brook and at 0.8 mile pass a trail sign to Notchland Inn. From here the trail climbs a little more steeply until you cross Nancy Brook at 1.6 miles. Along the way you will pass a number of intersecting trails; be sure to follow the yellow blazes to stay on Nancy Pond Trail.

At 1.9 miles pass the foundation of an old mill; beyond this the trail starts to get a good bit steeper. At 2.5 miles you cross back over Nancy Brook. Along the way you will pass by a number of bent trees and remnants of landslides. At 2.6 miles reach the bottom of Nancy Cascades, where a nearly vertical wall juts straight up above the pool that is usually shaded by the dense overhead canopy.

From the bottom of Nancy Cascades and continuing above along the trail rises a prime example of an old-growth high-elevation spruce-fir forest. From here the

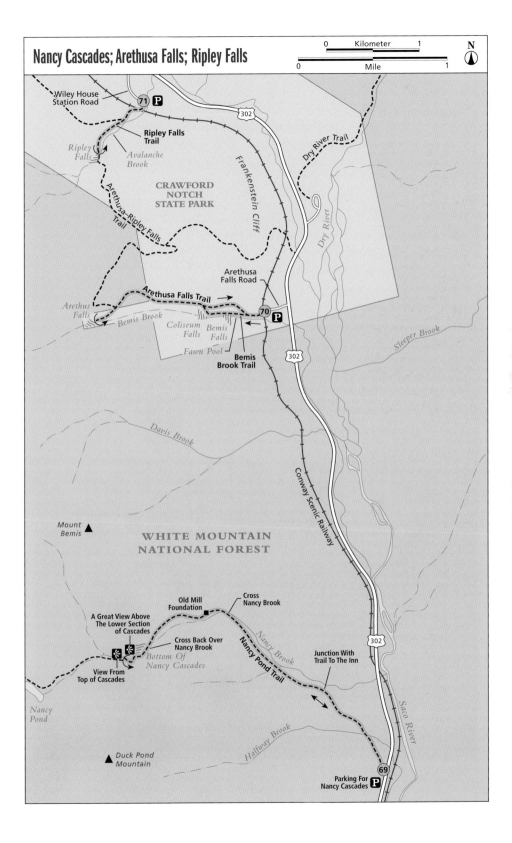

Nancy Cascades; Arethusa Falls; Ripley Falls

0 Kilometer 1

0 Mile 1

N

Wiley House Station Road

71 P

302

Ripley Falls Trail

Dry River Trail

Ripley Falls

Avalanche Brook

CRAWFORD NOTCH STATE PARK

Frankenstein Cliff

Dry River

Arethusa-Ripley Falls Trail

Arethusa Falls Road

Arethusa Falls Trail

70 P

Sleeper Brook

Arethus Falls

Bemis Brook

Coliseum Falls

Bemis Falls

Fawn Pool

Bemis Brook Trail

302

Davis Brook

Conway Scenic Railway

Mount Bemis

WHITE MOUNTAIN NATIONAL FOREST

Old Mill Foundation

Cross Nancy Brook

A Great View Above The Lower Section of Cascades

Cross Back Over Nancy Brook

Nancy Brook

Nancy Pond Trail

Junction With Trail To The Inn

302

Bottom Of Nancy Cascades

View From Top of Cascades

Nancy Pond

Saco River

Duck Pond Mountain

Halfway Brook

Parking For Nancy Cascades

69 P

trail gets much more rooty and rocky as it switchbacks up the steep hillside. After the first major switchback, reach a great view from the top of the lower portion of the cascades. Continue switchbacking up the mountain and at 2.9 miles (around 2,800 feet) see the top of the cascades through the woods. A short bushwhack leads to the top of the cascades, with great views to the east. From here Nancy Brook heads into the forest. You are 0.5 mile from Nancy Pond, a worthwhile excursion, especially since the trail above here is not nearly as steep. To get back to the parking area, return the way you came.

Miles and Directions

0.0 Start from the parking area and head up the Nancy Pond Trail.

0.3 Cross Halfway Brook.

0.8 Pass the junction of the trail to Notchland Inn.

1.6 Cross over Nancy Brook.

1.9 Pass a foundation of an old mill. Above this the trail gets significantly steeper.

2.5 Cross back over Nancy Brook.

2.6 Reach the bottom of Nancy Cascades (N44 06.911'/W71 23.158'). Continue up the trail as it climbs steeply up switchbacks along the brook.

2.7 Reach a great view above the lower cascades.

2.9 Reach the top of the cascades through a short off-trail bushwhack (N44 06.888'/W71 23.306'). Return back to the parking by descending the way you came.

5.8 Arrive back at the parking area.

Golden colored beech trees line the bottom of Nancy Cascades.

70 Arethusa Falls

This hike to one of the tallest waterfalls in New Hampshire should not be missed. The smaller falls along Bemis Brook are intimate and unique, rounding out this rewarding adventure.

See map on page 217.
Start: Upper parking lot on Arethusa Falls Road, 0.2 mile from junction with US 302
Distance: 3.0-mile lollipop
Hiking time: About 2 hours
Approximate elevation gain: 700 feet
Difficulty: Moderate to difficult
Beauty: Spectacular
County: Carroll
Land status: Crawford Notch State Park
DeLorme map: Page 44, F-4 (marked)
Other maps: Crawford Notch State Park Map: www.nhstateparks.org/uploads/pdf/Crawford

HikingMapAllWeb_2010.pdf; AMC White Mountains Trail Map: Crawford Notch–Sandwich Range and Moosilauke-Kinsmen; Map Adventures White Mountains Hiking Trails
Trail contact: Crawford Notch State Park; (603) 374-2272; www.nhstateparks.org/explore/state-parks/crawford-notch-state-park.aspx
Special considerations: This is one of the most popular waterfalls in New Hampshire; on a busy weekend you may have to park in the lower lot.

Finding the trailhead: (From North Conway) From the intersection of US 302 and NH 16 in Glen, a few miles north of North Conway, follow US 302 West for 14.5 miles to Arethusa Falls Road on the left. It is just past the Dry River Campground. The main parking lot is 0.2 mile up this road.

(From the north) Follow US 302 South for 14.5 miles from the intersection with US 3 in Twin Mountain and turn right onto Arethusa Falls Road. The main parking lot is 0.2 mile up this road.
GPS: N44 08.879' / W71 22.173'

The Hike

Be prepared for crowds—this is one of the most popular hikes in New Hampshire. Bemis Brook drops around 150 feet (estimates vary from 140 to 200 feet) creating Arethusa Falls, which plunges down in sheets along an almost vertical wall. It is truly stunning and you can get very close to the base of the falls, especially during low water. By adding the Bemis Brook loop to the hike, you will get to see a few other smaller falls that are very beautiful, and usually less crowded.

From the parking area, cross over the tracks; the trail begins to head uphill. After hiking 0.1 mile, reach the intersection with the Bemis Brook Trail. Turn left at this junction to access the lower falls along Bemis Brook. In 5 minutes reach the Fawn Pool, which in addition to being a beautiful shallow pool has a set of shallow ledges that create a wide cascade.

Just up the trail from this is Bemis Falls. This fall is actually two parts. Below the main drop is another set of shallow ledges similar to the Fawn Pool. However, these ledges wrap around in a semicircle, creating a series of cascades that flow through a natural amphitheater. Just above these cascades is another set of cascades that drop more steeply in short plunges.

Follow this trail upstream for another 0.15 mile. Here the trail takes a sharp right turn. At this turn is a great view of Coliseum Falls, a series of beautiful plunges ranging in height from 3 to 10 feet interspersed with wide pools. From here head up the very steep but short section of trail to the junction with the Arethusa Falls Trail. Continue straight ahead, following the sign for Arethusa Falls.

From this junction continue traveling uphill and away from the brook. Cross over two bridges and at 1.35 miles from the parking area reach the junction with the Arethusa-Ripley Falls Trail. Turn left at this junction and in 0.2 mile pop out onto wide, rock-strewn Bemis Brook below the main falls. You can wend you way uphill for a few hundred yards to get close to the bottom of the falls.

To return to the parking area, retrace your steps to the junction with the Bemis Brook Trail. Head left to continue on the Arethusa Falls Trail all the way back down to the parking area.

Miles and Directions

0.0 Start from the parking area, cross the tracks, and head left up the Arethusa Falls Trail.

0.1 At the junction, turn left onto the Bemis Brook Trail.

One of the benefits of visiting waterfalls during low water is the ability to get right up next to them. From this angle, the sheer immensity of Arethusa Falls becomes evident.

0.25 Reach the Fawn Pool (N44 08.826'/W71 22.434'). Continue up the trail.

0.3 Reach Bemis Falls (N44 08.833'/W71 22.488'). Continue up the trail.

0.5 Reach the viewpoint of Coliseum Falls (N44 08.830'/W71 22.669'). Head right as the trail climbs steeply.

0.6 Reach the junction with the Arethusa Falls Trail. Continue straight ahead.

1.35 At the junction with the Arethusa-Ripley Falls Trail, head left, following the sign for Arethusa Falls.

1.5 Reach the rocks below Arethusa Falls. Follow the streambed to the base of the falls.

1.55 Reach the base of Arethusa Falls (N44 08.801'/W71 23.546'). Retrace your steps, following the Arethusa Falls Trail back to the parking area.

2.5 At the junction with the Bemis Brook Trail, head left to continue following the Arethusa Falls Trail to the parking area.

3.0 Arrive back at the parking area.

SILVER AND FLUME CASCADES

Two beautiful roadside waterfalls in Crawford Notch State Park are well worth a pull-off. Near the north end of the park, just about a mile south of the Crawford Notch Visitor Center, Silver Cascade and Flume Cascade are two huge waterfalls visible from the road. If you cross the road, you can climb up to the base of both falls. Of the two, Silver Cascade is the more impressive, with at least 250 feet of vertical drop visible from the road.

Silver cascade pours for a long way down through a rock channel. Although visible by the road, it's worth taking a walk to the bottom for the most dramatic view.

71 Ripley Falls

A huge 100-foot waterfall that slides over a steep rock wall is the reward at the end of this short climb in Crawford Notch State Park.

See map on page 217.
Start: Parking area at end of Wiley House Station Road, 0.3 mile from junction with US 302
Distance: 1.2 miles out and back
Hiking time: About 45 minutes
Approximate elevation gain: 400 feet
Difficulty: Moderate
Beauty: Excellent
County: Carroll
Land status: Crawford Notch State Park
DeLorme map: Page 44, E-4 (marked)

Other maps: Crawford Notch State Park Map: www.nhstateparks.org/uploads/pdf/Crawford HikingMapAllWeb_2010.pdf; AMC White Mountains Trail Map: Crawford Notch–Sandwich Range and Moosilauke-Kinsmen; Map Adventures White Mountains Hiking Trails
Trail contact: Crawford Notch State Park; (603) 374-2272; www.nhstateparks.org/ explore/state-parks/crawford-notch-state-park .aspx

Finding the trailhead: Ripley Falls is located at the end of Wiley House Station Road, which is off US 302, 12.2 miles east of the intersection with US 3 in Twin Mountain and 17.1 miles west of the intersection with NH 16 in Glen. Wiley House Station Road is a right turn if you're coming from the west, a left if coming from the east. The trailhead is 0.3 mile up this road. **GPS:** N44 10.025' / W71 23.155'

The Hike

The area in and near Crawford Notch contains a fair number of New England's premier waterfalls. Most people know of Arethusa Falls, the tallest waterfall in the state, which is just a bit down the road, but Ripley Falls is a must-see as well. Technically you could call this a cascade, or horsetail, as the water slides along the surface of steeply angled granite, but the sheer size and continuous drop make it deserving of the "falls" moniker.

Although short, the hike is somewhat steep and very rooty and rocky. From the parking area, follow the white-blazed Ethan Pond Trail up into the woods as it shortly crosses the train tracks. This is actually part of the Appalachian Trail, and during late summer and early fall you may encounter hikers who have walked here from Georgia!

After going 0.2 mile, turn left onto the Arethusa-Ripley Falls Trail, marked with blue blazes. Continue along this trail for another 0.4 mile until you reach the base of Ripley Falls.

When the water is low, it flows down the right side (when looking up), but with greater volume the sheet expands farther left. You may need to head downstream a little bit to get a full picture of the falls. Although the Arethusa-Ripley Falls Trail does go to Arethusa Falls, it's a solid hike; you'd see both falls faster by taking the trails from their respective parking areas. Once you've had a chance to soak it all in, head back to the parking area the way you came in.

Miles and Directions

0.0 Start from the parking area and follow the Ethan Pond Trail up into the woods.

0.05 Cross the railroad tracks.

0.2 Head left onto the Arethusa-Ripley Falls Trail.

0.6 Reach the bottom of Ripley Falls (N44 09.755' / W71 23.519'). Return to the parking area on the same trails.

1.2 Arrive back at the parking area.

Ripley Falls is a giant cascades that is shrouded in shade during the late afternoon.

72 Glen Ellis Falls

Beautiful Glen Ellis Falls is one of the most popular waterfalls near Pinkham Notch, and rightfully so. It drops 64 feet and runs even through the drier months.

Start: Parking area on west side of NH 16, 0.6 mile south of Pinkham Notch
Distance: 0.5 mile out and back
Hiking time: About 20 minutes
Approximate elevation gain: 100 feet
Difficulty: Easy
Beauty: Excellent
County: Carroll
Land status: White Mountain National Forest
DeLorme map: Page 44, B-7 (unmarked)
Other maps: None

Trail contact: White Mountain National Forest–Androscoggin Ranger District; (603) 536-6100; www.fs.usda.gov/detail/whitemountain/about-forest/offices
Special considerations: Stay on the path; rocks above and below the falls can get very slippery. Parking can be tight on weekends. A White Mountain National Forest day-use or yearly parking pass is required. (You can pay at the trailhead.) Swimming is prohibited.

Finding the trailhead: A sign for the parking area for Glen Ellis Falls is visible on the west side of NH 16, 11 miles north of the intersection with US 302 and 11.3 miles south of the intersection with US 2 in Gorham. (The parking area is 0.6 mile south of Pinkham Notch.) **GPS:** N44 14.745'/W71 15.212'

The Hike

Pinkham Notch is one of the most popular spots in the White Mountains, and Glen Ellis Falls is probably the most popular waterfall in Pinkham Notch. Just down the road from the Pinkham Notch Visitor Center (and the trailhead to the Tuckerman Ravine Trail and Crystal Cascade, also listed in this book), the water from the Ellis River pours through a notch and plunges a dramatic 64 feet. The water flows strongly all year long, and above and below the falls you can see the beautiful green colored water.

From the parking area, follow the Glen Ellis Falls Trail, which goes through a tunnel under the road. You will see the Ellis River and, just a little farther down, a sign describing the geology of the falls. Check out the viewpoint above the falls, then head down a set of well-constructed stairs to the bottom. Be careful, as the spray makes the rocks slippery. This may be one of those waterfalls that you not only hear but feel—the sheer volume, especially after a rain, combined with the steep rock walls make the ground rumble. Return to the parking via the same trail.

Glen Ellis Falls; Crystal Cascade

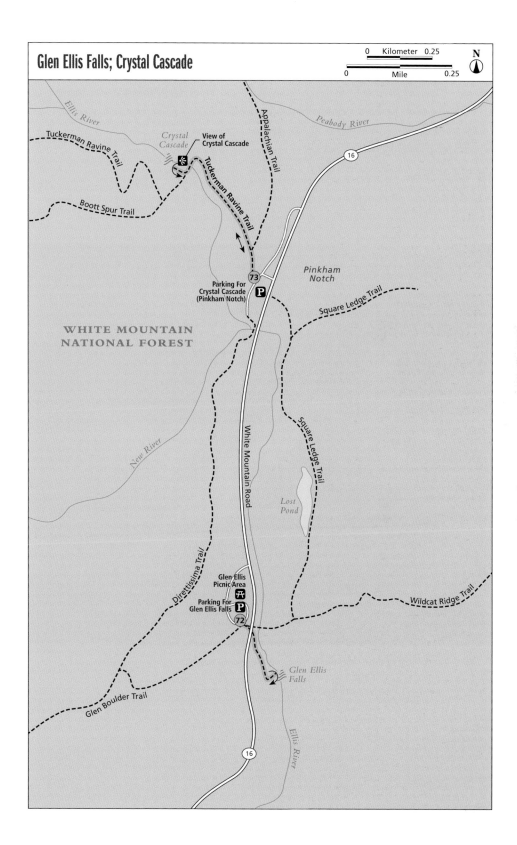

0   Kilometer   0.25

0   Mile   0.25

N

Ellis River

Peabody River

Tuckerman Ravine Trail

Crystal Cascade

View of Crystal Cascade

Appalachian Trail

16

Boott Spur Trail

Tuckerman Ravine Trail

Pinkham Notch

73

Parking For Crystal Cascade (Pinkham Notch)

P

Square Ledge Trail

WHITE MOUNTAIN NATIONAL FOREST

New River

White Mountain Road

Square Ledge Trail

Lost Pond

Glen Ellis Picnic Area

Direttissima Trail

Parking For Glen Ellis Falls

P

72

Wildcat Ridge Trail

Glen Boulder Trail

Glen Ellis Falls

16

Ellis River

Miles and Directions

0.0 Start from the parking area and head down the trail, which quickly goes under the highway.

0.25 Reach the bottom of Glen Ellis Falls (N44 14.643' / W71 15.135'). Return the way you came.

0.5 Arrive back at the parking area.

On the way down you can get a cool view from above the falls.

73 Crystal Cascade

The trail to this waterfall from Pinkham Notch eventually leads up Tuckerman Ravine. Most hikers will pass right by this cascade on their way up the mountain, but the short trip to the falls is well worth the small effort to get there.

See map on page 225.
Start: Behind visitor center at Pinkham Notch off NH 16
Distance: 0.8 mile out and back
Hiking time: About 30 minutes
Approximate elevation gain: 300 feet
Difficulty: Easy to moderate
Beauty: Very good
County: Coos
Land status: White Mountain National Forest
DeLorme map: Page 44, B-7 (Pinkham Notch marked, not falls)

Other maps: AMC White Mountains Trail Map: Presidential Range; Map Adventures White Mountains Hiking Trails
Trail contact: White Mountain National Forest—Androscoggin Ranger District; (603) 536-6100; www.fs.usda.gov/detail/whitemountain/about-forest/offices
Special considerations: Parking at Pinkham Notch can get very crowded on weekends, but unlike many locations in the White Mountains it is free.

Finding the trailhead: Parking for Crystal Cascade is at Pinkham Notch on NH 16, 10.6 miles south of the intersection with US 2 in Gorham and 11.8 miles north of the intersection with US 302 in Glen. The trail begins just past the visitor center at the sign for the Tuckerman Ravine Trail. **GPS:** N44 15.420' / W71 15.186'

The Hike

You may have heard of Tuckerman Ravine—a giant ravine known for some of the best, and steepest, backcountry open-bowl skiing east of the Rockies. On a nice spring weekend day, literally thousands of people pack the bowl to ski and watch others ski down the extremely steep chutes and cliffs. During summer, however, the Tuckerman Ravine Trail is one of the most popular and direct routes to the summit of Mount Washington, the tallest mountain in New England.

Even though hundreds of people climb this trail, you'd be surprised at how few stop to check out Crystal Cascade as they're huffing and puffing on their way to the summit. Nonetheless, the short trip to view Crystal Cascade is well worth it in its own right.

From the parking area, head up the main path to the Tuckerman Ravine Trail, which is just behind the visitor center. Follow the Tuckerman Ravine Trail for 0.4 mile as it makes two 90-degree turns just before reaching a very short spur trail to the view of Crystal Cascade. There is a rock wall at the viewing area, where you can see Crystal Cascade in all its glory. The top 70 feet are a beautiful example of a horsetail.

After this falls into a dark pool, the waterfall continues in another 30-foot drop, with one side a block falls and the other a shorter plunge that turns and cascades down to meet the bottom of the block fall. Return back down the trail to the parking area.

The visitor center is worth visiting; there are plenty of great books and maps, as well as employees who can answer your questions. There is also a canteen where you can grab a bite to eat.

Miles and Directions

- **0.0** Start from the parking area and follow the path behind the visitor center to the start of the Tuckerman Ravine Trail. In about 250 feet begin hiking up the Tuckerman Ravine Trail.
- **0.4** Reach the very short spur trail on the right to the viewing platform for Crystal Cascade (N44 15.648'/W71 15.423'). Return down the same trail.
- **0.8** Arrive back at the parking lot.

TUCKERMAN RAVINE

If you follow the Tuckerman Ravine Trail beyond Crystal Cascade, you will end up in Tuckerman Ravine. In winter this is the premier backcountry ski location in New England. A steep bowl with cliffs at pitches of more than 50 degrees, it is a fun challenge for any advanced skier. The Icefall is the toughest line down the bowl, requiring a mandatory cliff drop.

A long hike is required to get to the top. The bowl is named for Edward Tuckerman, who studied the vegetation in the area in the first half of the nineteenth century. Throughout the 1930s there were ski races here between Dartmouth and Harvard, among other notable races.

On a warm spring day, you are likely to see hundreds, if not thousands, of people sitting on the "lunch rocks" watching the hardy souls launch themselves down the mountain. Many people have died here, however. Tuckerman Ravine is a primary location for avalanches; in fact, it is one of the few places in the East where people can learn the skills necessary to travel safely in avalanche terrain.

Skiers and snowboarders can take the Sherburne Trail from the base of the ravine down to Pinkham Notch.

Many people miss this nice view of Crystal Cascade on their way up the Tuckerman Ravine Trail.

74 Eagle Cascade

This hike encounters Eagle Cascade, which, depending on the time of year, can be a fan of water or a stream that flows down a highly slanted slab high on a steep mountainside. The addition of walking along Bicknell Ridge and visiting deep, beautiful Emerald Pool make this a vigorous and rewarding afternoon adventure.

Start: Parking lot on east side of ME 113
Distance: 6.0-mile lollipop (includes spur to Emerald Pool and climb to Bicknell Ridge)
Hiking time: About 3.5 hours
Approximate elevation gain: 1,500 feet
Difficulty: Moderate to difficult
Beauty: Excellent
County: Coos
Land status: White Mountain National Forest
DeLorme map: Page 45, B-11 & 12 (unmarked)

Other map: Appalachian Mountain Club White Mountains Trail Map—North Country-Mahoosuc
Trail contact: White Mountain National Forest—Saco Ranger District; (603) 536-6100; www.fs.usda.gov/detail/whitemountain/about -forest/offices
Special considerations: Great swim hole at the Emerald Pool. As this hike requires some hiking on exposed terrain, turn around at Eagle Cascade if the weather is poor.

Finding the trailhead: The parking lot for the Baldface Circle Trail is located on the east side of ME 113, 17.3 miles north of the intersection with US 302 in Fryeburg, Maine, and 12.8 miles south of the intersection with US 2. **GPS:** N44 14.263'/W71 00.920'

The Hike

This hike has a little bit of everything. Eagle Cascade is a 50-foot cascade with varying personalities depending on the time of year. Bicknell Ridge provides outstanding views to the south and east. Top off the hike with a dip in beautiful and deep Emerald Pool, not far from the trailhead.

From the parking area, cross and then head north on the road for a few hundred feet; turn left into the woods on the Baldface Circle Trail. At 0.8 mile reach a junction with the path to the Emerald Pool on the right and the southern part of the Baldface Circle Trail on the left. Continue straight through this junction, crossing the brook at 0.9 mile, and continue to climb. At 1.4 miles continue straight on the Baldface Circle Trail as the Bicknell Ridge Trail comes in from the left. Cross the brook again in 0.1 mile and at 2.2 miles turn left onto the Eagle Cascade Link Trail.

Follow this trail for 0.3 mile to the base of Eagle Cascade, which will be either a fan or a ribbon of water, depending on the water flow. When you are ready, continue heading up this trail and soon cross the stream, with nice views of a winding cascade down below you. This trail is very steep, but do not be disheartened. At 3.0 miles pop out onto Bicknell Ridge at the junction with the Bicknell Ridge Trail. This rocky

Eagle Cascade; Brickett Falls

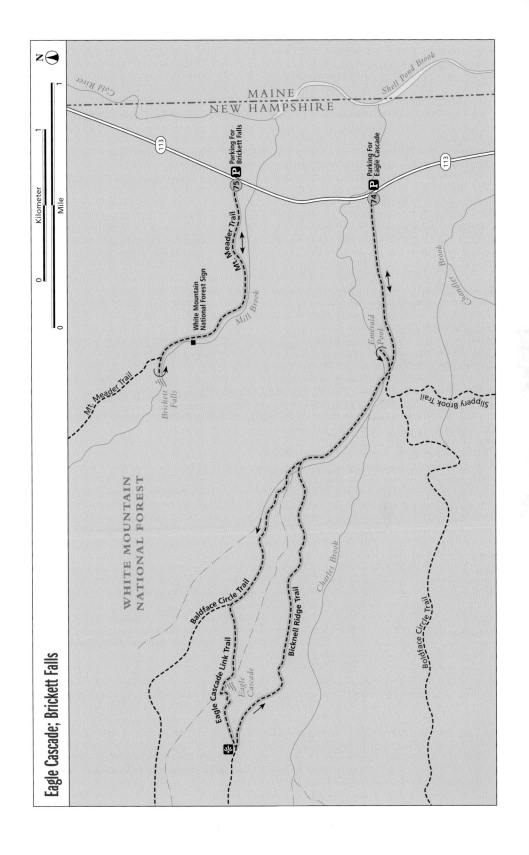

N

Kilometer
0   1

Mile
0   1

MAINE

NEW HAMPSHIRE

Cold River

Shell Pond Brook

113

Parking For
Brickett Falls

75

113

Parking For
Eagle Cascade

74

Mt. Meader Trail

White Mountain
National Forest Sign

Mill Brook

Brickett
Falls

Mt. Meader Trail

Emerald
Pool

Slippery Brook Trail

Chandler
Brook

WHITE MOUNTAIN
NATIONAL FOREST

Baldface Circle Trail

Charles Brook

Bicknell Ridge Trail

Eagle Cascade Link Trail

Eagle
Cascade

Boldface Circle Trail

ridge provides incredible views across the valley; you will want to hang out here to soak it all in.

Head left (downhill) on the Bicknell Ridge Trail, which at times can be a bit steep. At 4.4 miles you will return to the Baldface Circle Trail, where you will take a right and continue downhill. At 5.0 miles, take a left onto the spur toward Emerald Pool, which is just down the trail a tenth of a mile. The dark green pool, surrounded by rock walls will entice you to take a dip on a hot summer day.

Head back to the Baldface Circle Trail. Turn left and hike the remaining 0.8 mile back to the trailhead and parking area.

Miles and Directions

0.0 Start from the parking area, cross the street, and get on the Baldface Circle Trail, which is a few hundred feet north on the left.

0.8 Keep straight at the junction with the Emerald Pool Spur Trail and the south leg of the Baldface Circle Trail.

0.9 Cross Charles Brook.

1.4 Continue straight on the Baldface Circle Trail at the junction with the Bicknell Ridge Trail.

1.5 Cross a stream.

2.2 Turn left onto the Eagle Cascade Link Trail.

2.5 Reach Eagle Cascade (N44 14.798'/W71 03.351'). Continue uphill on this trail.

3.0 Turn left at the junction with the Bicknell Ridge Trail. Follow this back downhill.

4.4 Turn right onto the Baldface Circle Trail.

5.0 Turn left onto the spur for the Emerald Pool.

5.1 Reach the Emerald Pool. Head back to the Baldface Circle Trail.

5.2 Turn left onto the Baldface Circle Trail and head back to the trailhead.

6.0 Arrive back at the trailhead and parking area just beyond.

Even during times of low water, the sheer length of Eagle Falls is impressive.

75 Brickett Falls

Brickett Falls is a series of short cascades accessed by the Mount Meader Trail near Evans Notch. Although the falls is much more dramatic in spring, you'll find peace and tranquility here much of the year.

See map on page 231.
Start: "Mt. Meader Trail" sign on ME 113 across the street from parking
Distance: 2.2 miles out and back
Hiking time: About 1.5 hours
Approximate elevation gain: 400 feet
Difficulty: Moderate
Beauty: Good
County: Carroll
Land status: White Mountain National Forest
DeLorme map: Page 45, B-12 (marked)
Other map: AMC White Mountains Trail Map:
Carter Range–Evans Notch and North Country–Mahoosic
Trail contacts: White Mountain National Forest–Saco River Ranger District; (603) 536-6100; www.fs.usda.gov/detail/whitemountain/about-forest/offices
Chatham Trails Association; www.chatham trails.org/join.html; e-mail: president@chatham trails.org
Special considerations: A White Mountain National Forest day-use or yearly parking pass is required. (You can pay at the trailhead.)

Finding the trailhead: (From the south/Fryeburg, Maine) Take ME 113 North for 17.9 miles from the junction of ME 113 and US 302. Parking is on the right (east) side of the road just past Meader Road. The trail begins on the left (west) side of the road with a "Mt. Meader Trail" sign on an electric pole.

(From the north) From the junction of US 2 and ME 113 follow ME 113 South for 12.3 miles. Parking is on the left (east). The trail starts across the road at the "Mt. Meader Trail" sign on an electric pole. **GPS:** N44 14.763'/W71 00.900'

The Hike

These falls consist of short slides and cascades. Although the falls are highly seasonal, even in low water you will find peace and tranquility here. The Mount Meader Trail, which leads to the falls, starts across the street from the parking area. There is a small sign with an arrow posted on an electric pole.

Follow the trail into the forest. For most of the way, the trail is actually an old logging road. Stay on the main trail as other trails and old roads join and cross the trail. The trail begins to parallel Mill Brook. At 0.9 mile pass a sign for the White Mountain National Forest. At 1.0 mile you will see a sign bolted low down on an obscured tree for Brickett Falls, with an arrow pointing left. Take this left and reach the falls in 0.1 mile.

Explore the brook a bit; there are numerous cascades above the obvious drops. Return down the same trail. *Note:* The Mount Meader Trail continues to the summit of Mount Meader, as well as some nice ledges with viewpoints just below the summit.

Miles and Directions

0.0 Start from the parking area, cross the street, and look for a sign for the Mount Meader Trail. Enter the woods and follow this trail as other roads and trails come in from the sides.

0.9 Pass by a sign for the White Mountain National Forest.

1.0 Reach a signed junction for Brickett Falls. Head left to the falls.

1.1 Reach Brickett Falls (N44 15.061' / W71 01.878'). Return the way you came.

2.2 Arrive back at the road and the parking area across the street.

One section of Brickett Falls winds down over a mossy streambed.

76 Appalachia Falls

With at least five named waterfalls, along with a number of other falls and cascades, this loop hike provides a great opportunity to see a lot in a short distance. This is one of the best bangs for your buck in this book.

Start: Appalachia Trailhead parking on the south side of US 2
Distance: 2.6-mile loop
Hiking time: About 1.5 hours
Approximate elevation gain: 500 feet
Difficulty: Moderate
Beauty: Excellent
County: Coos
Land status: White Mountain National Forest
DeLorme map: Page 48, I-6 (not marked)
Other maps: AMC White Mountains Trail Map: Presidential Range; Map Adventures White

Mountains Hiking Trails
Trail contact: White Mountain National Forest—Androscoggin Ranger District; (603) 466-2713; www.fs.usda.gov/detail/whitemountain/about-forest/offices
Special considerations: The trailhead is also used for much longer hikes into the Presidential Range, and parking can fill up on weekends. A White Mountain National Forest day-use or yearly parking pass is required. (You can pay at the trailhead.)

Finding the trailhead: The Appalachia Trailhead parking lot is located on the south side of US 2, 5.3 miles west of the intersection with NH 16 in Gorham and 7 miles east of the intersection with NH 115. **GPS:** N44 22.288'/W71 17.354'

The Hike

The Appalachia Trailhead is the starting point for a number of long, steep trails that lead to the northern Presidential Range peaks of Mounts Madison and Adams, accounting for the huge number of vehicles often found here on weekends. However, just a short hike from the parking lot lie a multitude of beautiful waterfalls, worthy of a separate hike. There are a lot of trail junctions on this hike, but as long as you pay attention to the signs and map, you should have no problem.

From the parking area, follow the main trail into the woods and over the abandoned rail line. Almost immediately reach the junction of the Valley Way and Air Line Trails. Turn left onto the Valley Way; in another few hundred yards, reach another junction and turn left onto the Maple Walk. Continue along the Maple Walk until it meets up with the Fallsway at 0.25 mile. Head left (downstream) to reach Gordon Falls just a short way down the trail. This is a beautiful cascade with a nice pool.

Head back up the Fallsway Trail, past the junction of the Maple Walk and Sylvan Way as it parallels Snyder Brook. At 0.35 mile from Gordon Falls (0.65 from the parking area), reach Lower Salroc Falls, a multifaceted waterfall with a slide and a pool. Just beyond this is Upper Salroc Falls, where a horsetail flows through mossy rocks to the pool below.

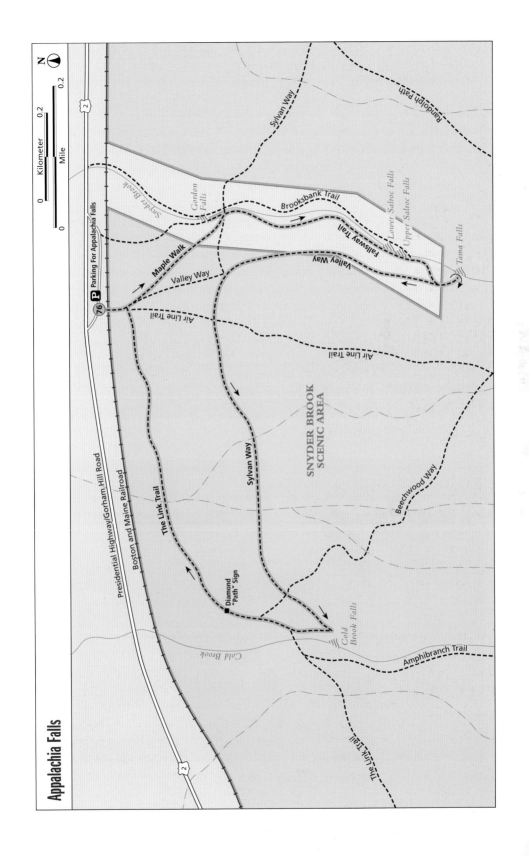

Appalachia Falls

Parking For Appalachia Falls

SNYDER BROOK SCENIC AREA

Sylvan Way

Randolph Path

Brooksbank Trail

Gordon Falls

Snyder Brook

Lower Salroc Falls

Upper Salroc Falls

Tama Falls

Fallsway Trail

Valley Way

Maple Walk

Valley Way

Air Line Trail

Air Line Trail

Sylvan Way

Beechwood Way

The Link Trail

Diamond "Path" Sign

Cold Brook Falls

Cold Brook

Amphibranch Trail

The Link Trail

Presidential Highway/Gorham Hill Road

Boston and Maine Railroad

Kilometer

0   0.2

Mile

0   0.2

N

Travel another 0.1 mile up Fallsway, past the junction with the Valley Way to a short spur trail down to Tama Falls, a dramatic 40-foot waterfall consisting of an upper section that cascades steeply into a small pool before immediately making a bend as it cascades down below a moss-covered vertical wall.

Head back down the Fallsway; at the junction a few hundred yards downstream, head left onto the Valley Way. Take this downhill for 0.3 mile and then head left at the junction with Sylvan Way. This travels 0.6 mile to the west as it crosses Air Line and Beechwood Way, as well as three streams, before making a short climb to Cold Brook Falls. Take a short spur down to the falls, where it drops 30 feet in a few short plunges. This dramatic waterfall, surrounded by dark jagged rocks with benches of ferns and moss, drops into a long pool. (***Note:*** Swimming is prohibited on Cold Brook.)

To round out the hike, head downstream on the yellow-blazed trail that parallels the brook, keeping the brook on your left. Pass a bridge that crosses Cold Brook; immediately after this, head right onto the Amphibranch Trail. This veers away from the stream and in 0.1 mile heads right at a small "Path" sign, with an arrow pointing to the right. This will take you all the way back to the Air Line Trail, where you will turn left and soon after take another left onto the Valley Way just before reaching the parking area.

Miles and Directions

0.0 Start from the parking area and take the main trailhead (on the east side of the parking area) toward the Valley Way.

Tama Falls is a beautiful example of a cascade.

0.05 Turn left onto the Valley Way.

0.1 Turn left onto the Maple Walk. (This will become Sylvan Way right before reaching the Fallsway.)

0.25 Turn left onto the Fallsway to get to Gordon Falls.

0.3 Reach Gordon Falls (N44 22.140' / W71 17.199'). Head back up the Fallsway. Continue past the intersection with Sylvan Way.

0.65 Reach Lower Salroc Falls (N44 21.898' / W71 17.268'). Continue up the Fallsway.

0.7 Arrive at Upper Salroc Falls (N44 21.882' / W71 17.277'). Continue up the Fallsway past the intersection with the Valley Way.

0.75 Turn left at the short spur to Tama Falls.

0.8 Arrive at Tama Falls (N44 21.832' / W71 17.307'). Head back up the spur and down Fallsway to the junction with the Valley Way.

0.9 Turn left onto the Valley Way.

1.2 Turn left onto Sylvan Way. Continue along Sylvan Way, passing over a number of stream and trail junctions.

1.8 Arrive at Cold Brook Falls (N44 21.991' / W71 17.911'). Take the path down to the brook for the best view. Turn around and head downstream on the yellow-blazed trail that parallels the brook.

1.9 Turn right onto the Amphibranch Trail just past the bridge on the left.

2.0 Turn right at the "Path" sign and continue following the Amphibranch Trail.

2.5 Turn left onto Air Line.

2.55 Turn left at the junction with the Valley Way.

2.6 Arrive back at the parking lot.

Get right down to the water to get the best view of Cold Brook Falls.

77 Giant Falls

An unexpectedly tall waterfall deep in the woods is the reward for the climb. Above the falls on the main trail is a nice northern New Hampshire view.

Start: Small parking pull-off on North Road, 1.3 miles from the junction with US 2
Distance: 3.6 miles out and back (includes 0.6-mile round-trip extension to viewpoint)
Hiking time: About 1.5 hours
Approximate elevation gain: 800 feet
Difficulty: Moderate
Beauty: Very good
County: Coos
Land status: Maintained by the Appalachian Mountain Club
DeLorme map: Page 49, G-10 (marked)

Other map: AMC White Mountains Trail Map: Carter Range–Evans Notch North Country–Mahoosuc
Trail contact: Appalachian Mountain Club; (603) 466-2721; www.outdoors.org/about/contact/; e-mail: AMCPinkhamInfo @outdoors.org
Special considerations: There are just a few parking spots across from the trailhead. Please respect the private property around the trailhead.

Finding the trailhead: Follow US 2 East for 3.4 miles from the eastern junction of US 2 and NH 16. Turn left onto North Road and follow this for 1.3 miles. A small parking pull-off is on the right, past Lead Mine Road but before Evans Road. A small sign for the Peabody Brook Trail is visible on the north (left) side of the road. **GPS:** N44 24.788' / W71 06.306'

The Hike

There is no definitive height for Giant Falls, as much of it is beyond view from the base. However, views from across the valley lead one to believe that the total height is in the multiple hundreds of feet. Regardless, what you can see from the trail is impressive, and a short climb beyond the spur to the falls provides a nice view of the northern Presidential Range.

The Peabody Trail begins across the street from the parking pull-off. Head up into the woods along an old logging road. At 0.15 mile take the right fork and soon cross a bridge. Stay left here as the trail continues to ascend on the east side of the brook. At 0.8 mile reach the first real trail junction. The Middle Mountain Trail comes in from the right; stay left, continuing to follow the Peabody Trail.

After this junction the trail begins to climb in earnest. At 1.2 miles reach the spur trail to the base of Giant Falls. This descends briefly and then continues to climb up along Peabody Brook, reaching the falls at 1.5 miles. In low water this is just a thin, steep cascade; but in spring or after a rain, Giant Falls truly lives up to its moniker. Return to the Peabody Trail.

Giant Falls

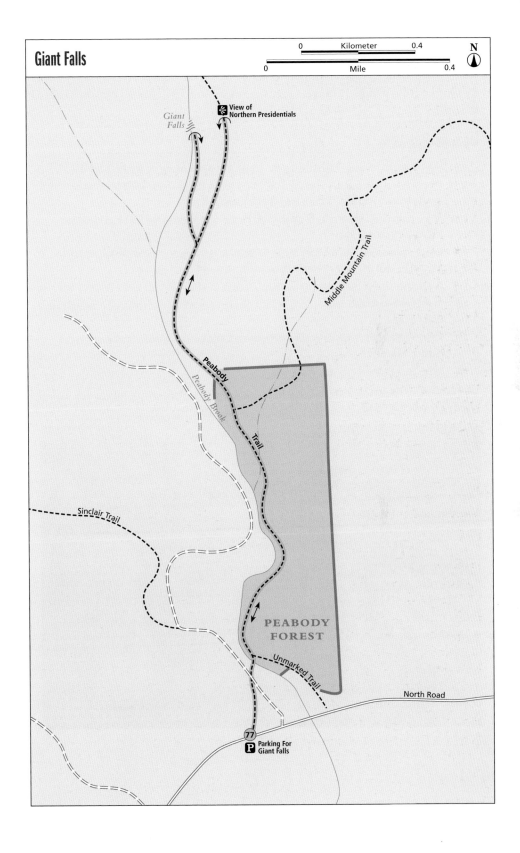

0   Kilometer   0.4

0   Mile   0.4

N

Giant Falls

View of
Northern Presidentials

Middle Mountain Trail

Peabody

Peabody Brook

Trail

Sinclair Trail

PEABODY
FOREST

Unmarked Trail

North Road

77

Parking For
Giant Falls

Since you made the effort to get up here, it's worth going the extra 0.3 mile to continue up along the Peabody Trail to an opening with a great long-range view of the northern Presidential Range. From here, head back down the Peabody Trail to the road.

Miles and Directions

0.0   Start from the parking pull-out, cross the street, and begin hiking up the Peabody Trail.

0.15   An unmarked trail comes in from the left; stay right on the Peabody Trail. Shortly after, cross a stream and stay to the left as the trail slowly climbs.

0.8   At a junction with the Middle Mountain Trail on the right, keep to the left to continue following the Peabody Trail.

1.2   Reach the junction with the spur to Giant Falls. Turn left here and follow the spur down to the stream and up along Peabody Brook to the base of Giant Falls.

1.5   Reach the base of Giant Falls (N44 25.892' / W71 06.436'). Return to the Peabody Trail.

1.8   To get to the trailhead, turn right. To get to a nice view, head left and continue climbing the Peabody Trail.

2.1   Reach a viewpoint, a clearing through the trees. Turn around and head back down to the road.

3.6   Arrive back at the road and parking pull-off.

In late fall, Giant Falls becomes a very slender giant.

78 Zealand and Thoreau Falls

Although it's a long journey out to Thoreau Falls, the hike is easy and the incredible view and unique curving falls make it well worth the effort. Zealand Falls, which is on the way, is also a beautiful falls formation, and the views from the Ethan Pond Trail are truly expansive.

Start: Parking area at end of Zealand Road
Distance: 10.1 miles out and back
Hiking time: About 4 hours
Approximate elevation gain: 500 feet
Difficulty: Moderate
Beauty: Spectacular
County: Grafton
Land status: White Mountain National Forest
DeLorme map: Page 44, C-E-2 (both falls marked)
Other maps: AMC White Mountains Trail

Map: Crawford Notch–Sandwich Range and Moosilauke-Kinsmen; Map Adventures White Mountains Hiking Trails
Trail contact: White Mountain National Forest–Pemigewasset Ranger District; (603) 536-6100; www.fs.usda.gov/detail/whitemountain/about-forest/offices
Special considerations: A White Mountain National Forest day-use or yearly parking pass is required. (You can pay at the trailhead.)

Finding the trailhead: To get to Zealand Road, turn right at the sign for Zealand Recreation Area off US 302, 2.2 miles east of the intersection with US 3 in Twin Mountain. Or turn left 27 miles west of the intersection with NH 16 in Glen. Cross over the river; the parking area is located at the end of the road in 3.4 miles. **GPS:** N44 13.488'/W71 28.699'

The Hike

Thoreau Falls is one of the most scenic waterfalls in New Hampshire. The trail takes you to the top of the falls, where you get expansive views to the Bonds. The waterfall curves around and down almost 100 feet to the valley below. Zealand Falls is not nearly as large, but the way the falls plunges over rectangular rocks, bouncing and changing direction as it does, makes this short side trip worthwhile. If you have the time, continue beyond the falls for a few hundred yards to check out the Appalachian Mountain Club's Zealand Hut.

From the parking area, follow the signs for the Zealand Trail. This is a rolling trail that gains elevation very slowly. At 1.7 miles cross over a marsh on a long boardwalk; continue along the trail, passing the A-Z trail, which comes in from the left at 2.3 miles. You reach a junction with the Ethan Pond Trail and the Twinway at 2.5 miles.

Turn right on the Twinway to get to Zealand Falls. Climb for 0.2 mile then take the short spur trail out to Zealand Falls. (Zealand Hut is just a few minutes farther up the Twinway.) Head back down to the intersection and turn right onto the white-blazed Ethan Pond Trail, part of the Appalachian Trail. Continue along the trail, an old railroad bed.

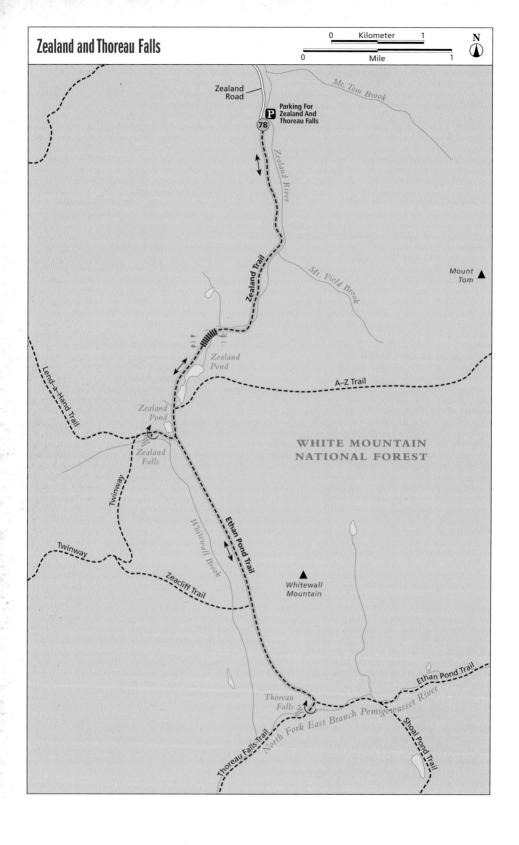

Zealand and Thoreau Falls

0 Kilometer 1
0 Mile 1

N

Zealand
Road

Parking For
Zealand And
Thoreau Falls

78

Mt. Tom Brook

Zealand River

Zealand Trail

Mt. Field Brook

Mount
Tom ▲

Zealand
Pond

A–Z Trail

Zealand
Pond

Lend-a-Hand Trail

Zealand
Falls

WHITE MOUNTAIN
NATIONAL FOREST

Twinway

Ethan Pond Trail

Whitewall Brook

Twinway

Zealcliff Trail

Whitewall
Mountain ▲

Ethan Pond Trail

Thoreau
Falls

North Fork East Branch Pemigewasset River

Thoreau Falls Trail

Shoal Pond Trail

Water pours from multiple directions over Zealand Falls.

After hiking for 1.0 mile on this trail, pop out into an open expanse, a giant rockslide on the side of Whitewall Mountain. Look up at the cliffs on Whitewall and down the valley for a great view of Mount Carrigain and the Hancocks to the south and Mounts Bond and Zealand to the west. At 2.1 miles from the Zealand intersection, you reach the Thoreau Falls Trail, which comes in from the right. Head right and in 0.2 mile reach the top of Thoreau Falls. Head back down the same trails to return to the parking area.

Miles and Directions

0.0 Start from the parking area and take the Zealand Trail south.

1.7 Cross over a marsh on a long boardwalk.

2.3 Pass the A-Z Trail junction, which comes in from the left.

2.5 Reach the junction with the Ethan Pond Trail and the Twinway. Turn right onto the Twinway.

2.7 Turn left onto the short spur trail to Zealand Falls.

2.75 Reach Zealand Falls (N44 11.744' / W71 29.613'). Head back down the Twinway to the junction with the Ethan Pond Trail.

3.0 Turn right onto the Ethan Pond Trail.

4.0 Reach an open section of trail near a giant rockslide.

5.1 Turn right at the junction with the Thoreau Falls Trail.

5.3 Arrive at Thoreau Falls (N44 10.166' / W71 28.331'). Head back along the Thoreau Falls Trail, then the Ethan Pond Trail, then the Zealand Trail to return to the parking area.

10.1 Arrive back at the parking area.

The sun in the west makes the ridges glow as seen from the top of Thoreau Falls.

HENRY DAVID THOREAU

Henry David Thoreau was an author, philosopher, and naturalist, among other things. He lived during the mid-nineteenth century and is probably best known for his book *Walden*, in which he discussed his reflections on life while practicing simple living for two years on Walden Pond in Massachusetts.

In many ways he is considered a father of environmentalism, as his writings on the natural world were unique in their time. He was also a traveler, exploring nature throughout New England, including Maine and Cape Cod, and Quebec. Although he is associated with the wilderness, his philosophies espoused an integration of civilization and the natural world.

Thoreau was an avid abolitionist and even practiced civil disobedience by not paying taxes for purposes he felt were unjust. Thoreau died young, at the age of 44, after several years of declining health that eventually left him bedridden.

Thoreau Falls is a fitting place to appreciate nature—and our place in it.

79 Huntington Cascades / Huntington Falls

With two sets of falls, the short hike to Huntington Cascades is another reason to visit Dixville Notch.

Start: Parking lot for Cascade Brook Picnic Area on NH 26 in Dixville Notch
Distance: 0.5 mile out and back
Hiking time: About 20 minutes
Approximate elevation gain: 150 feet
Difficulty: Easy to moderate
Beauty: Good

County: Coos
Land status: Dixville Notch State Park
DeLorme map: Page 50, C-6 (unmarked)
Other maps: None
Trail contact: Dixville Notch State Park; (603) 538-6707; www.nhstateparks.org/explore/ state-parks/dixville-notch-state-park.aspx

Finding the trailhead: (From the west) From the intersection of US 3 and NH 26 in Colebrook, take NH 26 East for 11.9 miles. Turn right into the parking lot for the Cascade Brook Picnic Area at the Dixville Notch Wayside Area. The trail begins at a chain in front of a wide gravel path.

(From the east) Follow NH 26 West for 9.7 miles from the intersection with NH 16 in Errol. Turn left into the parking lot for the Cascade Brook Picnic Area at the Dixville Notch Wayside Area. The trail begins at a chain in front of a wide gravel path. **GPS:** N44 51.394'/W71 17.178'

The Hike

It's just a short walk to these waterfalls. The lowest falls are easily accessible and consist of two side-by-side cascades of around 30 feet high that come together to flow through a narrow little gorge that is entirely coated in moss. The upper falls are viewable from above and consist of a long slender horsetail estimated at around 70 feet in length.

From the parking area, follow the wide gravel path as it winds around behind some picnic tables to a sign for "Huntington Falls." Continue along this path and soon reach the lower falls, just after you cross over the brook. Continue up the trail on this side of the brook and in a few hundred yards reach an outlook with a partially obscured view of the upper falls. Return the way you came.

Huntington Cascades/Huntington Falls

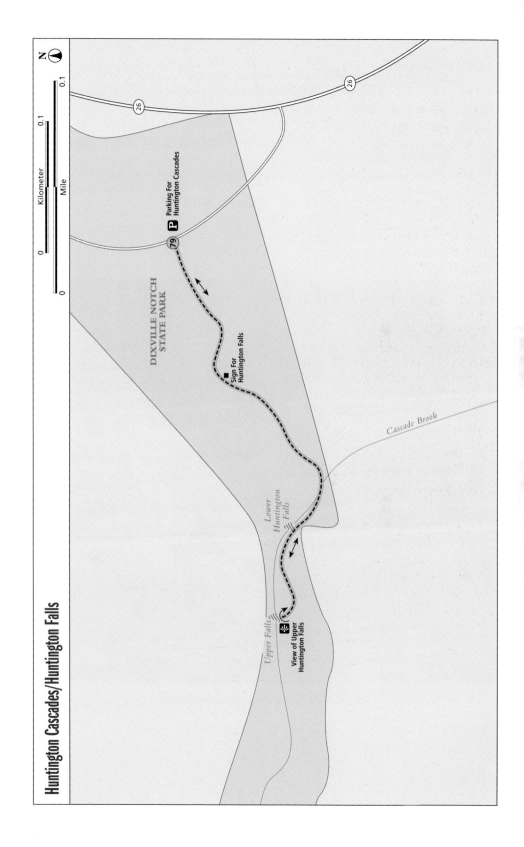

DIXVILLE NOTCH
STATE PARK

Parking For
Huntington Cascades

Sign For
Huntington Falls

Lower
Huntington
Falls

Cascade Brook

Upper Falls

View of Upper
Huntington Falls

N

Kilometer

Mile

0   0.1

0   0.1

Miles and Directions

0.0 Start from the picnic area parking lot and follow the wide gravel path as it bends around and behind the picnic area.

0.1 Reach a sign for "Huntington Falls."

0.2 Cross the brook and arrive at the lower Huntington Falls (N44 51.344' / W71 17.339'). Continue following the trail uphill.

0.25 Arrive at an outlook toward the upper falls (N44 51.343' / W71 17.391'). Return the way you came.

0.5 Arrive back at the parking lot.

The lower Huntington Cascades are surrounded by moss-covered rocks.

80 Beaver Brook Falls (Colebrook)

An unexpectedly large waterfall located just off the road near Colebrook, Beaver Brook Falls is well worth visiting if you're in the area. A short flat path provides a nice little loop to the base of the falls.

Start: Beaver Brook Falls Natural Area on NH 145
Distance: 0.2-mile lollipop
Hiking time: About 10 minutes
Approximate elevation gain: None
Difficulty: Easy
Beauty: Excellent
County: Coos
Land status: Beaver Brook Falls Wayside (state managed wayside area)
DeLorme map: Page 50, A-2 (marked)
Other maps: None
Trail contact: Beaver Brook Falls Wayside, managed by the New Hampshire Division of Parks and Recreation; (603) 538-6707; www .nhstateparks.org/explore/state-parks/beaver -brook-falls-wayside.aspx

Finding the trailhead: Visible from the road, Beaver Brook Falls is located at the Beaver Brook Falls Natural Area on NH 145, 2.4 miles north of the intersection of NH 145 and US 3 in Colebrook. **GPS:** N44 55.206'/W71 27.883'

The Hike

This is not only a beautiful waterfall but also a great rest stop and a perfect place for a picnic lunch, with restrooms and picnic tables in a large field. In addition to the short obvious trail, there are very steep informal trails that climb up along side the falls. Beaver Brook Falls is about 80 feet in height and in big water is a collection of horsetails and cascades that fall over a wide rocky ledge. In low water, however, it becomes a series of rivulets.

From the parking area, head across the field to a flat path that crosses the brook and comes to the base of the falls. There are shallow pools here at the bottom. You can rock hop across the stream below the falls and take a dirt path back to the parking area to create a loop.

Beaver Brook Falls (Colebrook)

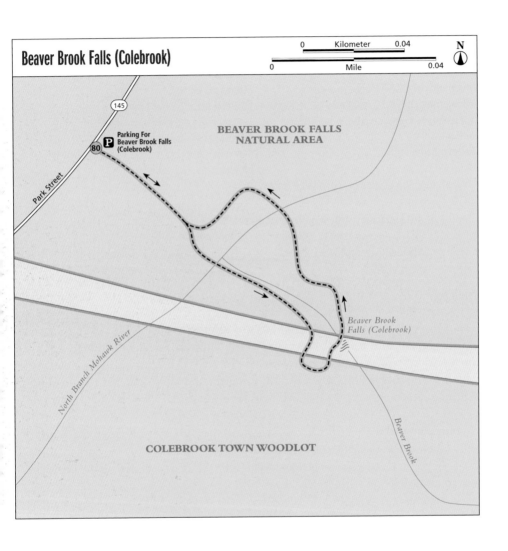

0   Kilometer   0.04

0   Mile   0.04

N

145

Parking For
Beaver Brook Falls
(Colebrook)

80

Park Street

BEAVER BROOK FALLS
NATURAL AREA

North Branch Mohawk River

Beaver Brook
Falls (Colebrook)

Beaver Brook

COLEBROOK TOWN WOODLOT

Miles and Directions

0.0 Start from the parking area and head across the field to a gravel path and a small bridge that leads to the base of the falls.

0.1 Reach the base of the falls (N44 55.168'/W71 27.811'). Cross the stream and head back on the dirt path to the parking area.

0.2 Arrive back at the parking area.

A boy fishes for (very) small trout at the bottom of Beaver Brook Falls.

81 Garfield Falls

The farthest-north New Hampshire waterfall featured in this book, Garfield Falls is a surprisingly large waterfall located seemingly in the middle of nowhere. Areas above and below the falls can be explored, and there's a great spot for cliff-jumping at a pool above the main falls and below a smaller set of falls.

Start: Parking area on East Branch Road
Distance: 0.7 mile out and back
Hiking time: About 45 minutes
Approximate elevation gain: 100 feet
Difficulty: Easy to view; moderate to difficult to get across the river and up above the falls
Beauty: Excellent

County: Coos
Land status: Private timberland but public allowed
DeLorme map: Page 53, H-10 (marked)
Other maps: None
Trail contact: N/A

Finding the trailhead: From the junction of NH 145 and US 3 in Pittsburg, travel north on US 3 for 11.6 miles. Turn right onto Magalloway Road and stay on the main road for 9.6 miles as it passes smaller roads. At 9.6 miles bear right onto East Branch Road and in 1.1 miles see a sign for the falls. Continue 1.4 more miles; the parking and trailhead are on the left near some boulders. **GPS:** N45 01.802'/W71 07.033'

The Hike

Getting to the view of this incredible 40-foot waterfall is easy, but with a little work you can get to the pools and cascades above the falls, as well as to the edge of the falls itself.

From the parking area, head down the obvious trail to the left. This nice graded trail descends at a moderate pace. In 0.25 mile reach a fantastic viewpoint across from the falls. Be careful, as you are at the edge of a cliff, but this is the best view of the entire falls. From here you can head down to the river, where you will see a number of other cascades below the falls.

If you are comfortable crossing rivers, do so and then ascend a steep but short trail on the other side. This takes you to a rock bench, where you can get a great view of the falls from the side. If you keep heading up the side, you will pass some large pools where on a nice day you are sure to find people swimming. Keep heading up the right bank to get to a clifftop view of the falls above the main plunge.

There is a deep pool below a large set of cascades a short ways above the main falls. People jump off a rock 10 feet above the pool; brave souls jump off the edge of the cliff a good 30 feet above the pool. This is not recommended, so do so at your own risk. Regardless, there are many great spots to explore above and below Garfield Falls. Return to the parking area by heading back up the trail you came down.

The best view of Garfield Falls is located on the way down to the stream.

Miles and Directions

0.0 Start from the parking area and head down the main obvious trail.

0.25 Reach viewpoint for Garfield Falls (N45 01.719' / W71 06.830').

0.3 Reach the river. Cross if you are comfortable and climb the steep trail on the other side to a rock bench next to the falls.

0.35 Arrive at the pool above the falls and take the trail to a great cliff-edge view of the upper falls. Return the way you came.

0.7 Arrive back at the parking area.

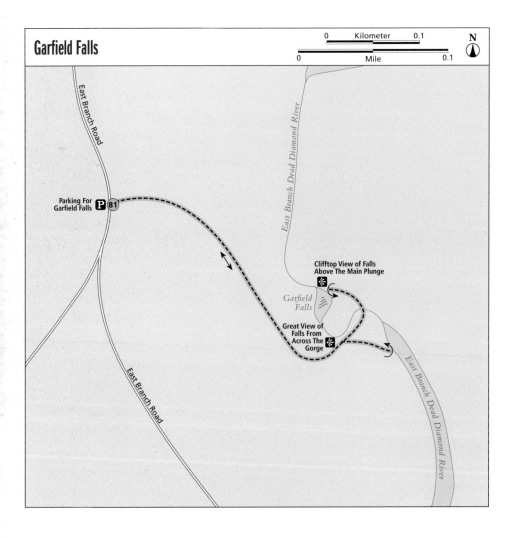

Maine

One of the best views of Smalls Falls is from the bridge that crosses over the stream just below the parking area (hike 89).

82 Bickford Slides

This rewarding hike leaves from the historic Brickett Place and takes you to a number of beautiful waterfalls and cascades along shaded Bickford Brook.

Start: Parking area off ME 113 at Brickett Place
Distance: 2.5-mile lollipop
Hiking time: About 1.5 hours
Approximate elevation gain: 700 feet
Difficulty: Moderate
Beauty: Excellent
County: Oxford
Land status: White Mountain National Forest, Caribou-Speckled Mountain Wilderness
DeLorme map: Page 10, C-1 (marked)
Other maps: AMC White Mountains Trail Map:

Carter Range–Evans Notch and North Country–Mahoosic; Map Adventures White Mountains Hiking Trails
Trail contacts: White Mountain National Forest–Androscoggin Ranger District; (603) 536-6100; www.fs.usda.gov/detail/whitemountain/about-forest/offices
Chatham Trails Association; www.chathamtrails .org/join.html; e-mail: president@chatham trails.org
Special considerations: WMNF day use or annual parking pass required.

Finding the trailhead: Parking for Bickford Falls is off ME 113, near the border of New Hampshire in the White Mountains. The parking for the falls, at Brickett Place, is 19.7 miles north of the junction with US 302 in Fryeburg and 10.6 miles south of the junction with US 2. **GPS:** N44 16.031'/W71 00.226'

The Hike

You will see a number of beautiful slides on this hike, and don't be discouraged if the trail gets very indistinct and rugged after crossing Bickford Brook.

From the Brickett Place parking area, look for signs to the Bickford Brook Trail. The trail is actually steepest in the beginning, but it quickly meets up with an old graded forest service road at 0.3 mile. This will head right but slowly curve around to the left as it gets into the Bickford Brook ravine. At 0.5 mile pass a sign saying you are entering the Caribou Speckled Mountain Wilderness. Continue along this path and at 0.7 mile hit a junction with the Blueberry Ridge Trail.

Turn right onto the Blueberry Ridge Trail and at 0.8 mile reach Bickford Brook. An informal trail on this side of the brook heads down for views of the lower slides. Cross the brook and see a sign for a trail heading to a view of the lower slides on that side of the river. Definitely check this out; the water pours down a 45-foot-long chute into a pool and then immediately drops another 25 feet as it cascades into a narrow gorge. Head back up to the trail junction.

From here follow the trail that heads up the brook, where the sign points toward the upper slides and the Bickford Slide Loop. (The Blueberry Ridge Trail continues

Bickford Slides

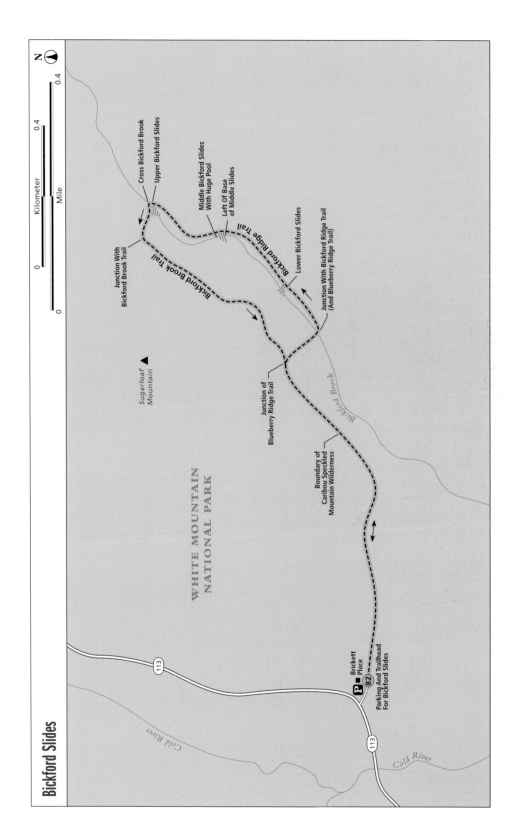

N

Kilometer
0   0.4
Mile
0   0.4

White Mountain National Park

Sugarloaf Mountain ▲

Cold River

113

113

Cold River

Brickett Place
P
82
Parking And Trailhead For Bickford Slides

Boundary of Caribou Speckled Mountain Wilderness

Junction of Blueberry Ridge Trail

Bickford Brook

Bickford Brook Trail

Junction With Bickford Brook Trail

Cross Bickford Brook
Upper Bickford Slides

Middle Bickford Slides With Huge Pool
Left Of Base of Middle Slides

Bickford Ridge Trail

Lower Bickford Slides

Junction With Bickford Ridge Trail (And Blueberry Ridge Trail)

straight up the hill away from the brook and eventually climbs to Blueberry Mountain.) This loop trail is rugged and indistinct at points, but if the brook is not far away, you are doing fine. In 0.3 mile you come to a short rugged spur trail that leads to the base of the middle slide. This slide pours down in a beautiful sheet through a V-shaped notch into a huge dark-green pool, excellent for swimming on a hot summer day.

Continue heading upstream, skirting a cliff along the side of the brook and shortly reaching the trail again. This is where the trail is the most indistinct and rugged, but in 0.1 mile you will reach the upper slide, which pours over mossy rock into a small but glistening pool. Above this the brook pours through a narrow gorge; just above that, cross the water and follow a path that angles back over to the Bickford Brook Trail. Head left and follow the trail 1.0 mile back down to the parking area.

Miles and Directions

0.0 Start from the parking area and head onto the Bickford Brook Trail, marked by a sign.

0.7 Turn right at the junction with the Blueberry Ridge Trail.

0.8 Reach Bickford Brook and cross over it. Head right at the trail junction for a view of the lower slides. (There is also an informal trail to view the slides on the near side of the brook.)

0.9 Reach the view of the lower slides (N44 16.102'/W70 59.534'). Return to the junction.

1.0 At the trail junction, take the trail that heads upstream and is marked by a sign for the Bickford Slides Loop.

1.3 Reach the bottom of Middle Bickford Slide (N44 16.279'/W70 59.293'). Continue up the rugged path on the right side of the brook.

1.4 Reach the bottom of the Upper Bickford Slide. Continue uphill.

1.45 Cross Bickford Brook directly above the upper slide.

1.5 Reach the junction with the Bickford Brook Trail. Turn left to head back down to the trailhead.

2.5 Arrive back at the trailhead and parking.

The middle Bickford Slides flow down through a notch into a beautiful pool of deep green.

83 Screw Auger Falls

Just off the road in Grafton Notch State Park, this is one of the most visited waterfalls in Maine. It deserves its popular reputation as one of the most beautiful as well.

Start: Parking area on ME 26 in Grafton Notch State Park
Distance: 0.2 mile out and back (almost roadside)
Hiking time: About 5 minutes
Approximate elevation gain: 50 feet
Difficulty: Easy (but can be tricky climbing down below)
Beauty: Excellent
County: Oxford
Land status: Grafton Notch State Park

DeLorme map: Page 18, E-2 (marked)
Other map: AMC Mahoosucs Map & Guide
Trail contact: Grafton Notch State Park; (207) 824-2912; www.maine.gov/cgi-bin/online/doc/parksearch/index.pl. Choose Select a Specific Place, then Select a park, and click on Grafton Notch State Park
Special considerations: There is a minimal day-use fee for Maine residents, slightly higher for nonresidents. Children 5 and under and Maine residents 65 and over get in free.

Finding the trailhead: Screw Auger Falls is located in Grafton Notch State Park on ME 26, 9.4 miles north of the junction with US 2 and 21 miles south of the junction with NH 16 in Errol, New Hampshire. **GPS:** N44 34.307' / W70 54.161'

The Hike

What makes Screw Auger Falls so popular? Well, it is a roadside waterfall and therefore very accessible, but more important, it's absolutely gorgeous. Here the Bear River has worn away the granite, creating unique rock formations and a sculpted gorge. There are a number of plunges and cascades, with the upper 30-foot plunge the most notable. Next to this upper plunge there is a naturally formed rock archway, or window.

Fences line the side of the gorge, and as you walk along there are numerous plaques with information about the gorge's geologic history and recent human history, including how in the mid-1800s the falls powered a mill used to cut lumber. There are cascades above and below the gorge, making a decent amount of exploration possible. Some people do wade here in summer.

There is no real hike to be done here, but if you walk along the edge and do some exploring, you can clamber down to the bottom of the gorge and make a 0.25-mile loop out of it. If you are planning on heading anywhere close to Grafton Notch, Screw Auger Falls should be on your must-see list.

Screw Auger Falls; Step Falls

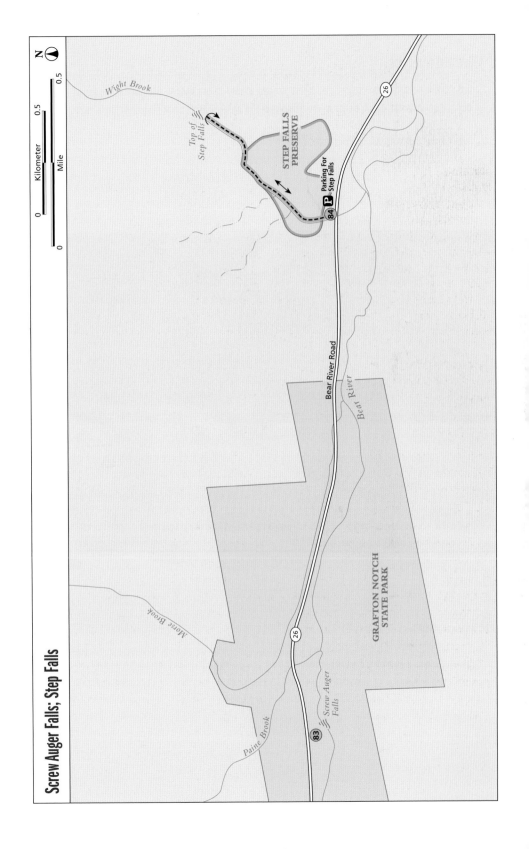

Miles and Directions

0.0 Start from the parking lot and head straight ahead to the river to walk along the fence.

0.1 If so inclined, climb down to the bottom of the gorge. Climb back up to the fence and return to the parking area.

0.2 Arrive back at the parking area.

Just below the main falls, the bottom of the rocky gorge is visible, and so is the way the water has sculpted the rocks over the past millennia.

84 Step Falls

One of my favorite waterfalls in New England, Step Falls is actually a series of falls that resemble a huge set of steps as the water plunges down more than 250 feet.

See map on page 263.
Start: Dirt parking lot on ME 26, just south of Grafton Notch State Park
Distance: 1.2 miles out and back
Hiking time: About 45 minutes
Approximate elevation gain: 250 feet
Difficulty: Easy to moderate
Beauty: Spectacular

County: Oxford
Land status: Mahoosuc Land Trust Preserve
DeLorme map: Page 18, E-2 (marked)
Other map: AMC Mahoosucs Map & Guide
Trail contact: Mahoosuc Land Trust; (207) 824-3806; http://mahoosuc.org/contacts.php

Finding the trailhead: Step Falls is located on ME 26, just south of Grafton Notch State Park; 7.9 miles north of the junction with US 2 and 22.5 miles south of the junction with NH 16 in Errol, New Hampshire. A dirt parking lot is accessed via a short dirt road on the east side of ME 26. There may or may not be a sign for the falls and the Step Falls Preserve. **GPS:** N44 34.288'/W70 52.239'

The Hike

The Grafton Notch State Park area (although these falls are just outside the park) is full of great waterfalls, and this might just be the best of the bunch. Although there is no single huge drop, the way these falls cascade from one step to another is truly dramatic. If you are into photographing waterfalls, there are endless opportunities here for creative compositions.

Note, however, that the character of these falls changes dramatically with less water. That being said, low water will allow you to get out on the riverbed and view the falls from angles not possible during heavy flow. There are numerous pools along the way, and since the falls are so long, you should have no problem finding your own "step" on which to sunbathe and get your feet wet.

Begin your hike by entering the only trail into the woods, passing a trail register and an information board. The trail wanders through the forest for a short while then begins climbing as it parallels Wight Brook. There are numerous spots to access the falls. At 0.6 mile reach the top of the falls and the end of the trail at the preserve boundary. Return to the parking area down the same trail.

Miles and Directions

0.0 Start on the trail that leaves from the north end of the parking lot.

0.6 Reach the top of the falls and the end of the trail (N44 34.602' / W70 51.878'). Return the way you came.

1.2 Arrive back at the parking lot.

A verdant forest can be seen lining the brook when looking downstream.

85 The Cataracts

The Cataracts are composed of two major falls and a flume. The lower falls is larger and is visible from a fenced area above. You can get down to the brook near the upper falls, and in low water there are many places to explore.

Start: Parking area before the bridge on Andover Road (East B Hill Road)
Distance: 1.2 mile out and back
Hiking time: About 30 minutes
Approximate elevation gain: 300 feet
Difficulty: Easy to moderate
Beauty: Excellent
County: Oxford
Land status: Mahoosuc Public Lands, managed by the Maine Division of Parks and Public Lands
DeLorme map: Page 18, D-2 (marked)
Other maps: The Maine Trail Finder (online): www.mainetrailfinder.com/trails/trail/cataracts-trail; AMC Mahoosucs Map & Guide
Trail contact: Western Region Lands Manager, Maine Division of Parks and Public Lands; (207) 778-8233

Finding the trailhead: At the junction of ME 5 and ME 120 in Andover, head west on Newton Street (which becomes Upton Road, East B Hill Road, and eventually Andover Road) for 5.4 miles. Parking is on the right before you cross a bridge. If you see Burroughs Brook Road on your right, you've gone too far. **GPS:** N44 38.481'/W70 51.355'

The Hike

This hike climbs up along Frye Brook. Head west up the road to the Cataracts Trail, on your left in a few hundred yards. After turning onto the Cataracts Trail, climb for 0.2 mile until you reach the bottom, and probably most impressive, waterfall. This plunge, known as The Churn, drops in a powerful narrow chute 50 feet into a deep gorge. A fence keeps people away from the edge, but if you're adventurous you can find a way down to the gorge to get a unique view.

Continue along the trail and in 0.1 mile reach the second falls, a long sloping cascade called The Cataract. Continue another 0.1 mile and to reach the final fall, The Flume, which pours 20 feet into a gorge next to a big rock wall. Along the way there are places to scramble down to the river and enjoy multiple swim holes. This can be a quick trip of just 20 minutes or a full afternoon if you want to explore.

When you are done, head back down the trail to the road. There is picnic table near the second fall, if you're inclined to stop and have a snack.

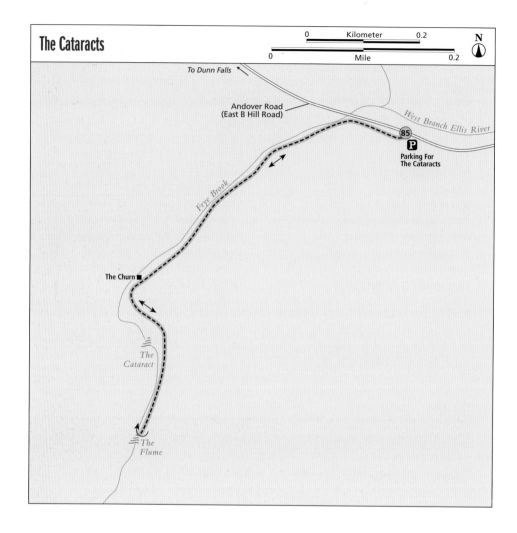

The Cataracts

0   Kilometer   0.2

0   Mile   0.2

N

To Dunn Falls

Andover Road
(East B Hill Road)

West Branch Ellis River

Frye Brook

85

Parking For
The Cataracts

The Churn

The
Cataract

The
Flume

Miles and Directions

0.0   Start from the parking area and head west up the road to the trailhead.

0.1   Turn left onto the Cataracts Trail.

0.4   Reach The Churn.

0.5   Reach The Cataract.

0.6   Reach The Flume. Return the way you came.

1.2   Arrive back at the parking area.

As the water pours through a narrow channel, it erodes the streambed and exposes the rocky ledge and roots of trees high above.

Water rushes down by The Cataract.

86 Dunn Falls

Both Lower and Upper Dunn Falls are incredibly beautiful and are just part of what makes this loop one of the highest recommended hikes in this book.

Start: Small dirt parking lot on Andover Road (East B Hill Road), just past the Appalachian Trail crossing
Distance: 2.3-mile loop
Hiking time: About 1 hour
Approximate elevation gain: 350 feet
Difficulty: Moderate
Beauty: Spectacular
County: Oxford

Land status: Protected land owned by the National Park Service and managed by the Maine Appalachian Trail Club
DeLorme map: Page 18, D-2 (marked)
Other maps: Appalachian Mountain Club Mahoosucs Map & Guide
Trail contact: Maine Appalachian Trail Club; www.matc.org; e-mail: info@matc.org

Finding the trailhead: At the junction of ME 5 and ME 120 in Andover, head west on Newton Street (which becomes Upton Road, East B Hill Road, and eventually Andover Road,) for 8 miles. Parking is in a small dirt lot on the right, across from a hiker sign and just past the Appalachian Trail crossing. **GPS:** N44 40.102'/W70 53.589'

The Hike

This hike is absolutely fantastic. You'll hit the two Dunn Falls as well as a number of beautiful cascades and pools as you wander through the dense forest. You will need to cross a few streams, so sandals or Crocs may be helpful.

From the parking area, head down (south) East B Hill Road for a few hundred feet. The entrance to the trail is on your right. This is the Appalachian Trail, and you want to head south on it. Walk down a hill, cross a brook, and turn left at a junction onto the blue-blazed Cascade Trail.

As you head downhill, the brook is on your right. You pass by a number of beautiful small cascades along the way and at 0.5 mile cross over the stream. After this crossing, the trail begins to climb for a bit before descending to the West Branch of the Ellis River at 0.7 mile. This can be a treacherous crossing when the water is high, so be aware.

Just a few hundred yards after this, reach a trail junction. Take the spur on the right and in 0.1 mile reach Lower Dunn Falls. This waterfall is very impressive; the river is compressed to fit through a narrow gap and pours 80 feet in a roiling mass before shooting out the bottom and finally falling over a much smaller cascade. The spray and sound coming from this waterfall are very dramatic.

When you have soaked it in (literally and figuratively) head back up to the trail junction and turn right, continuing uphill. In 0.2 mile hit the junction with the Appalachian Trail; this time turn right, heading north. You immediately cross back

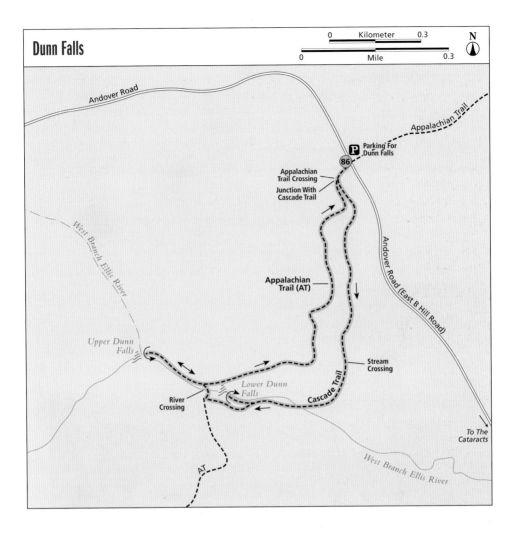

Dunn Falls

0   Kilometer   0.3

0   Mile   0.3

N

Andover Road

Appalachian Trail

P Parking For
Dunn Falls

86

Appalachian
Trail Crossing

Junction With
Cascade Trail

West Branch Ellis River

Appalachian
Trail (AT)

Andover Road (East B Hill Road)

Upper Dunn
Falls

Stream
Crossing

Lower Dunn
Falls

Cascade Trail

River
Crossing

To The
Cataracts

AT

West Branch Ellis River

over the river above the lower falls. The crossing is very doable, but it can feel a bit intimidating with the plunge falling just off to your right. (If you feel uncomfortable crossing here, you can head upstream a bit to cross.)

Immediately after crossing the river, turn left at a junction for a spur trail to the Upper Falls. (There is a sign, but it faces the other direction.) Follow this spur for 0.2 mile to reach the base of Upper Dunn Falls. Continue past the lowest drop to the base of the giant falls. This 70-foot waterfall pours down a steep ledge in beautiful form, meeting up with a small stream and bursting out from behind a wall. This access gets you right up against the falls, providing a great photographic opportunity. When you're ready, head back down the same trail to the junction with the Appalachian Trail.

Turn left (north) onto the Appalachian Trail and follow this uphill to the road and the parking area in 0.7 mile.

Miles and Directions

0.0 Start from the parking area and head south on the road; look for the Appalachian Trail crossing on your right.

0.05 Turn right onto the Appalachian Trail; in a few hundred feet turn left onto the Cascade Trail.

0.5 Cross the stream.

0.7 Cross the West Branch of the Ellis River.

0.75 Turn right onto the spur to Lower Dunn Falls.

0.85 Reach Lower Dunn Falls (N44 39.678' / W70 53.885'). Turn around and head back to the junction.

0.95 Reach the junction with the Cascade Trail; head uphill to the right.

1.15 At the junction with the Appalachian Trail, turn right (north) and immediately cross the river above Lower Dunn Falls.

1.2 Just across the river, turn left onto a spur trail to Upper Dunn Falls.

1.4 Reach Upper Dunn Falls (N44 39.751' / W70 54.090'). Turn around and head back to the Appalachian Trail.

1.6 At the junction with the Appalachian Trail, turn left (north) and follow the trail uphill back to the parking area.

2.3 Arrive back at the parking area.

At the lower part of Upper Dunn Falls, water merges from multiple directions through a notch in the rock wall. The moss on the slick rock walls reveals the waterline during extremely high runoff.

THE APPALACHIAN TRAIL

The hike to Dunn Falls is just one of the hikes in this book that use part of the Appalachian Trail (AT). Approximately 2,200 miles long, the AT runs a continuous path from Springer Mountain in Georgia to the summit of Mount Katahdin in Maine, following the spine of the Appalachian Mountain chain. Along its path the AT travels through Georgia, North Carolina, Tennessee, Virginia, West Virginia, Maryland, Pennsylvania, New Jersey, New York, Connecticut, Massachusetts, Vermont, New Hampshire, and Maine. There are public shelters along the whole route, spaced a day's hike or less apart.

After years of effort, the Appalachian Trail (officially the Appalachian National Scenic Trail) is now protected for almost its entire length through the National Park Service. The NPS has tried to maintain at least a 1,000-foot-wide corridor for the trail, even in populated areas.

Every year, thousands of people attempt to hike the trail from end to end in one straight shot. These hardy souls are called "thru-hikers." In 1948 Earl Shaffer was the first person to do this. A thru-hike usually takes from five to seven months. Hundreds finish every year, and almost 90 percent are "north-bounders" who hike from south to north. The trail is marked with white blazes along its entirety; trails that join the Appalachian Trail are marked with blue blazes.

Thru-hikers are all smiles on a gloriously sunny day as they dry their feet. Are their smiles due to the weather or the knowledge that they've come over 2,000 miles and have just a week or so to go before reaching the summit of Mount Katahdin, the end of the Appalachian Trail?

87 Angel Falls

This short hike takes you to one of Maine's tallest waterfalls, which appears to burst out of the forest as it falls to the bottom of a huge cliff.

Start: Parking on left side of dirt Bemis Road, 3.3 miles from junction with Houghton Road
Distance: 1.6 miles out and back
Hiking time: About 1 hour
Approximate elevation gain: 700 feet
Difficulty: Moderate (numerous stream crossings that can be tough in wet weather)
Beauty: Spectacular
County: Franklin
Land status: N/A

DeLorme map: Page 18, B-4 (marked)
Other maps: Maine Trail Finder (online): www .mainetrailfinder.com/trails/trail/angel-falls; TRAC Rangeley Hiking Trail Guide
Trail contact: Trails for Rangeley Area Coalition (TRAC); (207) 864-3951
Special considerations: The road to the trailhead is very rough and may be difficult in wet weather. Park on Bemis Road, not the smaller road down near the trailhead.

Finding the trailhead: Take US 2 to Mexico, which is right next to Rumford. Turn north onto ME 17 and continue 17.3 miles. Turn left onto Houghton Road. (It is easy to miss, so note that it is 1.5 miles south of the county line.) After Houghton Road crosses over a river, turn right onto Bemis Road. This is a rough dirt road. Continue 3.3 miles to some parking spots on the left. **GPS:** N44 47.386'/W70 42.420'

The Hike

Angel Falls is often reported as Maine's tallest waterfall, which it is not. But it still is very impressive as it shoots out of a notch, caressing a near vertical cliff before continuing along on Mountain Brook. The hike is straightforward (although the drive is a bit challenging), but there are numerous stream crossings, which can be a challenge in high water. Bring hiking poles, and be prepared to get your feet wet.

From the parking area, walk down the road for a hundred feet. Look for a dirt road on the left (possibly marked with a yellow sign for the falls) and head left, following the road around a bend to a gravel pit. The trail, marked by red blazes, begins here. Head directly into the woods, gradually losing elevation.

At 0.4 mile from the parking area, you need to ford Berdeen Stream. This shouldn't be too difficult unless the water is running high. After crossing the stream, head left, following the dirt road. In a few hundred yards turn right onto the trail marked by red blazes. Climb steadily until you reach Mountain Brook at 0.7 mile.

This is the first of three crossings within the next 0.1 mile, so keep an eye out for the trail and blazes on the opposite side of the brook. (There are some nice cascades here.) After your third crossing, the brook will be on your right. Climb for another 5 minutes and to reach the base of the falls. Apparently the falls gets its name from the

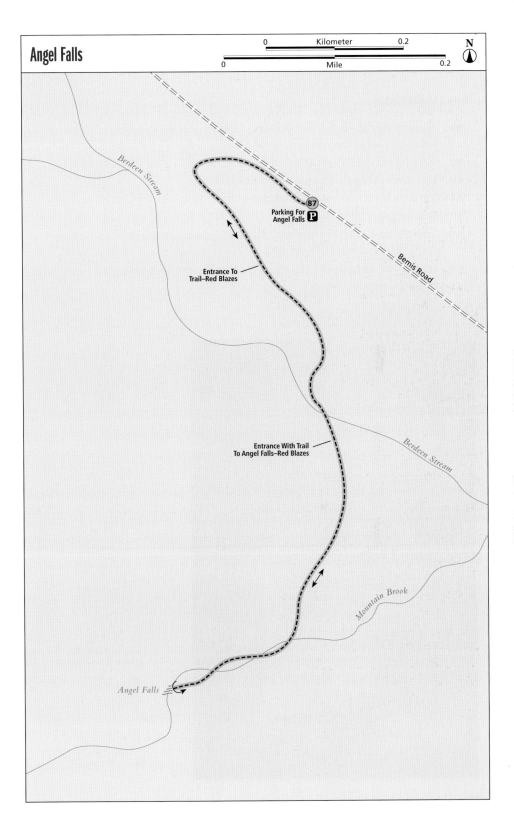

Angel Falls

0   Kilometer   0.2

0   Mile   0.2

N

Berdeen Stream

Bemis Road

87

Parking For
Angel Falls

Entrance To
Trail–Red Blazes

Entrance With Trail
To Angel Falls–Red Blazes

Berdeen Stream

Mountain Brook

Angel Falls

fact that in high water it takes on the shape of an angel's wing. Return to the parking area the way you came in.

Miles and Directions

0.0 Start from the parking area on Bemis Road. Continue along the road and turn left almost immediately onto a downward curving dirt road.

0.2 At the bottom of this gravel pit road, head into the woods on a trail marked by red blazes.

0.4 Cross Berdeen Stream. Continue left along the wide path.

0.45 Turn right onto the trail marked by red blazes.

0.7 Cross Mountain Brook.

0.75 Cross the brook again; very soon after this crossing, cross back over the brook. Continue up the trail with the brook on your right.

0.8 Arrive at Angel Falls (N44 47.011' / W70 42.581'). Return the way you came.

1.6 Arrive back at the parking area.

The light shining through a water droplet on the lens portrays Angel Falls in an appropriately heavenly manner.

88 Mosher Hill Falls

This hidden falls is remarkably picturesque, but be ready for a short but slippery bush-whack along the stream to reach the bottom of the falls.

Start: Parking area on Mosher Hill Road, just before the road crosses a stream
Distance: 0.4 mile out and back
Hiking time: About 20 minutes
Approximate elevation gain: 100 feet
Difficulty: Moderate
Beauty: Excellent
County: Franklin

Land status: N/A
DeLorme map: Page 20, C-1 (not marked)
Other maps: None
Trail contact: N/A
Special considerations: Some minor bushwhacking is required. You will be hiking up through a streambed, so if you want to keep your shoes dry, bring some good hiking sandals.

Finding the trailhead: At the junction of US 2 with ME 27 and ME 4 in Farmington, follow ME 27 west/ME 4 north for 2.3 miles. Head right onto ME 27 west and follow this for 4.3 miles before turning right onto Ramsdell Road. Go 0.5 mile before continuing on the road after a sharp left. In 1 mile turn right onto Mosher Hill Road; the parking area will be visible on the right, just before the road crosses the stream. The trail leaves from here. **GPS:** N44 44.734'/W70 06.739'

The Hike

This is one of those waterfalls that will blow away your expectations. (By telling you this, am I building up your expectations?) At the parking area you might think nothing is here. There are no big mountains, just a small lot, not even a sign marking the falls.

From the parking area, head straight into the woods, keeping the small stream on your left. In 0.1 mile you reach the top of the falls. From here you will get an idea of the drop but will not be able to see the entirety of the falls. Continue downhill, following a rough path over to the right and then back to the stream. Once you reach the water, work your way up the stream along the edge and rock hop until you come to the falls.

This very steep horsetail falls pours out of the forest. The right side of the falls plunges down as it barely caresses the rock wall; the left side bounces off small ledges on the way down, creating hundreds of beautiful sprays. At the bottom the brook makes a 90-degree turn and heads in a straight line down a beautiful riverbed lined with thick moss.

Lighting can be tricky deep in the gorge—the top may be in sun while the bottom is usually in shade. Because you are so close to the falls, blocked in by the gorge wall, you will need a very wide-angle lens to capture the whole thing. Return the way you came.

Dappled light creates interesting colors on the bottom of Mosher Hill Falls.

A large turtle awaits a curious photographer at the trailhead for Mosher Hill Falls.

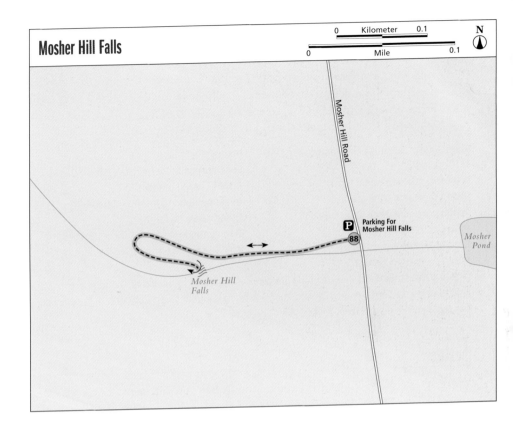

Mosher Hill Falls

Miles and Directions

0.0 Start from the parking area and head down the obvious path into the woods.

0.1 Arrive at the top of the falls. Head down a steep informal path to the right to get to the stream below.

0.15 At the streambed, start walking upstream.

0.2 Arrive at the bottom of the falls (N44 44.705' / W70 06.860'). Return the way you came.

0.4 Arrive back at the parking area.

89 Smalls Falls

Smalls Falls is anything but small, consisting of four main drops that are easily viewed. As a bonus, there's another stream just across the hill with some more cool cascades. If you're lucky, you may catch some whitewater kayakers like I did the last time I visited.

Start: Smalls Falls Rest Area on the west side of ME 4
Distance: 0.4-mile round-trip
Hiking time: About 10 minutes
Approximate elevation gain: 50 feet
Difficulty: Easy
Beauty: Excellent

County: Franklin
Land status: State rest area (Maine Department of Transportation)
DeLorme map: Page 19, A-1 (marked)
Other maps: None
Trail contact: Rangeley Lakes Maine; (410) 252-9488; www.rangeley-maine.com

Finding the trailhead: Parking at the Smalls Falls Rest Area is located on the west side of ME 4, 12.3 miles south of the junction with ME 16 in Rangeley, and 28.8 miles north of the junction with US 2 in Farmington. **GPS:** N44 51.484' / W70 30.923'

The Hike

You may not spend a lot of time hiking here, but you can spend hours checking out all the cool falls. The main attractions of Smalls Falls are the four waterfalls that tumble down through a colorful gorge, dropping more than 50 feet. You can see the three lowest falls from the bridge that crosses over the river from the parking lot.

From the parking area, head down the stairs and cross the bridge. From here, head right up a rooty trail for 0.1 mile to the top of the falls. There is a metal fence lining some of the cliff's edge, but you still should be able to get some great views.

The lowest falls is just a small cascade. The second falls up is possibly the most interesting; it plunges down into a circular pool. The far wall is sheer and curved, almost encasing the pool with high multihued walls. The third fall up is the largest, at 25 feet. Just below the lip it hits a ledge, sending whitewater a dozen or so feet out from the edge. Above this is another good-size cascade, and above and below these are a number of other smaller features.

If you show up on a nice day, you will find people swimming and picnicking here. The interesting colors in the rock are due to the fact that the schist contains layers of quartzite as well as pyrrhotite, an iron sulfide that gives it the reddish colors. The black comes from graphite, which is made from carbon. Other sulfides in the rock weather as well, giving it shades of orange and yellow.

If you cross the bridge and go straight instead of following the side of Smalls Falls, you will quickly come to an overlook of the Chandler Mill stream. There are a number of great falls and cascades here too, and even though it's just a few feet away,

Smalls Falls

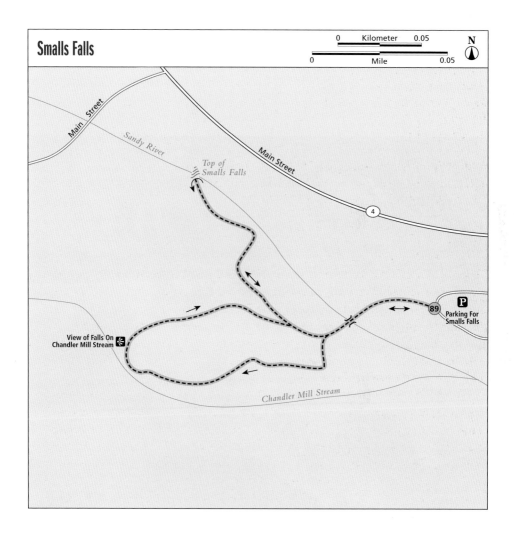

Kilometer
0   0.05

Mile
0   0.05

N

Main Street

Sandy River

Main Street

4

Top of
Smalls Falls

P
Parking For
Smalls Falls

89

View of Falls On
Chandler Mill Stream

Chandler Mill Stream

you'll most likely find some peace and quiet here. You may also witness whitewater kayakers dropping some pretty hairy falls on this side of the ridge.

Miles and Directions

0.0 Start from the parking area, head down the stairs, and cross the bridge.

0.1 Turn right and follow the trail along the side of Smalls Falls. Return the same way.

0.2 Back at the bridge, instead of heading left to cross over to the parking lot, head right and check out the falls along Chandler Mill Stream.

0.3 Reach the top viewpoint of Chandler Mill Stream. Return the same way, or cross the berm and meet up with the trail along Smalls Falls before crossing back over the bridge.

0.4 Arrive back at the parking area.

A kayaker launches off a waterfall on Chandler Mill stream, just a few hundred feet over the berm from the main Smalls Falls.

90 Houston Brook Falls

The beautiful wide falls are photo-worthy from both top and bottom.

Start: Parking next to transfer station on Ridge Road
Distance: 0.5 mile out and back
Hiking time: About 10 minutes
Approximate elevation gain: 100 feet
Difficulty: Easy to moderate

Beauty: Excellent
County: Somerset
Land status: N/A
DeLorme map: Page 30, D-3 (marked)
Other maps: None
Trail contact: N/A

Finding the trailhead: Follow US 201 North for 26.3 miles from the intersection with US 2 in Skowhegan. This is 0.5 mile south of where US 201 and ME 16 split. Go left (west) on Bridge Street over the Kennebec River, and at the junction go right onto Ridge Road. Follow this for 3.3 miles past a portion of Wyman Lake to a parking lot next to a transfer station. The trail begins at a sign for "Houston Brook Falls" affixed to a tree next to the road. **GPS:** N45 04.165' / W69 56.200'

The Hike

This powerful waterfall drops 30+ feet over jagged rocks. Some of the water drops in a continuous plunge while sections bounce from ledge to ledge, really adding to the unique character.

From the parking area near the transfer station, take the obvious trail on the left with a sign for "Houston Brook Falls." The trail is a little rough and rooty, so be careful. It may be muddy as well, so good footwear is advised. Descend about 75 feet in 0.2 mile and arrive at the edge of the falls. The trail along the edge is a bit rough but very doable.

From the top of the falls, you get a great view down Houston Brook and can get a glimpse of Wyman Lake, into which Houston Brook flows. Above the main set of falls are a number of beautiful cascades that are worthy of visiting in their own right. There are more cascades below the main falls as well. Return to the parking area the way you came.

The view from the top of Houston Brook Falls provides a glimpse of Wyman Lake, just downstream.

The powerful Houston Brook Falls create a bright backdrop to a riverside spruce tree.

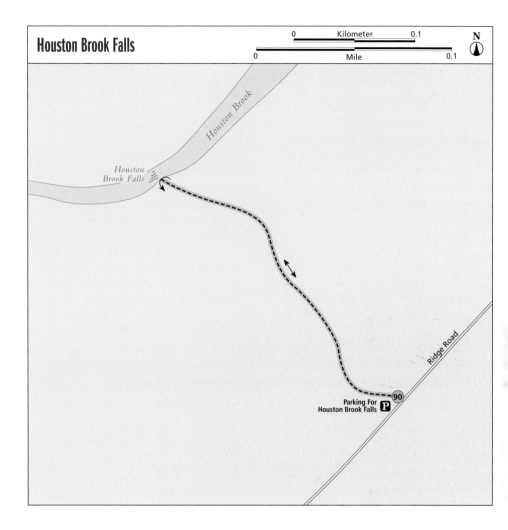

Miles and Directions

0.0 Start from the parking area and take the trail just to the left with the sign for "Houston Brook Falls."

0.2 Reach Houston Brook and the pool just below the main falls. You can clamber up the side of the falls to get a good view of the valley below and the cascades above.

0.25 Reach the top of the falls (N45 04.248' / W69 56.363'). Return the way you came.

0.5 Arrive back at the parking area.

91 Poplar Stream Falls

This lollipop hike visits two picturesque waterfalls, one more than 50 feet tall, as well as the Poplar Stream Hut.

Start: Small parking lot at Carriage Road Crossing 1
Distance: 4.4-mile lollipop
Hiking time: About 2.5 hours
Approximate elevation gain: 550 feet
Difficulty: Moderate
Beauty: Excellent
County: Franklin
Land status: Protected land, leased from the Penobscot Indian Nation
DeLorme map: Page 29, C-5 (marked)
Other map: Maine Huts & Trails Map: www

.mainehuts.org/maps/ (online Google map and place to order free paper map)
Trail contact: Maine Huts & Trails; (207) 265-2400; www.mainehuts.org/contact-us/
Special considerations: There are numerous trailheads for visiting these falls. The route described here leaves from the Carriage Road Crossing 1. A shorter out-and-back hike would be to use the Carriage Road Crossing 2, but that is down a long dirt road and somewhat difficult to find.

Finding the trailhead: From Kingfield, 23 miles north of Farmington on ME 27, follow combined routes ME 16/ME 27 North for 9.2 miles. Turn right onto Carriage Road and follow this for 0.6 mile to a small parking lot on the right at Carriage Road Crossing 1, which is 0.1 mile after the road becomes Double A Drive. **GPS:** N45 05.012' / W70 12.302'

The Hike

There are many trails here, and endless variations of hikes can be made to visit the falls. Some are shorter, but this is a nice relaxing route with the bonus of visiting the incredibly cool Poplar Stream Hut.

From the small parking area, cross the bridge and head left along the stream. At 0.1 mile the main trail comes in from the right; stay straight. At 0.6 mile the trail splits. Take the right fork onto the Maine Hut Trail and follow this as it gently ascends. At 1.8 miles cross over South Brook and head left.

Just a few hundred yards beyond, you hit the junction with the 0.1-mile spur trail to the Poplar Stream Hut. This beautiful hut is part of the Maine Hut System and is definitely worth a visit. After checking it out, return to the Maine Hut Trail and head right. Travel 0.5 mile and turn left at the signed junction toward the falls. In 0.1 mile (2.6 miles from the parking area) reach a junction. This can be a bit confusing, so make sure you are looking at your map.

First, head right for 0.1 mile and take a left to head down an eroded steep trail to the base of the smaller of the two falls. Here the 24-foot waterfall cascades over rocks as it makes a bend and pours into a large pool. You will see a bridge above the falls.

Poplar Stream Falls

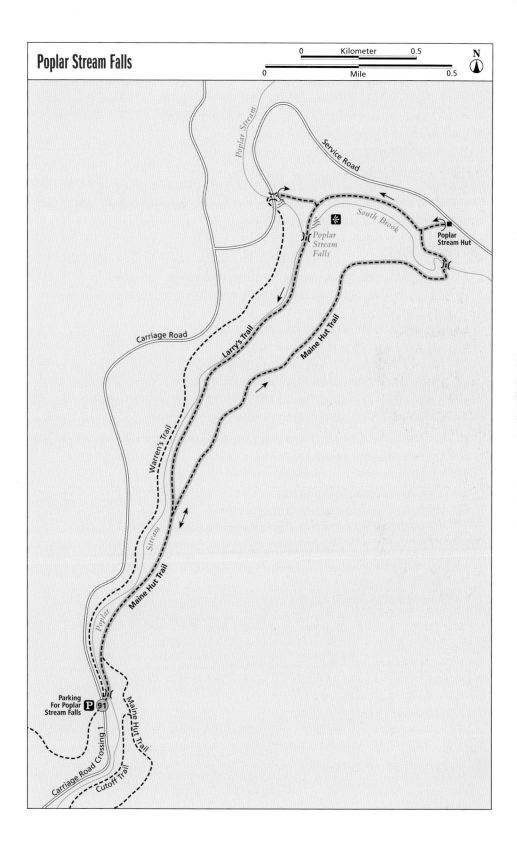

0   Kilometer   0.5

0   Mile   0.5

N

Poplar Stream

Service Road

South Brook

Poplar Stream Hut

Poplar Stream Falls

Carriage Road

Larry's Trail

Maine Hut Trail

Warren's Trail

Poplar Stream

Maine Hut Trail

Parking For Poplar Stream Falls

P 91

Maine Hut Trail

Carriage Road Crossing 1

Cutoff Trail

Retrace your steps back up the eroded trail, right onto the same spur trail. This time, when you reach the junction, head straight down a stone staircase to the jewel of this hike, 51-foot Poplar Stream Falls. This waterfall pours out of a notch in the rock, surrounded by curving rock walls as it fans out slightly and pours into South Brook just before it joins with Poplar Stream.

From here, continue following Larry's Trail as it parallels the stream and in a few hundred yards crosses over it on a bridge. Take Larry's Trail all the way back along Poplar Stream. It meets up with the Maine Hut Trail in 1.1 miles. Once on the Maine Hut Trail, go another 0.3 mile then take the trail on the right, which leads back to the bridge and the parking area just beyond.

Miles and Directions

0.0 Start from the parking area, cross over the bridge, and follow the trail upstream.

0.1 Join the Maine Hut Trail; continue following this for 0.3 mile to the intersection with Larry's Trail.

0.4 Stay right on the Maine Hut Trail and continue 1.4 miles.

1.8 Take spur trail to right to Poplar Stream Hut.

1.9 Reach Poplar Stream Hut. Head back down the spur trail.

2.0 Go right on the Maine Hut Trail.

2.5 Go left at the junction toward Larry's Trail.

2.6 Go right toward Warren's Trail.

2.7 At the next junction, turn left down a short steep eroded trail to the smaller falls.

2.75 Reach the falls under the bridge (N45 06.144' / W70 11.747'). Head back up the trail.

2.8 Go right, back to the junction with Larry's Trail.

2.9 At the junction, head straight/right to Poplar Stream Falls and Larry's Trail.

3.0 Reach Poplar Stream Falls. Continue along Larry's Trail.

3.1 Cross the bridge over Poplar Stream and continue along Larry's Trail.

4.0 At the junction with the Maine Hut Trail, go straight.

4.3 Turn right onto the spur trail that follows the stream and then heads over the bridge to the Carriage Road Crossing 1 trailhead.

4.4 Arrive back at the parking area at Carriage Road Crossing 1.

Poplar Stream Falls flows through a cleft in the rock before plunging into the dark water.

MAINE HUTS & TRAILS

The Poplar Stream Hut and the trails on this hike (along with the trail on the Grand Falls Hike) are maintained and operated by the Maine Huts & Trails nonprofit. The trail network is growing, but as of 2014 they have four "off the grid" huts with bunkhouses and maintain more than 80 miles of trail in western Maine. The huts are reached via hiking or skiing, and delicious meals are served. The hope is that the trail network and number of huts will continue to expand. Check out www.mainehuts.org for more information.

Poplar Stream Hut is one of four huts currently open along the Maine Huts & Trails system.

92 Grand Falls

The drive to the trailhead is much longer than the hike itself, but the huge 40-foot-tall, 120-foot-wide falls is well worth the time to visit.

Start: Parking lot/boat launch at end of dirt Lower Enchanted Road
Distance: 1.1 miles out and back
Hiking time: About 30 minutes
Approximate elevation gain: 100 feet
Difficulty: Easy
Beauty: Very good
County: Somerset
Land status: N/A

DeLorme map: Page 29, A-5 (marked)
Other map: Maine Huts & Trails Map: www.mainehuts.org/maps/ (online Google map and place to order free paper map)
Trail contact: Maine Huts & Trails; (207) 265-2400; www.mainehuts.org
Special considerations: There are parking spots above the lower lot with access trails to the trail down to the river.

Finding the trailhead: Follow US 201 North 49 miles from the intersection with US 2 in Skowhegan. (This is 3 miles north of the bridge over the river in Forks.) Go left onto Lower Enchanted Road, a long rough dirt road. Set your odometer to 0 here. At 4.2 miles keep right, at 4.7 miles turn left, at 7 miles stay straight through a four-way intersection, at 8.9 miles turn left, and at 9.6 miles stay right. Follow this road to 13.7 miles, just past a small clearing where you can park. To park at the closest spot to the falls, follow the road down to the right, where it ends in a fairly large lot/boat launch right next to the river. **GPS:** N45 18.036′/W70 13.297′

The Hike

On this hike you will get a great view of one of the largest waterfalls in this book (in terms of width and flow.) From the parking area (boat launch) near the river, follow the trail across the road that heads along the stream. You will see a sign for the Maine Hut Trail with an arrow pointing to "Grand Falls 0.6 mi." In 0.1 mile cross a bridge on your left.

After you cross, a short spur trail to your left leads to a picnic table near the river, just in case you are looking for a nice place to have lunch. Continue straight ahead on a snowmobile trail as it follows the Dead River upstream. In 0.2 mile turn left onto a trail with a sign pointing to the Grand Falls Waterfall. From here you cross a small wooden bridge and then climb up a hill on stone steps. Now up on a promontory, the trail loops around as you get a few different views directly above the falls. You will even be able to feel the spray up here.

At 40 feet high and 120 feet wide, this block-style falls is truly impressive. The water level can dramatically change the character of the falls—it can be entirely covered by water or showing exposed rock in the middle with falls on the right and left sides of the formation. If you head back upstream, you can access the top of the falls, although getting down to river level requires a scramble. To get back, retrace your steps to the bridge and the parking area.

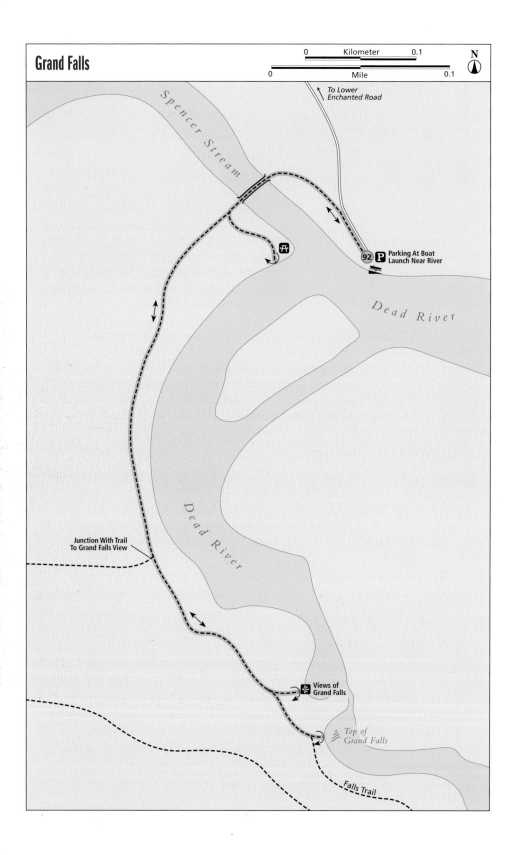

Grand Falls

0   Kilometer   0.1

0   Mile   0.1

N

To Lower
Enchanted Road

Spencer Stream

92 P Parking At Boat
Launch Near River

Dead River

Dead River

Junction With Trail
To Grand Falls View

Views of
Grand Falls

Top of
Grand Falls

Falls Trail

Miles and Directions

0.0 Start from the parking area and take the Maine Hut Trail upstream to a bridge.

0.1 Go left over the bridge.

0.15 Continue straight onto a snowmobile trail.

0.35 Turn left onto a trail to the Grand Falls View.

0.5 Reach the views to Grand Falls (loop on promontory).

0.55 Head upstream to the top of Grand Falls (N45 17.805'/W70 13.332'). Return the way you came.

1.1 Arrive back at the parking area.

The power of Grand Falls, even in fairly low water as seen here, is a sight to behold.

93 Moxie Falls

One of the tallest waterfalls in Maine, Moxie Falls provides great views from above. A steep but fun bushwhack to the stream and pools below the falls will give you a view few other people get.

Start: Signed parking for Moxie Falls off Lake Moxie Road
Distance: 2.2 miles out and back (includes bushwhack to stream)
Hiking time: About 1 hour
Approximate elevation gain: 200 feet
Difficulty: Easy to top; difficult scramble to bottom
Beauty: Spectacular
County: Somerset

Land status: Moxie Falls Scenic Area, managed by the Maine Department of Conservation (gift from Coburn Lands Trust)
DeLorme map: Page 40, E-3 (marked)
Other map: Maine Trail Finder—Moxie Falls (online): www.mainetrailfinder.com/trails/trail/moxie-falls
Trail contact: Maine Division of Parks and Public Lands, Southern Region Parks Manager; (207) 624-6077

Finding the trailhead: Follow US 201 North 48.6 miles from the intersection with US 2 in Skowhegan to The Forks. Turn right onto Lake Moxie Road just before the Kennebec River Bridge and follow this to an intersection in 2.1 miles. Go left and follow the "Moxie Falls" signs. **GPS:** N45 21.243'/W69 56.422'

The Hike

A truly impressive waterfall, this is one of the few 80-plus-foot waterfalls in New England that is not a horsetail or cascade. It is a very popular falls, and rightfully so. The boardwalk viewing platforms across from the falls provide great views.

From the parking area, follow the obvious path to the falls. The trail is wide and flat. At 0.5 mile reach a dirt road and a sign for "Moxie Falls Scenic Area." Continue straight ahead as the trail begins to gently slope downhill. Eventually you hit some stairs and a boardwalk. At 0.8 mile reach the first view from the boardwalk of the stream and small cascades above the main falls. Over the next 0.2 mile there are multiple viewing platforms along the boardwalk, all with great views—first next to, then across from, the falls.

Up to this point the hike is easy, but if you want a unique perspective on the falls, you can make a steep scramble down to the stream. At 1.0 mile, just beyond the final viewing platform, a few informal trails head down the steep slope to the stream below. There is no right way, so just use your judgment and hold on to roots, trees, and rocks to aid your descent. Once at the bottom you will discover a number of 5- to 10-foot cascades and can work your way up to the cascade just below the main pool. Return the way you came.

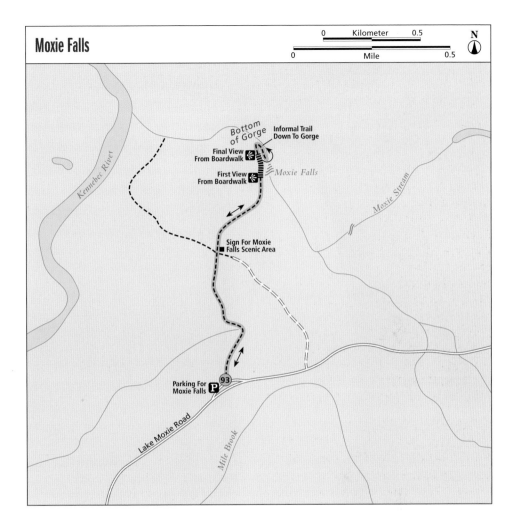

Moxie Falls

Bottom of Gorge

Informal Trail Down To Gorge

Final View From Boardwalk

First View From Boardwalk

Moxie Falls

Kennebec River

Moxie Stream

Sign For Moxie Falls Scenic Area

Parking For Moxie Falls **P** **93**

Lake Moxie Road

Mile Brook

Miles and Directions

0.0   Start from the middle of the parking area and head straight down the obvious wide gravel path.

0.5   Cross a dirt road and reach a sign for "Moxie Falls Scenic Area." Continue straight ahead.

0.8   Reach the stairs and the first view from the boardwalk.

0.95 Reach the end of the boardwalk and the final view.

1.0   Head down one of many very steep informal paths to the stream below.

1.05 Reach Moxie Stream. Walk along the rocks upstream to the cascades below the main falls.

1.1   Reach the highest cascade below the main falls. Return the way you came.

2.2   Arrive back at the parking area.

There are numerous viewpoints where an observer can witness the sheer immensity of Moxie Falls.

MOXIE, THE SODA OF MAINE

You may know the definition of moxie, which means "energy, courage, or determination." However, if you're up in Maine, pick up the soda called Moxie, which in 2005 was designated the official drink of Maine. It was created in 1876 as a cure-all by Augustin Thompson, who was born in Union, Maine. It is both bitter and sweet and contains gentian root, which is used in the making of cocktail bitters. Pick up a Moxie in Maine, or elsewhere in New England, and try it for yourself. You're bound to have an opinion, one way or the other!

94 Gulf Hagas

This long hike deep in the Maine woods is one of the grandest Maine adventures. With big cliffs and cool waterfalls all along the way, you'll want to spend a whole day here.

Start: Parking lot on Katahdin Iron Works Road (KI Road)

Distance: 9.2-mile lollipop (includes most spur trails to outlooks)

Hiking time: About 6 hours

Approximate elevation gain: Varies, but ~2,000 feet

Difficulty: Difficult

Beauty: Spectacular

County: Piscataquis

Land status: Protected land owned by the National Park Service, managed by the Maine Appalachian Trail Club, Katahdin Ironworks (KI)

Jo-Mary Multiple-Use Forest

DeLorme map: Page 42, D-1 (marked)

Other map: North Maine Woods Gulf Hagas Map: www.northmainewoods.org/images/pdf/gulf-hagas-map.pdf

Trail contact: Maine Appalachian Trail Club; www.matc.org; e-mail: info@matc.org

Special considerations: There is a gate fee for each person in the party. The gate that allows people in is open from early May through Columbus Day. There is a significant river crossing.

Finding the trailhead: (From Millinocket) Take ME 11 South for 26 miles from the junction with ME 157 in downtown Millinocket. Turn right onto the dirt Katahdin Iron Works Road (KI Road) and follow this for 6.4 miles to the gate station. Beyond the gate, turn right at 0.1 mile and then fork left at 2.2 miles, following signs for "Gulf Hagas Parking." In 1.2 miles take another left at a fork; in another 3 miles park in a large lot on the right.

(From Greenville) Take Pleasant Street for 0.5 mile east where it becomes East Road. Follow this for 3.6 miles until it becomes the Katahdin Iron Works Road (KI Road); continue approximately 8 more miles to the Hedgehog Checkpoint. Follow KI Road for 1.9 more miles and go right at the intersection. The trailhead is on the left in just over 3 miles. **GPS:** N45 28.662' / W69 17.115'

The Hike

Gulf Hagas is an incredible location filled with many interesting features focused on a deep gorge. There are a number of named waterfalls and countless other features both in the river and above it along the Rim Trail. This is a long, hard hike but one of the most rewarding in Maine. The route described here follows the Appalachian Trail to the Rim Trail to the Pleasant River Tote Trail. Not all features are listed here, but the main waterfalls and trail junctions are described. (Map point numbers refer to the numbers on the Gulf Hagas Trail map, available at the entrance station.)

Note: Trail mileage here includes the spur trails.

Gulf Hagas; Hay Brook Falls

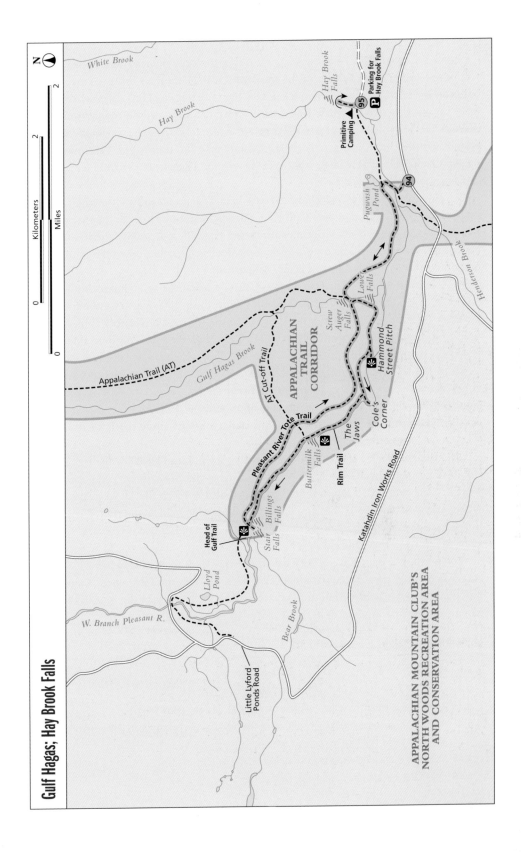

APPALACHIAN MOUNTAIN CLUB'S
NORTH WOODS RECREATION AREA
AND CONSERVATION AREA

White Brook

Hay Brook

Hay Brook

Hay Brook Falls

Parking for
Hay Brook Falls

Primitive Camping

95

94

Puguash Pond

Henderson Brook

Appalachian Trail (AT)

Gulf Hagas Brook

AT Cut-off Trail

APPALACHIAN
TRAIL
CORRIDOR

Screw Auger Falls

Lowe Falls

Pleasant River Tote Trail

Hammond Street Pitch

Cole's Corner

Buttermilk Falls

Rim Trail

The Jaws

Katahdin Iron Works Road

Head of Gulf Trail

Stair Falls

Billings Falls

Lloyd Pond

Bear Brook

W. Branch Pleasant R.

Little Lyford Ponds Road

N

Kilometers

Miles

0   2   2

0   2

From the main Gulf Hagas parking area, take the only obvious trail. In 0.2 mile you must ford the West Branch of the Pleasant River. In summer this is an easy ford, but in heavy rain or early summer, it can be a big undertaking. This is also where you meet up with the Appalachian Trail. Once across, continue on the trail as you pass through the Hermitage, an area with large old white pine trees that's owned by The Nature Conservancy. At 0.4 mile (Map Point 1) take the trail to the left, following the Appalachian Trail. (Heading right takes you to the Pleasant River and Hay Brook campsites and falls beyond.)

At 1.5 miles (Map Point 2) the Appalachian Trail heads off to the right. Stay straight and take the bridge over Gulf Hagas Brook. You soon come to the first viewpoint of Screw Auger Falls. Continue ahead and take the spur trail to the left to the base of Screw Auger Falls. (This is a fairly steep descent.) Farther down the Rim Trail is another spur to a lower part of Screw Auger Falls.

Continue along the Rim Trail and at 2.4 miles reach the spur trail to the Hammond Street Pitch, the deepest part of the gorge (over 100 feet.) Continue along the Rim Trail and at 2.8 miles pass a shortcut to the Pleasant River Tote Trail. At 3.0 miles you reach the short spur trail to Cole's Corner Viewpoint. Continue along the Rim Trail, passing a number of great viewpoints, all of which are worth checking out.

At 3.4 miles pass a number of great clifftop viewpoints of The Jaws, where the gorge narrows considerably; at 3.6 miles reach another view above The Jaws. In another 0.4 mile you get to a viewpoint of Buttermilk Falls and just beyond pass another shortcut to the Pleasant River Tote Trail. Continue along the Rim Trail as it passes more viewpoints.

At 5.0 miles reach a short spur to a fantastic viewpoint of a rock ledge just above Billings Falls. At 5.2 miles reach a short spur down to the river, where you get a great view of Stair Falls. Just a few hundred feet beyond this, reach the Head of the Gulf, where you will start your journey back. Continue along the Rim Trail and at 5.4 miles reach the intersection of the Pleasant River Tote and Head of Gulf Trails. Turn right to return to the trailhead.

Follow the Pleasant River Tote Trail all the way back to the bridge above Screw Auger Falls, then take the Appalachian Trail back through the Hermitage. Continue following the Appalachian Trail until you ford the river again; take the spur to the left to return to the parking area.

Miles and Directions

0.0 Start from the parking lot on the trail down to the river.

0.2 Cross the West Branch of the Pleasant River.

0.4 At the trail junction, head left to follow the Appalachian Trail (Map Point 1).

1.5 At this trail junction, stay straight and cross the brook as the Appalachian Trail turns off to the north (Map Point 2).

1.55 Head left at the junction onto the Rim Trail (Map Point 3).

1.75 Reach the first spur to Screw Auger Falls.

1.8 Reach lower spur to Screw Auger Falls.

2.4 Reach the spur to Hammond Street Pitch. Continue climbing along the Rim Trail.

2.8 Reach the first shortcut to the Pleasant River Tote Trail on your right (Map Point 4). Stay on the Rim Trail.

3.0 The spur trail to Cole's Corner viewpoint is on the left.

3.4 Reach one of a number of viewpoints of The Jaws.

3.6 Arrive at another view of The Jaws.

4.0 Reach a short spur to a view of Buttermilk Falls.

4.1 Pass the second shortcut to the Pleasant River Tote Trail on your right (Map Point 7).

5.0 Reach the spur trail to a rock outcrop with a view to Billings Falls.

5.2 Arrive at the short trail to Stair Falls.

5.25 Reach the Head of the Gulf.

5.4 At the junction with the Head of Gulf and Pleasant River Tote Trails, head right on the Tote Trail.

7.7 Reach the bridge over Gulf Hagas Brook. Just beyond, rejoin the Appalachian Trail, this time heading southbound (straight) on the AT.

9.0 Cross back over the West Branch of the Pleasant River. On the south side, take the spur trail to the left to return to the parking lot.

9.2 Arrive back at the parking lot.

The lowest part of Screw Auger Falls pours through an interesting chasm.

95 Hay Brook Falls

You can walk to this unique falls from the trail along Gulf Hagas. Or you can make an adventurous drive to a campsite right next to the falls.

See map on page 299.
Start: Parking area off the KI Road, across the road from Hay Brook Campsite
Distance: 0.4 mile out and back
Hiking time: About 5 minutes
Approximate elevation gain: 50 feet
Difficulty: Easy
Beauty: Very good
County: Piscataquis

Land status: Owned by KI Jo-Mary Multiple-Use Forest
DeLorme map: Page 42, D-1 (marked)
Other maps: None
Trail contact: North Main Woods, Inc.; (207) 435-6213; www.northmainewoods.org/contacts.html; e-mail: info@northmainwoods.org
Special considerations: There is a gate fee for each person in the party. The road to Hay Brook Falls is very rough.

Finding the trailhead: (From Millinocket) Take ME 11 South for 26 miles from the junction with ME 157 in downtown Millinocket. Turn right onto the dirt Katahdin Iron Works Road (KI Road) and follow this for 6.4 miles to the gate station. Beyond the gate, turn right at 0.1 mile and then fork left at 2.2 miles, following signs for "Gulf Hagas Parking." In 1.2 miles go right at a fork with signs pointing to "Hay Brook and the Hermitage." Follow this for 2.2 miles; fork left, cross a bridge, and continue 0.2 mile. Turn left at a sign marking "High Bridge Campsite #3" and follow this for 0.4 mile, Turn left at a sign for "Hay Brook Campsite" and go 1.4 more miles to a parking area on the left. The trail to the falls is just beyond the campsite across the road.

(From Greenville) Take Pleasant Street for 0.5 mile east onto East Road. Follow this for 3.6 miles until it becomes the Katahdin Iron Works Road (KI Road); continue approximately 8 more miles to Hedgehog Checkpoint. Follow the KI Road for 1.9 more miles and then go right at the intersection. Look for signs pointing to "Hay Brook and the Hermitage" in just over 6 miles; turn left here. Continue 2.2 miles; fork left, cross a bridge, and go 0.2 mile. Turn left at a sign marking "High Bridge Campsite #3" and follow this for 0.4 mile. Turn left at a sign for "Hay Brook Campsite" and go 1.4 more miles to a parking area on the left. The trail to the falls is just beyond the campsite across the road. **GPS:** N45 28.994'/W69 16.493'

The Hike

The hardest part of this hike is getting here. This is actually a pretty nice waterfall, and if you are visiting Gulf Hagas, it is definitely worth the extra hour or so to visit these falls.

From the parking area, follow the dirt road beyond where you parked another 100 yards to a camping area with a few nice spots. If you plan ahead, this could be a great place to stay for a Gulf Hagas trip, but you will need to make a reservation.

Once you are at the camping spot, just follow the brook upstream along an obvious path. You soon reach the falls, which drop a total of 30 feet or so. The falls bounce down a few ledges, creating small pools, and actually change direction before reaching the bottom. Return down the same trail.

Miles and Directions

0.0   Start from the parking area and follow the dirt road to the primitive campsites.

0.1   Reach the campsites. Take the path that follows the brook upstream.

0.2   Arrive at Hay Brook Falls. Return the way you came.

0.4   Arrive back at the parking area.

Hey Brook Falls is a nice reward for a very short hike.

96 Big and Little Niagara Falls

This is a great family hike in the southern part of Baxter State Park. Both Big and Little Niagara Falls provide ample room for exploration next to surprisingly wide falls.

Start: Day-use lot at the Daicey Pond Campground on Daicey Pond Road in Baxter State Park

Distance: 2.5 miles out and back

Hiking time: About 1.5 hours

Approximate elevation gain: 200 feet

Difficulty: Easy

Beauty: Excellent

County: Piscataquis

Land status: Baxter State Park

DeLorme map: Page 50, D-4 (Big Niagara Falls marked)

Other maps: Baxter State Park Kidney & Daicey Ponds Trailhead Map: www.baxterstateparkauthority.com/pdf/maps/KidneyDaicey.pdf; National Geographic Trails Illustrated Map—Baxter State Park

Trail contact: Baxter State Park Authority; (207) 723-5140; www.baxterstateparkauthority.com

Special considerations: Baxter State Park requires an entrance fee per vehicle. Dogs are not allowed in the park.

Finding the trailhead: Big and Little Niagara Falls are accessed via the southern entrance (Tongue Pond Gatehouse). Take I-95 to exit 244 onto ME 157. Head west for 11 miles to Millinocket. In Millinocket bear right at the second traffic light, then bear left at the next intersection. Follow Millinocket Road to Baxter State Park. You will pass Northwoods Trading Post after 8 miles; the gatehouse is 8 miles farther along the paved road. There are signs to the park.

Once in the park, follow the Park Tote Road 10.4 miles from the gatehouse, take a left onto Daicey Pond Road and follow this for 1.4 miles. Park in the day-use lot at the Daicey Pond Campground. The trail begins at the intersection with the Appalachian Trail. **GPS:** N45 52.937' / W69 01.918'

The Hike

Visiting these two significant falls is an easy hike and makes a great outing for young and old alike.

From the parking area, head toward the Appalachian Trail sign on the left, which directs you to the trail and the waterfalls. Hike south on the Appalachian Trail, keeping right at the junction with the Daicey Pond Nature Trail. In 0.9 mile reach a signed trail junction. Head right on this spur trail to Little Niagara Falls.

From here you can explore both above and below the falls, where an imposing vertical rock wall that faces downstream abuts the falls. Head back up the trail to the junction; turn right to continue following the Appalachian Trail to the south. In 0.3 mile reach a signed junction for a spur trail to Big Niagara Falls. Head right and soon reach the falls, which drop 20 feet in a roar of water. There are plenty of large boulders to sit on and watch the waterfall while enjoying some lunch. Return to the parking area by heading back up the Appalachian Trail.

Big and Little Niagara Falls; Katahdin Stream Falls

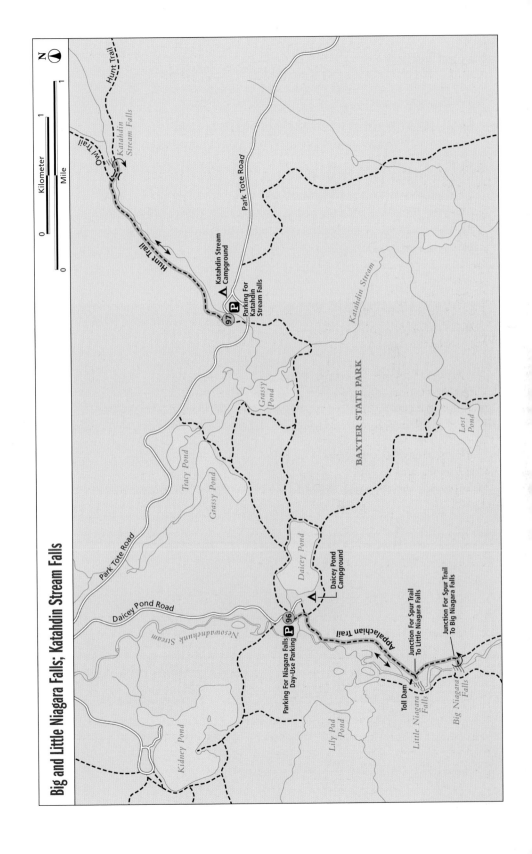

Miles and Directions

0.0 Start from the parking area and head south on the Appalachian Trail.

0.1 Keep right at the junction with the Daicey Pond Nature Trail.

0.9 Go right at the junction with the spur trail to Little Niagara Falls.

1.0 Reach Little Niagara Falls (N45 52.339' / W69 02.371'). Head back to the Appalachian Trail.

1.1 Head right (south) on the Appalachian Trail.

1.3 Turn right onto the spur to Big Niagara Falls.

1.35 Reach Big Niagara Falls (N45 52.161' / W69 02.255'). Return on the same trail.

1.4 At the junction with the Appalachian Trail, head left (north) to return to the parking area.

2.5 Arrive back at the parking area.

A giant vertical rock wall creates a unique juxtaposition against Little Niagara Falls.

97 Katahdin Stream Falls

Just part of the way up the Hunt Trail, which summits Mount Katahdin, these beautiful falls are easily visible from the trail. If you're up for it, try to summit Mount Katahdin, but be sure to head out early.

See map on page 305.
Start: Day-use parking at Katahdin Stream Campground on Park Tote Road in Baxter State Park
Distance: 2.5 miles out and back
Hiking time: About 1.5 hours
Approximate elevation gain: 600 feet
Difficulty: Moderate
Beauty: Excellent
County: Piscataquis
Land status: Baxter State Park
DeLorme map: Page 50, D-5 (marked)
Other maps: Baxter State Park Abol Trailhead

Map: www.baxterstateparkauthority.com/pdf/maps/Abol.pdf; National Geographic Trails Illustrated Map—Baxter State Park
Trail contact: Baxter State Park Authority; (207) 723-5140; www.baxterstateparkauthority.com
Special considerations: Baxter State Park requires an entrance fee per vehicle. Katahdin Stream day-use parking is limited, so you should register ahead online or show up to the gate very early to get a spot. Dogs are not allowed in the park.

Finding the trailhead: Katahdin Stream Falls is accessed via the southern entrance (Tongue Pond Gatehouse) to Baxter State Park. Take I-95 to exit 244 to ME 157. Head west for 11 miles to Millinocket. In Millinocket bear right at the second traffic light, then bear left at the next intersection. Follow Millinocket Road to Baxter State Park. You will pass Northwoods Trading Post after 8 miles; the gatehouse is 8 miles farther along the paved road. There are signs to the park.

Once in the park, follow the Park Tote Road 8 miles from the gatehouse; park in the day-use lot near the road at the Katahdin Stream Campground. **GPS:** N45 53.319'/W68 59.903'

The Hike

Depending on the time of year you do this hike, you may encounter Appalachian Trail "thru-hikers" who have walked here all the way from Georgia. In fact, the Hunt Trail is their final climb, as the summit of Mount Katahdin is the terminus of the Appalachian Trail. If you climb to Katahdin Stream Falls, you will be doing 2,177 miles less than these thru-hikers!

From the Katahdin Stream Campground, begin by walking up the road. Meet up with the trail and pass an info sign and trail register. The trail parallels Katahdin Stream as you climb at a moderate pace for 1.1 miles. At this point cross a log bridge over the stream. There are some nice cascades visible from this bridge. (There is also an outhouse here if you need to make a pit stop.)

Now on the other side of the stream, head up the trail at a steeper angle; in 0.1 mile there's a short spur to a beautiful outlook over the falls. Katahdin Stream Falls comprises three main drops, each about 20 feet in height. Even in late summer this stream has a good flow. There is no way to get to the bottom of the falls, but higher up you may be able to make your way down to the top of the falls. Return the way you came.

If you have the time—and energy—the climb up Mount Katahdin is well worth the effort. Mount Katahdin is an incredibly beautiful, challenging, and unique mountain with terrain unlike anything else east of the Mississippi River.

Miles and Directions

0.0 Start from the day-use parking lot and follow the campground road up to the Hunt Trail trailhead.

0.1 Pass a trail register and info board. Continue up the Hunt Trail.

1.0 Reach the junction with the Owl Trail. Stay on the Hunt Trail.

1.1 Reach a bridge that crosses over the stream. Continue climbing up this trail, now on the other side of the stream.

1.2 Reach the short spur trail to an excellent view of Katahdin Stream Falls.

1.25 Reach the view of Katahdin Stream Falls (N45 53.742' / W68 58.949'). Return the way you came.

2.5 Arrive back at the parking area.

The grandeur of Katahdin Stream Falls is visible from just off the Hunt Trail up Mount Katahdin.

98 Howe Brook Falls

Howe Brook falls is a nice hike on the north side of Baxter State Park that passes a number of cascades and pools before reaching the main attraction. With a lake and canoe rentals next to a campground at the trailhead, this would make a great family outing.

Start: Day-use parking area for South Branch Pond Campground in Baxter State Park
Distance: 6.2 miles out and back
Hiking time: About 3 hours
Approximate elevation gain: 700 feet
Difficulty: Moderate
Beauty: Excellent
County: Piscataquis
Land status: Baxter State Park
DeLorme map: Page 50, A-1 (marked)
Other maps: Baxter State Park South Branch

Pond Trailhead Map: www.baxterstatepark authority.com/pdf/maps/SouthBranch.pdf; National Geographic Trails Illustrated Map—Baxter State Park
Trail contact: Baxter State Park Authority; (207) 723-5140; www.baxterstatepark authority.com
Special considerations: Baxter State Park requires an entrance fee per vehicle. Dogs are not allowed in the park.

Finding the trailhead: Howe Brook Falls is accessed via the northern (Matagamon) gate to Baxter State Park. Take exit 264 off I-95 in northern Maine. Turn briefly onto ME 158 West; join up with ME 11 and follow this north for 9.3 miles into the town of Patten. Go left onto ME 159/Shin Pond Road and continue 9.8 miles, passing Lower Shin Pond. From here the road becomes Grand Lake Road. Follow this for 16.3 miles to the Matagamon Gate at Baxter State Park. From the gate, follow the Park Tote Road for approximately 7 miles before turning left on the road to South Branch Pond Campground. Continue approximately 2 miles to a day-use parking lot at the campground. **GPS:** N46 06.518'/W68 54.057'

The Hike

Howe Brook Falls sits in the valley between North Traveler and Traveler Mountains in the north part of Baxter State Park. This is a great hike for families. In addition to camping at the South Branch Pond Campground (with reservations), the campground also rents out canoes that you can take from the trailhead to a small beach 1.0 mile along the trail. This multi-modal trip means this 6.0-mile hike can become a 4.0-mile hike plus a 2.0-mile canoe trip.

From the day-use parking area, walk all the way through the campground. The Pogy Notch Trail begins near Campsite 19. Turn onto the Pogy Notch Trail and walk through the woods, keeping the pond on your right. After 0.1 mile, the North Traveler Trail comes in from the left; stay straight. At 0.9 mile reach the edge of the pond, where you would park the canoe if you were using one. Continue on this trail for another 0.1 mile.

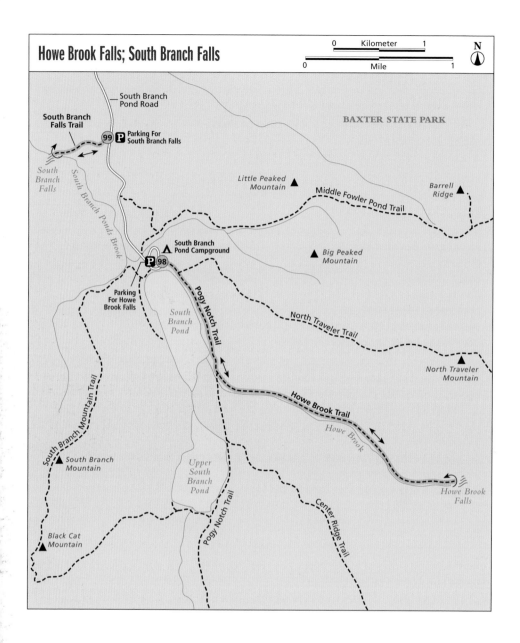

Howe Brook Falls; South Branch Falls

0   Kilometer   1

0   Mile   1

N

South Branch
Pond Road

BAXTER STATE PARK

South Branch
Falls Trail

99 Ⓟ Parking For
South Branch Falls

South
Branch
Falls

South Branch Ponds Brook

Little Peaked
Mountain ▲

Middle Fowler Pond Trail

Barrell
Ridge ▲

▲ South Branch
Pond Campground

Ⓟ 98

▲ Big Peaked
Mountain

Parking
For Howe
Brook Trail

South
Branch
Pond

Pogy Notch Trail

North Traveler Trail

North Traveler
Mountain ▲

South Branch Mountain Trail

Howe Brook Trail

Howe Brook

South Branch
Mountain ▲

Upper
South
Branch
Pond

Howe Brook
Falls

Pogy Notch Trail

Center Ridge Trail

Black Cat
Mountain ▲

At 1.1 miles from the parking area, reach the junction with the Howe Brook Trail, on which you continue straight. In 0.2 mile reach a small waterfall and a big beautiful pool. Continue climbing up this trail, passing a number of nice pools and cascades. At 3.1 miles from the parking area, arrive at Howe Brook Falls, a medium-size waterfall that drops as a sheet over highly slanted bedrock into a large pool overhung by a tree. Return the way you came.

Miles and Directions

0.0 Start from the day-use parking area and head through the campground to the Pogy Notch Trailhead.

0.2 Take the Pogy Notch Trail along the pond.

1.0 Reach the canoe landing area at the end of the pond. Continue on the trail.

1.1 At the trail junction, head straight onto the Howe Brook Trail.

1.3 Reach the lower falls and pools along Howe Brook.

3.1 Arrive at the upper falls on Howe Brook (N46 05.282' / W68 51.482'). Return the way you came.

6.2 Arrive back at the parking area.

A shadow of the surrounding trees is visible on the main upper Howe Brook Falls.

99 South Branch Falls

Although there are no major waterfalls here, the unique geology, cascades, and slides are worth a trip if you're in Baxter State Park and looking for a short easy hike.

See map on page 310.
Start: Parking area on road to South Branch Pond Campground in Baxter State Park
Distance: 1.0 mile out and back
Hiking time: About 30 minutes
Approximate elevation gain: 200 feet
Difficulty: Easy
Beauty: Good
County: Piscataquis
Land status: Baxter State Park
DeLorme map: Page 51, A-1 (not marked)

Other maps: Baxter State Park Abol Trailhead Map: www.baxterstateparkauthority.com/pdf/maps/Abol.pdf; National Geographic Trails Illustrated Map–Baxter State Park
Trail contact: Baxter State Park Authority; (207) 723-5140; www.baxterstatepark authority.com
Special considerations: Baxter State Park requires an entrance fee per vehicle. Dogs are not allowed in Baxter State Park.

Finding the trailhead: South Branch Falls is accessed via the northern (Matagamon) gate to Baxter State Park. Take exit 264 off I-95 in northern Maine. Turn briefly onto ME 158 West and then join up with ME 11. Follow this north for 9.3 miles into the town of Patten. Go left onto ME 159/Shin Pond Road and continue 9.8 miles, passing Lower Shin Pond. From here the road becomes Grand Lake Road. Follow this for 16.3 miles to the Matagamon Gate at Baxter State Park. From the gate, follow the Park Tote Road for approximately 7 miles before turning left on the road to South Branch Pond Campground. Continue 1.2 miles to a small parking area on the right. **GPS:** N46 07.222' / W68 54.368'

The Hike

These falls are not large, but they are unique. From the parking area, head straight into the woods on the South Branch Falls Trail. After hiking 0.5 mile, head to your right to reach the falls, which slide through an angled flume. Upstream of this flume is a little 3-foot plunge falls. You can also have a good time wandering around on the ledges. This is an ideal hike if you are staying at the South Branch Pond Campground, as it is appropriate for all ages.

Miles and Directions

0.0   Start from the parking area and head down the South Branch Falls Trail.

0.5   Reach South Branch Falls (N46 07.129' / W68 54.886'). Return the way you came.

1.0   Arrive back at the parking area.

South Branch Falls do not drop very far, but nonetheless have a unique flow through a rocky channel.

100 Sawtelle Falls

Make the short trip to the small but powerful Sawtelle Falls if you're on your way to the northern entrance to Baxter State Park.

Start: Parking pull-off after bridge on Scraggly Lake Road (Sawtelle Road)
Distance: 1.0 mile out and back
Hiking time: About 25 minutes
Approximate elevation gain: 50 feet
Difficulty: Easy
Beauty: Good

County: Penobscot
Land status: N/A
DeLorme map: Page 51, A-4 (marked)
Other maps: None
Trail contact: N/A
Special considerations: None.

Finding the trailhead: Take exit 264 off I-95 in northern Maine. Turn briefly onto ME 158 West and then join up with ME 11. Follow this north for 9.3 miles into the town of Patten. Go left onto ME 159/Shin Pond Road and continue 9.8 miles, passing Lower Shin Pond. From here the road becomes Grand Lake Road. Continue straight on this for 6.8 miles and then turn right onto Scraggly Lake Road, which may also be called Sawtelle Road. Go 1.6 miles; park on a pull-off on the right after crossing a bridge. The trailhead is just ahead on the right. **GPS:** N46 09.393' / W68 39.489'

The Hike

Although this is not an amazing waterfall, accessed via a very easy hike, you'll be surprised by its power. You are pretty much guaranteed to have this one to yourself. From the parking area, look for a trail in the woods on the right. It is about 200 feet beyond the bridge you crossed and appears initially to be a rugged four-wheel-drive dirt road.

Take the trail through the woods, passing a small meadow. The trail can be very muddy; you may need to veer through the woods a bit to avoid large puddles. In 0.5 mile reach a view that is right next to the falls. It is possible to scramble down to the river to get a view from below, but it is anything but easy and safe to do so. Return the way you came. If you are visiting Sawtelle Falls, you should also visit nearby Shin Falls, a much larger and more interesting waterfall.

Sawtelle Falls; Shin Falls

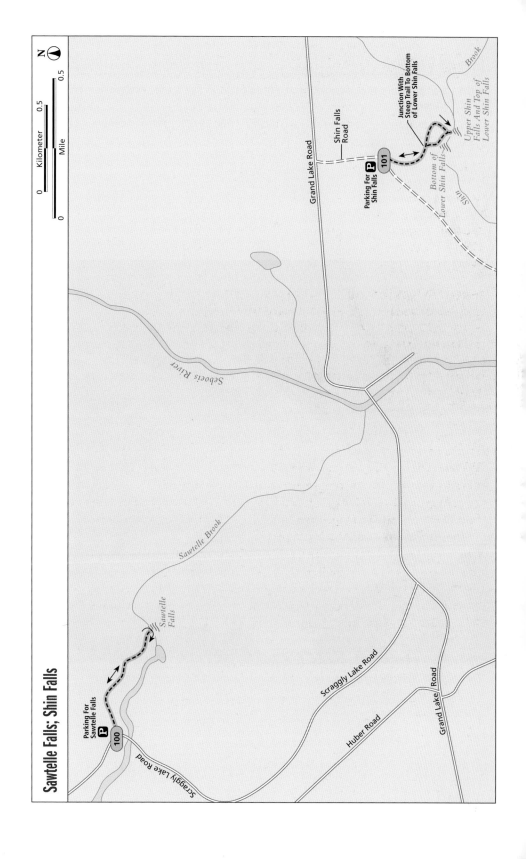

N

| 0 | Kilometer | 0.5 |
| 0 | Mile | 0.5 |

Sawtelle Brook

Sebocis River

Sawtelle Falls

Scraggly Lake Road

Parking For Sawtelle Falls 🅿 **100**

Huber Road

Scraggly Lake Road

Grand Lake Road

Grand Lake Road

Shin Falls Road

Parking For Shin Falls 🅿 **101**

Junction With Steep Trail To Bottom of Lower Shin Falls

Upper Shin Falls And Top of Lower Shin Falls

Bottom of Lower Shin Falls

Shin Brook

Miles and Directions

0.0   Start from the parking area and head right onto the trail that is a few hundred feet past the bridge.

0.5   Reach the edge of Sawtelle Falls (N46 09.267' / W68 39.026'). Return the way you came.

1.0   Arrive back at the parking area.

The height of Sawtelle Falls is not very high, but the power of the water is tremendous.

101 Shin Falls

Shin Falls is actually composed of two separate falls, both accessible via a short hike. It's well worth the visit, especially if you are entering Baxter State Park from the north.

See map on page 315.
Start: Parking area on Shin Falls Road, 0.2 mile from junction with Grand Lake Road
Distance: 0.8-mile lollipop
Hiking time: About 20 minutes
Approximate elevation gain: 150 feet
Difficulty: Moderate

Beauty: Excellent
County: Penobscot
Land status: N/A
DeLorme map: Page 51, A-4 (marked)
Other maps: None
Trail contact: N/A

Finding the trailhead: Take exit 264 off I-95 in northern Maine. Turn briefly onto ME 158 West and then join up with ME 11. Follow this north for 9.3 miles into the town of Patten. Go left onto ME 159/Shin Pond Road and continue 9.8 miles, passing Lower Shin Pond. From here the road becomes Grand Lake Road. Continue straight on this for 5.1 miles before taking a left onto a dirt road appropriately named Shin Falls Road. Parking is on the left in 0.2 mile. **GPS:** N46 08.536' / W68 36.938'

The Hike

From the parking area, follow the trail into the woods. There is a "Shin Brook Falls" sign posted high up in a tree. Follow this trail for 0.3 mile as it curves around to the east. Pass a trail on your right as you begin to curve around; pass a number of indistinct trails as well. You also pass an obvious trail on your right, currently marked with orange tape.

At 0.3 mile turn right onto a trail that leads to the river. It is currently marked with blue tape. When you reach another junction near the river, go straight/left and soon pop out at the upper falls. Looking downriver you will see you are near the top of the lower falls. This is a powerful river (do not be deceived by the "brook" in the name), and the water here is a roiling mass. Backtrack a tiny bit and then head left, keeping Shin Brook to your left. Stay left at another junction and follow the steep trail beside the falls down to the bottom. From here you get a glimpse of the 30-foot horsetail falls that pounds the water, sending up a large spray.

Just beyond the bottom of the lower falls, there is a steep 0.1-mile trail up to the main trail. Once you reach this flat trail, turn left and follow it back to the parking area.

Miles and Directions

0.0 Start from the parking area and take the trail directly into the woods. Continue following this main trail, passing a few junctions on the right.

0.3 Turn right onto the trail to Upper Shin Falls (currently marked with blue tape).

0.35 Turn left onto a spur out to Upper Shin Falls. Backtrack to this junction.

0.4 Head left, keeping the brook on your left.

0.45 At the next junction, near the top of Lower Shin Falls, stay left and take the trail down along the side of the brook.

0.5 Reach the bottom of Lower Shin Falls. Take the steep trail up to the right.

0.6 At the top of the steep trail, head left to return to the parking area.

0.8 Arrive back at the parking area.

Although the falls are in the shade, the spray below creates a beautiful glow as the early morning light reflects off the small airborne water droplets.

PHOTOGRAPHY TIP: USE A FAST SHUTTER SPEED

Just as using a slow shutter speed can create an image of moving water that is different than what our eyes see, so too does using a fast shutter speed. By stopping the action, we are able to see ripples, splashes, waves, and droplets as unique and seemingly crystalline structures. Capturing a brief moment in time allows us to see the world in new ways.

To get a shot of rapidly moving and spraying water to be sharp, you must use a shutter speed of at least 1/500 of a second, preferably at least 1/2000 of a second. This may involve opening up your aperture and raising your ISO. Put your camera on continuous shooting and fire away, as you won't know what you've got until you review the images. You won't need a tripod for this type of shooting; the shutter speed is fast enough to discount any slight movement of the camera. The faster the water is moving, and the closer you are to it, the faster your shutter speed will need to be.

Shin Falls is a very powerful waterfall. In the early morning, just the upper part of the falls catches the sunlight.

Hike Index

Abbey Pond Cascades, 127

Angel Falls, 274

Appalachia Falls, 236

Arethusa Falls, 219

Bailey Falls, 119

Bailey's Ravine, 29

Bartlett Falls, 130

Bash Bish Falls, 49

Basin-Cascade Trail Falls, 204

Beaver Brook Cascades (Moosilauke), 189

Beaver Brook Falls (Colebrook), 251

Beaver Brook Falls (Keene), 172

Bickford Slides, 258

Big and Little Niagara Falls, 304

Big Falls, 160

Bingham Falls, 143

Blackledge Falls, 32

Bolton Potholes, 136

Brickett Falls, 234

Bridal Veil Falls, 210

Buttermilk Falls (CT), 18

Buttermilk Falls (VT), 92

Campbell Falls, 42

Cascade Falls (VT), 95

Chapman Falls, 27

Chesterfield Gorge, 169

Crystal Cascade (NH), 227

Diana's Baths, 213

Doane's Falls, 70

Dunn Falls, 270

Eagle Cascade, 230

Emerson Falls, 138

Enders Falls, 35

Falling Waters, 207

Falls of Lana, 116

Flume Gorge / Flume Pool Loop, 200

Garfield Falls, 254

Garwin Falls, 163

Gerry Falls, 101

Giant Falls, 240

Glen Ellis Falls, 224

Glen Falls, 113

Grand Falls, 291

Gulf Hagas, 298

Hamilton Falls, 89

Hay Brook Falls, 302

Hell Brook Cascades (Lower), 146

Hidden Falls, 98

Honey Hollow Falls, 134

Houston Brook Falls, 283

Howe Brook Falls, 309

Huntington Cascades / Huntington Falls, 248

Huntington Gorge, 132

Indian Well Falls, 12

Jay Branch Gorge / Four Corners, 158

Jefferson Falls / Brewster River Gorge, 155

Jelly Mill Falls / Old Jelly Mill Falls, 79

Katahdin Stream Falls, 307

Kent Falls, 20

Livermore Falls, 182

Lost River Gorge, 193

Lye Brook Falls, 84

March Cataract Falls, 58

Money Brook Falls, 62

Mosher Hill Falls, 277

Moss Glen Falls (Granville), 125

Moss Glen Falls (Stowe), 140

Moxie Falls, 294

Nancy Cascades, 216

Old City Falls, 110

Pikes Falls, 81

Poplar Stream Falls, 286

Profile Falls, 179

Purgatory Falls, 166

Quechee Gorge, 103

Race Brook Falls, 45

Ripley Falls, 222

Royalston Falls, 75

Sabbaday Falls, 196

Sawtelle Falls, 314

Screw Auger Falls, 262

Shin Falls, 317

Smalls Falls, 280

South Branch Falls, 312

Spirit Falls, 73

Spruce Brook Falls, 15

Step Falls, 265

Stepstone Falls, 39

Sterling Falls Gorge, 149

Tannery and Parker Brook Falls, 67

Terrill Gorge, 152

Texas Falls, 122

The Cataracts, 267

Thundering Falls / Thundering Brook Falls / Bakers Falls, 107

Trues Ledges, 175

Twin Cascade, 64

Wadsworth Big and Little Falls, 23

Wahconah Falls, 52

Waterville Cascades, 185

Windsor Jambs, 55

Zealand and Thoreau Falls, 243

About the Author

Eli Burakian is an outdoors enthusiast, writer, and photographer based in Vermont. He photographed a number of books in the Knack series, including *Knack Hiking and Backpacking*. His other books include *Moosilauke: A Portrait of a Mountain* and *Best Easy Day Hikes Green Mountains*. In addition to his writing and photography pursuits, he is the Dartmouth College Photographer in Hanover, NH. An avid long-distance backpacker, Eli makes it a priority to go on at least one big adventure each year. Visit him at BurakianPhotography.com.

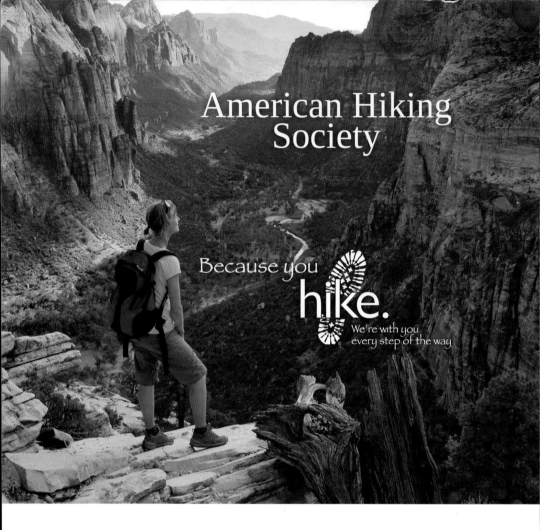

American Hiking Society

Because you **hike.**
We're with you every step of the way

As a national voice for hikers, **American Hiking Society** works every day:

- Building and maintaining hiking trails
- Educating and supporting hikers by providing information and resources
- Supporting hiking and trail organizations nationwide
- Speaking for hikers in the halls of Congress and with federal land managers

Whether you're a casual hiker or a seasoned backpacker, become a member of American Hiking Society and join the national hiking community! You'll enjoy great member benefits and help preserve the nation's hiking trails, so tomorrow's hike is even better than today's. We invite you to join us now!

American Hiking Society